Cricket Nurseries of Colonial Barbados

The Elite Schools, 1865–1966

Keith A. P. Sandiford

The Press University of the West Indies
Barbados • Jamaica • Trinidad and Tobago

The Press University of the West Indies
1A Aqueduct Flats Kingston 7 Jamaica W I

ISBN 976–640–046–6

Printed in Canada

CATALOGUING IN PUBLICATION DATA
Sandiford, Keith A.P.
Cricket nurseries of colonial Barbados : the elite schools, 1865–1966 / Keith A.P. Sandiford.

p. cm.
Includes bibliographical references and index.
ISBN 976–640–046–6

1. Cricket – Barbados. 2. Lodge School (Barbados) – Cricket. 3. Harrison College (Barbados) – Cricket. 4. Combermere School – (Barbados) – Cricket. I. Title.
GV928.B35S36 1998 796.358'09729'

Cricket Nurseries of Colonial Barbados

Contents

List of Illustrations *vi*
Preface *viii*
Abbreviations *xi*

1 Cricket in Barbados: The Context 1

2 The Lodge School: Cradle of Cricket in Barbados 36

3 The Overwhelming Influence of Harrison College 72

4 The Role of Combermere School 106

5 Epilogue: *Quo Vadis?* 146

Select Bibliography 163

Index 171

Illustrations

Page no.

2 Horace Deighton, headmaster of Harrison College, 1872–1905
13 Frank M. King (1926–90), perhaps the first true Barbadian cricket professional
23 George N. Francis (1897–1942), who was selected only four times for Barbados
24 George Challenor (1888–1947), the father of modern Barbadian batsmanship
26 The 'Three Terrible Ws' who dominated West Indies cricket from 1945 to 1960
27 Gordon Greenidge, the finest of all Barbadian opening batsmen
28 Sir Garfield Sobers, the greatest cricketer of them all
31 Charles Griffith, who terrorized batsmen during the 1960s
40 Clifford Goodman (1869–1911), one of the world's best bowlers in the 1890s
41 Percy Goodman (1874–1935), the first great Barbadian batting hero
44 'Tim' Tarilton (1885–1953), held the Barbadian record (1,885 runs) for many years
49 Leslie Arthur 'Bessie' Walcott (1894–1984), easily the most famous of all Barbadian cricket masters
51 John Goddard (1919–87), the outstanding Lodge School athlete of the 1930s
52 'Charlie' Taylor, one of the most generous of the Lodge's benefactors
53 The Lodge School XI, 1936–37
55 The Lodge School XI, 1944–45
57 Roy Edwin Marshall (1930–92), the Lodge School star of the 1940s
59 The Lodge School XI, 1956–57
61 David Allan, the finest wicketkeeper thus far produced by the Lodge
75 Arthur Somers Cocks (1870–1923), a source of inspiration to hundreds of Harrisonians
77 Sir H.B.G. Austin (1877–1943), the father of West Indies cricket
81 'Snuffie' Browne (1890–1964), one of the leading West Indian cricketers during the 1920s

83 The Harrison College XI, 1930–31
89 Thomas Noel Peirce (1916–88), a great Barbadian captain and administrator
94 The Harrison College XI (1946–47)
96 'Cammie' Smith, who once struck a whirlwind 300 against Police
97 Robin Bynoe who should have played more often for the West Indies
98 David Holford, the most successful of all Barbadian captains
108 Revd A.E. Armstrong (1881–1963), who promoted cricket and athletics at Combermere
109 Stanton O'C. Gittens (1911–94), who played on six championship teams
119 Herman Griffith (1893–1980), Empire's heart and soul for more than 50 years
116 The Combermere School XI, 1927–28
118 'Mannie' Martindale (1909–72), the fastest bowler of his generation
122 The Combermere School XI, BCA first division champions, 1940–41
125 Sir Frank Worrell (1924–67), the greatest Combermerian of them all
128 Denis Atkinson who earned a memorable draw by the sweat of his brow
131 Rawle Brancker who toured England with the West Indies in 1966
133 Wes Hall, the fastest bowler in the world during the 1960s
134 'Peter' Lashley, who has masterminded the Instant Money Game since 1978
149 The 1957 West Indies Cricket team in England
152 Desmond Haynes who exceeded 7,000 runs in Test cricket
159 Joel Garner, the greatest star produced by Foundation School

Preface

This book is the natural offspring of three articles published recently in *Cricket Lore* on the contribution to Barbadian cricket made by the three oldest and most important secondary schools in that island. These essays have been updated and considerably expanded. The chapter on Combermere is, in large part, a repetition of the text for the magazine on Combermerian cricket which that school had planned to publish (but eventually did not) as part of the celebrations of its three-hundredth anniversary in 1995. A lengthy chapter is presented here on cricket in Barbados to provide a broader context for those chapters on Combermere, Harrison College and the Lodge School. This is, in essence, a reworking of items already published in *Banja: A Magazine of Barbadian Life & Culture* and the *Canadian Journal of History*. The epilogue is mainly an attempt to suggest ways in which the rich cricketing tradition in Barbados may be maintained.

Altogether, the story of Barbadian cricket remains an epic. I still marvel at the thought that such a small community could have done so well in any discipline for such a long time, notwithstanding its relative paucity of men and money. On the cricket field, Barbados could have challenged any nation on even terms for most of the period since World War II. Few other communities can make that boast. Perhaps New South Wales during the 1950s might have done reasonably well against the full might of England or even the combined remainder of Australia. In that same decade, too, Surrey, under Stuart Surridge and Peter May, could probably have done the same. But neither of those teams remained so consistently powerful for more than a decade. They suffered the normal consequences of periodic reconstruction. Barbados always seemed capable of replacing its veteran stars with younger lions, eager to demonstrate their equality with the rest of the world.

This ability to reconstruct without apparently breaking stride has recently been copied by the West Indian Test teams which did not lose a major series between 1980 and 1995. In one glorious spell of 19 years (1976 to 1995), the West Indies played unbeaten with the exception of one brief and unhappy visit to New Zealand. From the time that first-class cricket was introduced to the Caribbean in 1865, Barbados has been a dominant force and its periods of slump have been brief and infrequent. It is this sociological miracle that has led scholars such as Professor Hilary Beckles and Dr Brian Stoddart in recent years to examine Barbadian society and culture very closely. The search for explanations of the cricket cult has led naturally to the academic institutions and it is almost impossible to write about Barbadian cricket without somehow reflecting on Barbadian education. This examination of the nurseries, then, is as natural and as important as a scrutiny of the sport itself. It adds to common knowledge a considerable store of details and statistics about Barbadian cricketers in the hope of providing concrete data to form the basis of further sociological analysis by other scholars.

The Cricket Nurseries of Colonial Barbados is written with the firm belief that sociology and history must, to a considerable degree, be grounded on simple arithmetic. It is not enough to declare that three Barbadian schools wielded a disproportionate influence in the days before independence. Their influence can to some extent be quantified and thus be more precisely evaluated. This book is also intended to fill a gap in West Indian cricket literature. Although the story of Barbadian cricket is so exceptional, it has never really been told in sufficient detail. Apart from Bruce Hamilton's pioneering *Cricket in Barbados*, written more than 50 years ago, one can point only to the *100 Years of Organised Cricket in Barbados 1892–1992*, produced by the Barbados Cricket Association as part of its centenary celebrations. These are the only two books dealing exclusively thus far with the miracle that is cricket in Barbados. There are, of course, a number of excellent articles on the subject, and those by Stoddart are certainly worthy of special mention, but surely this wonderful epic deserves much more than that.

Most of the factual cricket details presented here have been gleaned from the files of the *Combermerian*, the *Harrisonian* and the *Lodge School Record*. These school magazines were published with great regularity in former times, but have been much scarcer since the 1960s. The prohibitive cost of publication has limited the schools to a few scattered editions over the past 35 years or so. The dearth of more recent news is reflected in the chapters themselves, which tend to become much more sweeping and general when dealing with the age of independence. Curiously, the same period (1966 to the present) is marked by a notable decline in the standard of cricket at these schools. This phenomenon defies adequate explanation. The most that can be said, for the moment, is that all the secondary schools are now concentrating on a more general physical education programme and the singular focus on cricket has more or less disappeared. This, of course, is not as tragic as some commentators would like to suggest. It is time that young Barbadians became more proficient in athletics, basketball, field hockey, golf, soccer, swimming and tennis. The society must understand, however, that such proficiency in other sports can only be purchased at a price. The energy previously devoted to cricket must now be more evenly dissipated. In any case, most sporting fortunes are cyclical. Periods of boom and slump typically alternate. If the state of Barbadian cricket is not now as healthy as it once was, there is always the chance that it will be so again in the near future.

The writing of any book is impossible without the accumulation of debts. This study has depended to a large extent on the encouragement and cooperation of the staff of the Barbados National Archives and the headteachers of Combermere, Harrison and the Lodge. Mr David Williams, especially, was most helpful in the search for archival materials in Black Rock, St Michael. Messrs Charles Alleyne, Ronald Hughes and Patrick Frost were kind enough to review earlier drafts of some of the chapters and to offer constructive criticisms. Mr Richard Hill, editor of *Cricket Lore*, and Mr Clive W. Porter, editor of the *Journal of the Cricket Society*, readily granted permission to reproduce several passages previously published by them. For all of these kindnesses I am very grateful. Grants from the Social Sciences and Humanities Research Council of Canada and from the University of Manitoba also provided assistance of a more tangible sort.

Winnipeg, Canada
July 1997

Abbreviations

AA	Arrow of Achievement
BBC	British Broadcasting Corporation
BCCC	Barbados Cricket Challenge Cup
BCA	Barbados Cricket Association
BCL	Barbados Cricket League
BET	Barbados External Telecommunications
BLP	Barbados Labour Party
BWU	Barbados Workers' Union
CBE	Commander of the Order of the British Empire
CCR	Centre for Cricket Research
CIBC	Canadian Imperial Bank of Commerce
CLICO	Colonial Life Insurance Company
DLP	Democratic Labour Party
GSC	Garrison Sports Club
GSM	Gold Crown of Merit
ICC	International Cricket Council
IMG	Instant Money Game
LCC	London County Council
MCC	Marylebone Cricket Club
NBA	National Basketball Association
OBE	Officer of the Order of the British Empire
ODI	One-Day International
QRC	Queen's Royal College
UWI	University of the West Indies
WICBC	West Indies Cricket Board of Control
YMPC	Young Men's Progressive Club

1

Cricket in Barbados

The Context

Barbados has long been world famous for its cricket. It is the one area in which this small island has held its own against the mightiest of neighbours. Cricket fans and historical sociologists have marvelled at the fact that a nation of roughly 265,000 souls, occupying an area no more than 430 km^2 (166 square miles), has been capable of playing this game better than the Englishmen and the Australians who were the first to modernize it. This extraordinary phenomenon sprang from the fact that Barbadians, from as early as the nineteenth century, adopted cricket as their peculiar national symbol. Cricket gradually became more important to them than literature or the arts. The sport, to this day, means much more to them than does soccer to the Brazilians or curling to the Scots. Amazing proficiency on the cricket field has thus become the most vital feature of the Barbadian identity.[1]

This cricketing craze owes much to the soldiers, priests, politicians and educators who left England in the nineteenth century with the view of civilizing the far-flung empire. They equated the spread of civilization with the adoption of Christianity, an appreciation for the classics, and the growth of cricket – the famous three Cs, as they have often been called. Thus cricket, like commerce, followed the British flag to most quarters of the globe. This "civilizing" mission was eminently successful in places as far apart as Australia, India, New Zealand and the West Indies.[2] In the Caribbean, it was the educators who did most to establish the cult of cricket and it was an incredibly long list of Barbadian headmasters who virtually transformed the three leading secondary schools (Combermere, Harrison College and the Lodge) into cricket factories during the last century before independence (1966).[3]

From as early as the 1860s the secondary schools and churches in Barbados deliberately began to use cricket as a socializing and civilizing agent. In those days the schools were dominated by headmasters who had come from Victorian Britain steeped in the public school ethos which then placed great store on team sports. Priests, such as Revd Theodore Clarke, Revd S. Farr, Revd T. Lyall Speed, Revd T. Watts and Revd W.T. Webb, combined with scholars, such as William Burslem, Horace Deighton and Charles Tracey, to lay very firm cricketing foundations in late Victorian Barbados.[4]

THE INFLUENCE OF HORACE DEIGHTON

Among such educators, by far the most important was Deighton, headmaster of Harrison College from 1872 to 1905, who made cricket an integral feature of the curriculum and exalted it as a prime medium for the inculcation of all the requisite civic virtues. Convinced that there was a direct link between mental acuity and physical fitness, Deighton firmly believed that there was no possibility of a strong mind being accompanied by a feeble body. He himself was a mathematics graduate from Oxford, where he had shone as a cricketer, athlete and oarsman. He continued to play cricket himself, taking part in games between the masters and the boys and attending with his immediate family most of the sporting fixtures. In 1882, he inaugurated the Annual Past vs Present match and in the 1890s played a leading role in the establishment of the Barbados Cricket Challenge Cup (BCCC) Committee. The longest serving (and perhaps the most influential) headmaster of Harrison College, Deighton did not retire from that post until he had reached the ripe age of 75.[5]

Horace Deighton, headmaster of Harrison College, 1872–1905

Deighton deliberately attempted to transform Harrison College into a replica of an English public school. He introduced many of the practices then in vogue at Eton and Harrow, including the publication of a regular school magazine. *The Harrisonian* thus came into being during his tenure as headmaster. He also succeeded in making Harrison College a very successful cricket, soccer and athletics institution. Under him, the school became one of the most important cricket nurseries in the entire world. During his 33 years at that school, literally hundreds of fine cricketers received their grounding in the game under his direction. Deighton personally had much to do with the careers of such fine cricketers as Francis Gardiner Austin, H.B.G. (later Sir Harold) Austin, John Gardiner Austin, Clyde Keith Bancroft, Howell Wood Barnes, Alfred Browne, Clement Browne, Chester Browne, C.R. 'Snuffie' Browne, George Challenor, Carleton Howell Clarke, Hallam Cole, G.B.Y. 'Gussie' Cox, G.A. (later Sir Gerald Aubrey) Goodman, Ernest Hinkson and Stephen Rudder.

But Deighton's influence did not end here. Several of his students went on to become teachers and headmasters in Barbadian schools where they continued to spread the cricketing gospel that he had done so much to establish. It seems clear, in fact, that the three leading secondary schools made by far the most significant contribution to the development of the cricket cult in Barbados. In spreading the gospel of athleticism, they studiously copied the approach and methods of the leading public schools of Victorian Britain. The majority of the latter had put enormous store on physical education. In an age dominated by muscular Christianity and social Darwinism, British teachers and parents had stressed the importance of games in the development of character. Hence playing-fields, gymnasia and swimming pools had gradually become more important to them than class rooms and curricula.[6] The Victorians had seen games not only as a means of strengthening the body but also of teaching moral and spiritual values. They had consequently glorified play and transformed it into work largely because their Puritan ethics had devalued relaxation. To the Victorians, recreation never meant fun and games. It meant the constructive regeneration of mind and body. As a result, such sports as cricket, soccer and rowing became vital features of the public school curricula. The universities also became involved in perpetuating the games ethic, and their graduates eventually disseminated muscular Christian ideas all over the empire.[7]

The Triumph of Muscular Christianity

As some of these graduates and alumni migrated to Barbados, they established cricket clubs and encouraged Barbadian youths to play the game. The alumni of Barbadian schools behaved in exactly the same manner. It was the enthusiasm displayed by the Lodge School and Harrison College alumni especially which ultimately produced regular and organized cricket in the island. Most of the founders of the new cricket clubs were Old Lodge Boys and Old Harrisonians and it was they who established the BCCC in 1892 and administered it for more than 40 years. The alumni of the three élite schools eventually founded the Barbados Cricket Association (BCA) in 1933 and made it work far more successfully than the vast majority of cricket leagues and associations elsewhere.[8] And the Barbados Cricket League (BCL), established in 1937, was the brainchild of a handful of Old Combermerians.[9] It was some of the same Old Combermerians, too, who had founded Empire in 1914.[10]

The significance of such early pioneers of the cricket cult as Burslem, Deighton and Tracey, lay not only in the fact that they popularized cricket. They also produced and reproduced several generations of scholar–athletes who kept the cricket craze alive long after they themselves had died. For more than a century after its emergence as a first-grade secondary school in the late 1870s, Harrison College was dominated by muscular Christians who continued to preach Deighton's message, almost literally in Deighton's own words. There is not much difference, for instance, in the Speech Day Addresses delivered by Deighton in his last days and those given, say, by Albert Williams, the first non-white headmaster of Harrison College, during the 1970s. Both Deighton and Williams, themselves scholar–athletes, devoted considerable space to sports in their annual speeches and both were convinced that the achievements of their boys on the cricket field were a sound reflection of the physical, spiritual and mental health of their school. They therefore encouraged all the lads to play cricket and urged their parents to make it possible for the boys to do so. It did not matter that Williams was addressing a totally different audience in a vastly different sociocultural context.[11]

Deighton appointed scholar–athletes like himself to teach at Harrison College. He considered it just as important for his appointees to be well grounded in the classics as to be endowed with athletic skills. The most famous example in this regard was Arthur Somers Cocks, another Oxford graduate, who was an excellent athlete and cricketer. Deighton appointed him in 1892 and he spent his last 31 years in Barbados making an incalculable contribution to Barbadian cricket and soccer. Settling down comfortably in his adopted country, Somers Cocks married one of Deighton's daughters and devoted the rest of his life to the cause of Harrison College. In due course, he succeeded to the headship in 1922 and steered the good ship Harrison in much the same direction and manner that Deighton had steered it. Somers Cocks, who captured 53 wickets in his 10 matches for Barbados during 1894–1902, was one of the best new-ball bowlers in the

Caribbean at the turn of the century. Not surprisingly, he inspired a host of Harrisonians to play the game.[12]

To appreciate fully the pervasive influence of men like Deighton and Somers Cocks, one must also bear in mind that many of the most famous headmasters in the history of Barbadian education were trained at Harrison College when these two educators were there. Gussie Cox, for instance, was a Harrison College pupil in Deighton's time. He returned to teach at his alma mater after graduating with a classics degree from Codrington College in the early 1890s. After an association with Harrison that amounted to more than 30 years, he took his classical and cricketing skills to Combermere, where he served as headmaster from 1926 to 1934. Gussie remains one of the most celebrated scholar–athletes in Barbadian legend and history. He left a huge imprint on both Harrison College and Combermere, contributing enormously to the development of cricket at those institutions.[13] In their prime, Cox and Somers Cocks made Harrison College a very competitive team in both cricket and soccer in Barbados.

The case of Oliver DeCourcey Emtage, perhaps the greatest headmaster in the history of the Lodge School, is similar. He, too, was a Deighton product who preached the cricketing gospel at two Barbadian schools and ensured that the game prospered at the Lodge during his long reign there from 1898 to 1931. All of his successors at that school, from 1932 to the 1980s, had either been trained by him or by Deighton or by tutors who had themselves been trained by one or by both of them. The headmasters of the Lodge School from 1946 to 1985, in fact, were all notable scholar–athletes who tried their utmost to keep the cult of cricket alive. W.A. Farmer, Arthur Ralph Vernon Newsam, P.McD. Crichlow and C.E. Aurelius Smith were all products of the system that Deighton and Emtage had securely set in place. The incomparable Farmer, indeed, was one of the greatest talents in the history of Barbadian athletics.[14]

Revd T. Lyall Speed, who administered Combermere School from 1879 to 1896, had been, like Gussie Cox and Somers Cocks, a Deighton appointee at Harrison College for some years. He, too, was a scholar–athlete, who had gained selection to the very first team to represent Barbados in intercolonial cricket. He and Deighton, in fact, played exciting cricket together for Harrison against the Officers of the 35th Regiment in 1876.[15] He naturally took his cricketing interests to Combermere and ensured that the game took very hearty root there.[16] His immediate successor (1897–1925) was G.B.R. Burton, an Old Harrisonian trained by Deighton, who preached the gospel of muscular Christianity even though he himself had never been a good athlete.[17] Gussie Cox's successor as headmaster of Combermere was Revd Arthur Evelyn Armstrong, another Deighton product, who played a great deal of club cricket in his youth (for Pickwick and St Ann's) and saw no reason to discourage Combermerians from participating in that sport. In fact, it was during Armstrong's headship (1934–46) that his school enjoyed its greatest athletic triumphs. Combermere not only won the BCA first division title in 1940–41 but won four inter-school athletic championships between 1936 and 1940.[18] An important member of Armstrong's staff was Stanton O'Connor Gittens, another Old Harrisonian scholar–athlete, who played cricket and soccer for Barbados and eventually became headmaster of Combermere in 1961. Over the mild objections of his own governing body, Armstrong also appointed J.E. Derek Sealy, a West Indian Test player, to the Combermere staff for the express purpose of bolstering the school's cricket programme during the 1930s.[19] When Sealy migrated to Trinidad in the early 1940s, Armstrong proceeded to replace him with Harold Gittens Brewster, one of the most famous athletes ever to attend Combermere.

The Cricket Cult Firmly Established

It was educators such as Armstrong, Deighton, Emtage and Speed who trained those Barbadian cricketers who desperately wished to continue playing the game following their departure from school. The alumni then took cricket with them, as an essential ingredient in their cultural and social baggage, wherever they went in their adulthood. Not surprisingly, therefore, the cricket cult has held the imagination of all Barbadians from Deighton's day to this. It has spread from the churches and the schools to the civil service, the courts of law and business firms. The language of commerce, politics, and even religion is dominated by cricket metaphors, similes and allusions. All the boys are encouraged to play the game in the firm belief that it will make them better Christian gentlemen and more loyal Barbadian citizens. When Test matches are being played in the island, half holidays are routinely declared by all sectors within the work place, and headteachers readily curtail the hours of study to allow both their students and themselves to watch Barbadian heroes perform in the greatest sporting arena of all. An exciting Test match invariably brings all other business to a standstill in Barbados. No other activity has quite succeeded in galvanizing this community in such a hypnotic fashion.

The leading Barbadian heroes are cricketers past and present. Cricket triumphs are the crux and essence of Barbadian legend. George Challenor, dead since 1947, lives on triumphantly in the collective memory; while the image of Sir Grantley Adams, the great politician who survived until 1971, has already begun to fade. The idols of the present generation are Sir Garfield Sobers, Wesley Hall, Malcolm Marshall, Joel Garner, Gordon Greenidge and Desmond Haynes; and the more mature Barbadians have not yet forgotten the marvellous exploits of the three 'Terrible' Ws, who, in their own individual ways, gave such artistic expression to Barbadian independence and ingenuity in the last days of colonialism. The elderly still speak in awe of the exploits of 'Mannie' Martindale and 'Foffie' Williams.

The primacy of cricket is little short of a miracle, since the society has also had the choice of playing a much simpler and cheaper game like soccer. But soccer never quite achieved the mass appeal over Barbadians as it did in other developing communities in the New World. Perhaps this was due to soccer's image in Britain itself during the late Victorian age. Snobbish middle class Englishmen considered it the working man's game; and it was snobbish middle class Victorians who went forth to preach the gospel of cricket and the classics to the colonists. They considered it more fashionable to play cricket which had a richer and more distinguished heritage than soccer. The latter sport, after all, was really a recent product of the Industrial Revolution and its first official rules dated back only to the 1860s. In any case, soccer already had a reputation for evoking emotional and violent excesses on the part of fans and spectators as well as players.[20]

THE EARLY CRICKET CLUBS

Cricket, in fact, established itself as the main form of Barbadian recreation after the abolition of slavery, even before the introduction of Association football in Britain. Clubs sprang up, mainly around the British soldiers, who manned the Garrison in the Drill Hall and encouraged the white natives to participate. Such early clubs as St Ann's and St Michael's, which existed during the first half of the nineteenth century, did not survive very long; nor did Belleville, which rose and fell during the 1890s; but most of the Barbadian cricket clubs established in the second half of the nineteenth century (like Leeward, Pickwick, Spartan, Wanderers and Windward) most certainly did.[21] They have remained in existence to this day.

When these cricket clubs first appeared, they naturally reflected the environment in which they were born. Barbadian society, during the Victorian age, was grotesquely racist and snobbish. Class and complexion lay at the very base of Barbadian ethical values. As they were then inextricably linked, fine distinctions were routinely made between the slightest gradations of colour. Thus the socio-economic pyramid descended from lily white, through yellowish-brown, to jet black.[22]

The Barbadian society was then dominated by a small minority of wealthy planters and businessmen. They controlled in equal measure the political machinery, the schools, the police and legal systems, the church, the newspapers, the vestries, the sugar industry and sport. Cricket in nineteenth century Barbados mirrored the interests and values of this élite. This was evident even in the manner in which the annual seasons were arranged. In accordance with the needs of the sugar plantocracy, the season had to begin in July and end in February and thus, illogically, to coincide with the worst possible weather. This quirk in the schedule, however, seems to have produced some positive results. It taught Barbadian cricketers how to adjust to sticky wickets and thus contributed materially to the production of some of the finest batsmen in the entire world during the period 1890–1970.

Not surprisingly, the early cricket clubs followed traditional patterns. They were established to serve the interests and aspirations of a select few. Consequently, all of the earliest cricket clubs in the island were white. Wanderers, founded in 1877, was deliberately intended to cater to the wealthiest members of the community. It therefore included merchants, planters and the most successful lawyers and doctors (who had also bought several acres of land). Its membership was comprised of such influential merchants as the Arthurs, Austins, Brydens, Carringtons, Challenors, Collymores and DaCostas. Planters like the Hinksons, Inces, Masons, Piles and Skeetes gravitated towards that club. So too did such legal luminaries as the Chandlers and Jackmans. Successful solicitors, such as the Evelyns, and prominent doctors, such as John Hutson, did likewise.[23]

Thanks to the efforts of Thomas Birt Evelyn, a local solicitor with important connections, Wanderers was able to use a portion of the Bay Estate as its headquarters. Evelyn was not the owner of this estate; he was simply serving as the agent for the absentee landlord. But despite its enormous wealth and influence, Wanderers did not legally possess its own playing fields until it moved from the Bay Land to Dayrells Road in 1952. At the Bay, it boasted only a small pavilion and never erected proper boundaries or fences. The villagers' houses surrounded the boundary, especially on the western and southern flanks, and their windows were constantly in danger of being damaged by hard-hit balls. Slightly more fortunate were those on the eastern and northern fringes, even though houses on Beckles Road and Culloden Road were occasionally struck. Still, Wanderers long remained one of the most exclusive of all West Indian clubs.[24]

Wanderers versus Pickwick

Wanderers, then, represented money and means. It excluded successful whites, such as the Tariltons, for instance, who sprang from clerical or bureaucratic roots. But it welcomed individuals who had just arrived from England. This seemed to give William Bowring, for example, a more distinctive stamp of gentility. Horace Deighton and Arthur Somers Cocks, two Englishmen on the Harrison College staff, also gained admission, which might otherwise have been difficult had they been white Barbadian natives. They were certainly neither wealthy planters nor merchants. So the emphasis was on colour and class, and the general opinion then was that the Englishman born and bred in the 'Mother Country' was naturally whiter than his Barbadian counterpart. This was the determining boundary between Wanderers and Pickwick, another white club, founded in 1882.

Pickwick was a definite response to the exclusivity of the Wanderers clique. With no possibility of admission into the latter organization, middle class whites (who had learnt their cricket on the playing fields of Harrison and the Lodge) now had to establish a cricket club of their own. Smaller planters and merchants, like the Bancrofts, Goddards, Goodmans and Hoads, found a haven in Pickwick which also provided a refuge for white teachers, priests, plantation managers and foremen, accountants and civil servants. With most of the clerical and bureaucratic skills (as provided by the Barclays, Brownes and Coles) moving in the direction of this club, it soon found itself much better administered than the wealthier Wanderers. Representing the best clerical and managerial minds in the country, Pickwick steadily emerged as the administrative leaders of Barbadian cricket. Thus, while Wanderers remained too long in the small confines of the pasture on the Bay Estate, Pickwick established itself early in the Fontabelle district at the spacious Kensington Oval which shortly became the headquarters of cricket in Barbados, thanks in the main to the foresight of three families in particular: the Goodmans, Hoads and Goddards. From the 1890s onwards, all first-class cricket matches in Barbados took place at Kensington. The administration of Wanderers remained so chaotic, in fact, that H.B.G. Austin often found himself paying the club's bills out of his own pocket while he was serving as its president during the first quarter of the twentieth century.[25]

Class antagonisms had much to do with the bitter rivalry which at once developed between Pickwick and Wanderers. They waged an epic civil war for about 70 or 80 years until it became illegal to exclude members from admission on the basis of class or colour, or both. The new laws, in fact, shattered the foundations of these two old clubs at one blow. After 1960, the Pickwick–Wanderers confrontations consequently lost a good deal of their original intensity. But, in the early days, these matches invariably drew large and excited crowds both to Kensington and the Bay. Curiously, while the gladiators were uniformly white, the majority of the boisterous spectators were black. The local residents cheered unabashedly for their team, even though they could have entertained no hope of ever representing it.[26] They simply looked upon the club as an important village institution which represented *them*.

As both Pickwick and Wanderers were meant to serve an urban clientele, Leeward and Windward soon had to be created to meet the needs of rural whites. They were formed in the early 1890s and joined the Challenge Cup competition in 1893. Leeward established its headquarters at Hannay's in St Lucy in the far north, while for many years Windward occupied the Codrington College grounds in St John. They played the game in a lighthearted spirit and became famous for their hospitality.[27] As late as the 1950s, schoolboys anxiously looked forward to the excursions to these two country grounds. They were invariably well fed and generously treated.

THE ADVENT OF ORGANIZED CLUB CRICKET

During the 1880s and early 1890s, the Alleyne School, Codrington College, Combermere School, the military Garrison, Harrison College, the Lodge School, Pickwick, the Pilgrim School, St Andrews, St Ann's, St Michael's and Wanderers played frequently among themselves. But the sport lacked organization until the BCCC was established. This was the brainchild of Douglas Ince, the Wanderers captain, who thought that the triangular tournament, staged at the Bay Estate Grounds in 1891 between Barbados, Demerara (later known as British Guiana) and Trinidad, might have been better organized had there been some kind of central administration in Bridgetown. Hence the emergence of the notion of a Barbados Challenge Cup committee to formalize the cricket competition that had previously been regular but haphazard. The BCCC was initially led by such cricketers and former players as Horace Deighton, Herbert Emtage, Aubrey Goodman, Dr John Hutson (its first chairman), and F.B. Smith (who had the distinction of captaining the first team ever to represent Barbados in 1865). It was this committee which arranged the first regular season during 1892–93 and promulgated the first set of rules governing organized cricket in the island.[28]

A regular competition thus came into being with Belleville, Codrington College, the Garrison, Harrison College, the Lodge School, Pickwick and Wanderers playing one-day games each Saturday roughly from July to February. Belleville, Codrington College and the Garrison withdrew from the competition in 1893 and were replaced by such new teams as Leeward, Spartan and Windward. While the Belleville and Codrington clubs remained in oblivion thereafter, Garrison (or Regiment) reappeared periodically, depending on the availability of cricketers among the English soldiers stationed on the island. However, the Garrison Sports Club (GSC) which flourished in the 1940s and actually won the first division title in 1947 before disappearing altogether, was a product of World War II, drawing its members from the Barbados Regiment, a part of the South Caribbean Force.[29]

As the Challenge Cup competition was then geared specifically to meet the needs of the small white minority of the island's population, everything was done to exclude working class blacks. Thus one of the BCCC's laws explicitly debarred 'professionals' from participation, which automatically excluded groundsmen and manual labourers. For much too long, unfortunately, the competition was governed by considerations of class and colour. Racial and social barriers remained solidly in place until they began to break down under the pervasive influence of the anti-discrimination laws which were enacted by the Grantley Adams government in 1957.[30] Adams, who was later granted a knighthood, was the first premier of Barbados before becoming the first (and only) prime minister of the West Indian Federation (1958–62). He had himself been a good wicketkeeper/batsman for Spartan and Barbados during the 1920s.[31]

The Establishment of Spartan

Spartan was the first cricket club to consider the interests of middle class blacks in Barbados. It came into being in 1893, thanks to the initiative of such remarkable coloured men as Sir Conrad Reeves, J. Challenor Lynch, and the Brownes, Clairmontes, Pilgrims, Rudders and Stroudes. Men like Graham Trent Cumberbatch, who was assistant inspector of schools in the 1890s, helped to establish Spartan because there was no possibility of their entry into Pickwick. But Spartan itself proved no less snobbish than the white clubs of that era. Many bourgeois members refused to admit less fortunate blacks and there was considerable resistance to the lobby which forced Delmont Hinds upon the others in 1899. Those liberals who wanted to admit Herman Griffith in 1913 thus found the task a lot more difficult.[32]

Avowedly representing middle class blacks and creoles, Spartan played its matches on the small Belleville ground in St Michael. Its best player was George Learmond, an Old Combermerian, who eventually achieved the unique distinction of playing intercolonial cricket for three Caribbean territories. The Spartan decision to elect Learmond its first captain was a most instructive one. In the first place, Learmond was only 18 years old, while his colleagues were much more experienced. Secondly, he was a foreigner. He had come to Barbados from Demerara to profit from the more practical curriculum which Combermere was then offering. Learmond was also white. Apparently, the conservative Spartan membership could not yet conceive of the radical notion of 'black captaincy'.[33]

The early history of Spartan is dwarfed by the notorious 'Fitz Lily affair' which tells a great deal about late Victorian attitudes in Barbados. Delmont Cameron St Clair Hinds, then generally known as 'Fitz Lily', had worked as a Pickwick groundsman while serving his apprenticeship as a painter in his youth. He was still only 19 years old in 1899. By the regulations then in vogue he was ineligible to participate in the Cricket Cup competition as the committee considered him a 'professional'. The Challenge Cup Committee, in fact, branded as 'professionals' all groundsmen, as well as other black manual labourers, in a deliberate attempt to restrict the sport mainly to white 'gentlemen'. Hinds was clearly one of the best cricketers in the Caribbean at that time and naturally he wanted to further his cricket career. He therefore left his job at Kensington and applied for admission to Spartan. The Spartan membership was much divided over the issue but eventually some remarkable lobbying brought the great Fitz Lily into the fold.[34]

Hinds' election to Spartan provoked an incredible uproar. The majority of the Pickwick and Windward cricketers refused outright to play against him and even some of the Spartan members could not be persuaded to play *with* him. This kind of racism and snobbery destroyed the whole of the 1899–1900 season. The net result was that Spartan actually won the first division title for the first time that year because its major opponents often took the field without their key players. The cup committee thereupon strengthened its rules to prevent any repetition of what many considered to have been chicanery on the part of the Spartan club. The new regulations made it impossible after 1900 for former groundsmen or 'professionals' to take part in the Challenge Cup competition. It did not matter, of course, that there was not a single professional cricketer (as the term was then used in England) in Barbados at that time. Barbadian groundsmen were never in the same category as the so-called ground staff, employed by the

Marylebone Cricket Club (MCC) at Lord's. The first really professional cricketer in Barbados was probably Frank McD. King, a fiery fast bowler, who was hired as head groundsman by Major Cecil Noott, the Combermere headmaster, for the express purpose of coaching cricket at the school and playing in the BCA first division with the Combermerians during the 1950s.

Frank M. King, (1926–90): perhaps the first true Barbadian cricket professional

In all fairness, however, it has to be said that some white liberals, such as the Goodmans, Hoads, A.B. St Hill and George Walton, objected to the policy of segregation and tried their best to remove the barriers between Pickwick and the groundsmen. Attempting to undo some of the mischief caused by the 'Fitz Lily affair', Clifford Goodman arranged a friendly match between Pickwick and Fenwick (the most famous working class cricket club of the era) in November 1899. In his own team he also included two blacks, Stephen Rudder and G.T. Cumberbatch from Spartan. For this he received fulsome praise from another white liberal, the editor of the *Barbados Globe*, who remarked that the "stubborn refusal of certain members of the Pickwick to take part in any game in which poor coloured men are engaged is a persistent exhibition of artificial greatness that finds no place where intelligence encamps". He consequently found Goodman's determination to change this attitude most praiseworthy.[36] Clifford's elder brother, Aubrey, then president of the Pickwick Cricket Club, also made an impassioned plea to his colleagues in 1900 for sportsmanship and fair play, insisting that "cricket should be played without regard to class, colour or creed".[37] His plea apparently fell upon deaf ears since Clifford, who had led the club with great success for six years, was promptly replaced by the more conservative Clement Browne.

The Barbadian daily newspapers at the turn of the century all appeared more progressive in their racial attitudes than the cricket establishment. In 1896, for instance, the *Advocate* was seriously suggesting that W.T. Burton should be selected to represent Barbados against the English touring teams of 1896–97 in the same way that Trinidad had chosen J. 'Float' Woods to play for them against the Slade Lucas XI in 1895, and the *Globe* gave consistent support to Hinds and Spartan during the stormy campaign of 1899–1900.[38] Fenwick, consisting entirely of very poor working men, was by far the most powerful team in the colony for most of period 1895–1905 but none of its matches against the BCCC clubs were regarded as official. Even when it was clear, in 1900, that Hinds and William Shepherd were the finest cricketers in Barbados, they were both excluded from the team that toured Trinidad and won the intercolonial championship that year.[39] This was all the more regrettable since Hinds had just starred in regular BCCC competition. These were not decisions with which the local press agreed, although white men still controlled the media. And it was in vain that the editor of the *Advocate* pleaded in 1903 for a more intelligent utilization of the island's cricket resources. He was very excited by the introduction of a new cricket league for manual labourers, especially since "the Island has never been in a worse position for representative cricketers". He strongly urged the Challenge Cup committee to tap into Barbadian working class talent as other Caribbean colonies had already begun to do.[40]

The Exclusion of Lower Class Blacks

The stringent rules upon which the more reactionary BCCC so long insisted reflected the harsh realities of life in Barbados during the late Victorian period. The island was then dominated by the white minority who retained very strict laws in order to preserve their social, political and economic hegemony. Thus blacks were deliberately excluded as much as possible from politics through the retention of an absurdly high franchise qualification, from economic empowerment through the simple policy of high interest rates and restricted credit, and from organized cricket through the operation of an incredibly absurd definition of amateurism. As late as 1938, among an estimated total population of 193,082 there were only 6,381 Barbadian voters, the vast majority of whom were white.[41]

The result of all of this was that, at the turn of the century (and for several decades thereafter), very few Barbadian blacks had the right to vote in any kind of elections and very few of them had full access to organized cricket. Even so great a cricketer as George Nathaniel Francis, one of the finest fast bowlers in the world during the 1920s, was never allowed to participate in BCCC or BCA competition. It was this situation that eventually drove some of the best of the black cricketers out of the island altogether. Such excellent fast bowlers, for instance, as W.T. Burton, Archie Cumberbatch and J. 'Float' Woods, sought greener pastures in Demerara, Trinidad and elsewhere. Oliver Layne and William Shepherd also migrated, as did Hinds himself in the early years of the twentieth century.[42] This situation had distressed even the white editor of the *Barbados Advocate* as early as 1897 when (in comparing the Barbadian and Trinidadian approaches) he angrily remarked that:

> [h]ad 'Archie' [Cumberbatch] been here he would not have been played against the English team. He would have been perhaps led to believe that such would be the case. He would have been trotted round to play in practice matches and as much work would have been got out of him as possible. But when the time came for the selection to be made his name would not be found among the men chosen to represent the island. And, moreover, although a professional, it would be a toss up whether the Committee would ever think of rewarding him for the time they had him working for them. In Trinidad he receives more generous treatment. His ability is openly acknowledged, and he is given the chance of proving his mettle against the great English amateurs. If then Trinidad adopts him we cannot in justice dispute their claim.[43]

Despite such overt racial discrimination and injustice, however, Barbadian blacks played cricket so well indeed that, Fenwick, the so-called 'professional' team, which included Hinds, William Jones, Oliver Layne and Shepherd, often defeated the best players from the white clubs in exhibition matches. At the turn of the century, Fenwick was definitely the most powerful cricket squad in Barbados. It was often used by the Challenge Cup committee in trial matches against Barbadian teams just before intercolonial tournaments. Early in 1899, for example, a practice match was arranged at Kensington Oval between A.B. St Hill's XI (already selected to tour Trinidad) and a team of groundsmen, led by Shepherd. The latter won easily, routing the Barbados XI for 111 and responding with 146/7. Hinds, still employed by Pickwick, scored 50 not out after taking 5 wickets for 34 runs.[44] But it was not until a local businessman, Frederick N. Martinez, subsidized the Frame Food Competition during the first decade of this century that lower income Barbadian blacks found a regular outlet for their cricketing skills. This competition gradually languished, largely due to the lack of middle class support, but in 1903 it at once attracted such clubs as Fenwick, Gleeville, Holy Trinity, Hunters, Hyde Park, Police, Printers, Quakers, Railway, Sportmans, St Martins, United, West India Regiment and Wranglers. The registration of as many as 13 teams to participate in the second season (1904) bore eloquent testimony to the degree of zeal which rural as well as urban blacks had already mustered for the sport.[46]

The Emergence of Empire

Even lower middle income blacks in those days found it difficult to participate in organized cricket. When, for example, such a fine fast bowler as Herman Griffith applied for admission into Spartan in 1913 he found the doors closed. The majority of the Spartan members considered him too poor to enter. This attitude so distressed the progressive minority, led by Chris Brathwaite, Lionel O. Gittens, Benjamin Gilkes, E. Morris and G.C. Williams, that they seceded altogether from Spartan and founded a cricket club of their own. Thus it was that Empire came into being in 1914.[47] It took two years of frantic lobbying for Empire to gain admission to the Challenge Cup competition. Its application was consistently rejected by the representatives of Pickwick and Spartan even though Harrison College and Wanderers were prepared to accept it. In 1916, when Arthur Somers Cocks was serving as chairman of the Committee of Management which considered Empire's application, he personally broke the deadlock by supporting the new club. Thus, although Empire celebrated its 75th anniversary in 1989 with much fanfare, its inaugural season in the cup competition was actually 1916–17. Occupying a small lot in Bank Hall and owning a small pavilion in keeping with its limited means, Empire came to symbolize the triumph of character and justice over wealth and snobbery. For years it regarded Spartan as its most hated enemy and its contests with that club matched the Pickwick–Wanderers rivalry in their vigour and keenness.[48]

Improvement and Expansion

For several seasons, judging from the scores, the standard of play in the early days of Barbadian first division cricket was not particularly high as the bowlers were totally dominant. Pitches were not as well prepared then as was the case later on and many of the games had to take place during the rainy season, so that one could expect wickets to be tricky about as often as they were true. This tradition of playing cricket on uncertain strips apparently helped in the development of superior batting techniques. Consequently, the best batsmen in the early history of Caribbean cricket, with the notable exception of the Jamaican George Headley, were invariably Barbadians. By far the most powerful (BCCC) club in those days was Pickwick, led by the Goodman brothers, who took their club to 12 first division titles during the first 17 years of the competition.[49]

Despite its restrictive codes, the BCCC still had to cope with the problem of expansion during the Edwardian era. The sport became so popular that a second division had to be established in 1903.[50] The existing clubs now had more members than could be accommodated in a single competition. This expansion also allowed Combermere School to enter. The school had no grounds of its own, and (in accordance with the Scheme of Government then)[51] its pupils were not permitted to compete for the Island and Barbados Scholarships or to write the higher certificate examinations. The majority of its pupils therefore had to leave school before the age of 18, while those at Harrison College and the Lodge could soldier on until they were almost 20. Still, it was everywhere agreed that Combermere, as the leading second-grade secondary school in Barbados, had to have a cricket XI. This was in keeping with the universal notion at that time that cricket, at the secondary education level, was as essential as the classics. As Combermere could not compete with the older clubs in the senior competition, the second division was thought to be its proper place. Thanks to the participation of some of its teachers, the school consistently performed well at the junior level, but it was not before the 1928–29 season that Combermere was promoted to the first division.[52]

Expansion was accompanied, almost inevitably, by improvement. The quality of the batting reached the point where matches could no longer be finished in a single Saturday. Even the decision, reached in 1896, to commence play at noon failed to produce satisfactory results.[53] It was thus decided to allot two days to first division games and to allow two full innings. As this regulation proved no more satisfactory than the first, it was shortly resolved to extend the first division matches to three Saturdays and the second division games to two. Despite these changes, the improved batting (and occasionally the weather) still produced too many draws. In fact, during the early 1920s, the batting became so strong that when Pickwick and Wanderers once played a match to a finish, to determine the first division championship, it took some six weeks to complete it. This memorable encounter, played at the Bay, lasted from 8 January to 19 February 1921. Wanderers emerged victorious after the two teams had amassed no fewer than 1,799 runs.[54]

THE BEGINNINGS OF INTERCOLONIAL COMPETITION

Barbados was not the only Caribbean territory to play cricket during the nineteenth century. The game was flourishing also in Antigua, Demerara, Grenada, Jamaica, St Vincent and Trinidad. Intercolonial tournaments, involving Barbados, Demerara and Trinidad, began as early as 1865.[55] These preliminary encounters, like so many of the later ones, were dominated by Barbados. It was not until the early 1890s that Jamaica began to take part in intercolonial cricket. That island was too isolated geographically from the other British West Indian colonies and it took too much time and money to travel there. Even as late as 1913, the captain of a touring MCC team was left to regret that his squad could not visit Jamaica, since it involved "a nine-day voyage to that island from the rest of the West Indies and such a break in the tour programme was impractical".[56] Barbadian cricketers, though, had no difficulty exchanging occasional visits with teams from Antigua, Grenada and St Vincent at the turn of the century. These friendly tournaments did much to encourage the growth of cricket in the eastern Caribbean.[57]

Visits by teams from England, beginning in 1895, also stimulated the growth of West Indian cricket. Local teams provided such stiff resistance to the early English tourists that competent critics, including P.F. (later Sir Pelham) Warner, urged the West Indies to select a composite team to tour England in 1900. Thereafter regular exchanges between English and West Indian touring teams culminated in the granting of Test match status to the West Indies in 1928. There was abundant talent in the Caribbean but the West Indians did not have the experience of playing first-class cricket on a sustained, daily basis. They were more accustomed to playing one day each week during the local season. It took some time therefore before they could make an impression on the international stage. But they were still manifestly superior to the South Africans who achieved Test match status as early as 1889. It is clear that had not the West Indians been perceived by the MCC as a 'black team', they would have been promoted many years earlier. The supreme irony here, of course, is that the majority of the West Indian cricketers who toured England in 1900 and 1906 were actually white.[58]

The Rise of the Barbados Cricket League

The flourishing of Barbadian cricket during the twentieth century is one of the epics of Caribbean sociology. Despite the various obstacles placed deliberately in their path by the BCCC and later the BCA, the local blacks continued to play the game with increasing enthusiasm and sophistication. Occasional friendly matches among themselves, after the collapse of the Frame Food Competition, were the order of the day until the Barbados Cricket League (BCL) was created by Chris Brathwaite, J. Mitchie Hewitt and J.T.C. Ramsay in the late 1930s. The basic idea behind this new league was to provide opportunities for underprivileged blacks, especially in the rural districts, to participate in organized cricket. The BCL prospered at once, immediately attracting some 20 teams and growing to about 100 within 30 years. By 1960, it had produced so many talented players that the government began to regard it as a valuable institution performing a useful community service. The BCA also invited it to field a composite team to participate in its own regular competition after having played exhibition matches against its leading stars for about two decades. The BCA–BCL game was one of the important trials each year before the final selection of the island side. The full significance of the BCL can more readily be appreciated when it is recalled that it provided several international stars with the springboard from which their illustrious careers were ultimately launched. It was the BCL which produced such heroes as Clairemont Depeiza, Charles Griffith, Vanburn Holder, Conrad Hunte, Frank King, Seymour Nurse, Garfield Sobers and Everton Weekes. It was also able to boast of having been represented at the national level by Othniel Downes, Ormond Graham and Kenneth Goddard, among a host of others.[59]

The Explosion of the Barbados Cricket Association

The emergence of the BCL is one interesting yardstick by which the growing popularity of cricket in Barbados can be measured over the past 50 or 60 years. No less revealing is the growth of the BCA itself. Established in 1933, it replaced the old cup committee and assumed control over organized cricket in Barbados from then until now. In 1951, it still catered only to 17 clubs. By 1985 this number had increased to 50, and it had also added an intermediate level to its first and second divisions. In 1996 the BCA could claim as many as 78 "affiliated clubs and school".[60] As several of these institutions have two and sometimes three teams participating simultaneously in organized cricket, this means, in effect, that on some Saturdays there are more than 200 BCA and BCL games taking place all at once in an island that is one of the smallest cricket centres in the world.

This is the basic arithmetic of Barbadian cricket. This tiny nation can boast an average of more than one club per square mile. No other community can show such total commitment to any other sport. This is enough to explain why the Barbadian cricketers have dominated the Shell Shield and Red Stripe competitions ever since their inception in 1966, why Barbadians have been so successful as cricket professionals in Australia, England, South Africa and sometimes Europe, and why the Barbadian contingent has traditionally been the major element in West

Indian Test teams. It is this kind of arithmetic that also helps to explain why the West Indian teams have been so consistently powerful during the past three or four decades.

There is some more Barbadian cricket arithmetic that is equally impressive. It concerns the BCA. This organization could attract only 99 members as late as 1947. But it could claim as many as 1,321 at 31 March 1996 after having reached an all-time peak of 1,350 during 1989–90. In 1969, its president, Eric D. Inniss, was still complaining that the BCA was attracting no more than 200 life members despite the low cost (Bd$120) of such memberships. In 1993, however, the BCA boasted as many as 463 life members and this number has since risen to 527. In 1953, the BCA's total assets were estimated at Bd$107,000. They have since swollen to more than Bd$7.5 million.[61] No other sports club or institution in the Caribbean has been so astonishingly successful since World War II. By making excellent use of such devices as the Instant Money Game (IMG), the BCA has managed to show continuing profits over the past 30 years and to make substantial additions and renovations to the Kensington Oval.[62]

The headquarters of Barbadian cricket was once a drab venue eliciting laughter and negative comment from unkind and critical visitors. It has recently been beautified and enlarged. In addition to the old Pickwick Pavilion and George Challenor Stand, there are now modern grandstands erected to honour the Three Ws, Sir Garfield Sobers, Wes Hall and Charlie Griffith, Mitchie Hewitt and Eric Inniss. The scoreboards have been enlarged and modernized and there is far more comfortable space now for both the press and the public. To accommodate the anticipated throng for the 1994 England–West Indies Test, a new stand (as yet unnamed) was erected close to the main scoreboard. The Kensington Oval is still not the most spacious or most beautiful Test arena in the Caribbean but is considerably larger and more imposing than it once was.

Something of the significance of cricket in Barbadian life may be gleaned from the fact that, even during the days of acute depression between 1930 and 1945, the BCA had to admit additional teams such as Carlton, Police and the Young Men's Progressive Club (YMPC). The strength of the game was by no means undermined by the prolonged economic slump and, like their predecessors, these new teams were consciously intended to represent specific constituencies. Carlton and YMPC were deliberately established to cater to the lower middle income whites and nearly whites, for whom there was no space in Pickwick or Wanderers. These two new clubs were intended to absorb the dozens of junior clerks in Bridgetown who had begun to take a keen interest in the game. Thus

Carlton, the brainchild of W. St Clair Hutchinson, was comprised chiefly of Edgehills, Greenidges, Hutchinsons and Marshalls, while YMPC, founded by Theorold Barnes, W.H. Carter, A.N. Jones and E.C. Queree, contained the Archers, Burkes, Clarkes, Hoyoses and Lucases.[63] While white officers, like Captain Wilfred Farmer, might have been able to find a haven in Pickwick, there was no obvious place in Barbadian cricket for the rank and file of the local constabulary, who had previously participated in the Frame Food Competition. Nor could Pickwick absorb the increasing number of lower middle income whites after 1930. Hence the emergence of so many additional clubs whose non-black members would obviously have felt uncomfortable in Empire and Spartan and who did not relish the prospect of joining the rural clubs.[64]

Ascendancy of the Blacks

This otherwise bleak period proved an important one in the history of Barbadian sport. It witnessed the emergence of a new generation of black cricketers, determined to carry on the class struggle on the cricket pitch and to make their mark in this arena in the same way that young black leaders like Grantley Adams, Chris Brathwaite, Wynter Crawford, Hugh Springer, Frank Walcott and Clennell Wickham were then doing in the fields of journalism and politics. Indeed, many of these same political leaders contributed directly to the creation and growth of the BCL and Empire as well as the Barbados Labour Party (BLP) and the Barbados Workers' Union (BWU). They clearly saw the cricket battle as essentially an element in the overall and broader social struggle. They ultimately won both the battle and the war as blacks have steadily come to dominate most areas of Barbadian life.

Then came the generation of the Three Ws, who emerged to leave an indelible imprint on all forms of West Indian cricket. When World War II ended, Frank Worrell was 21, Everton Weekes 20, and Clyde Walcott 19; but already they had established themselves as the stars of the future. Worrell, in fact, had made a magnificent triple century against Trinidad in 1944 before reaching the age of twenty. He was the youngest player (19 years, 199 days) ever to have achieved this feat.[65] Walcott had become a fixture on the Barbadian team after having made his début on his sixteenth birthday.[66] And Weekes had forced his way into the Barbados XI by batting brilliantly for Westshire in the BCL and then for GSC in the BCA.[67] Three other young players, John Lucas, Keith Walcott and C.B. 'Boogles' Williams, also showed exceptional promise at this time but were destined to be overshadowed.

Social rules, values and attitudes changed dramatically in Barbados after World War II. The radical movements of the interwar period could no longer be denied after the war effort itself had given such a substantial boost to progressive ideas. Hence the relaxing of those outdated rules governing the political franchise as well as the exercise of the right to collective bargaining. The rise of the BLP and the BWU undermined the pillars of white authority and, by 1955, ministerial government under a black premier had suddenly become a reality.

The domination of modern Barbadian cricket by blacks is in keeping with developments in the political sphere. When universal adult suffrage was introduced in 1951, the new electorate promptly began to support black candidates. The result is that the Barbadian legislature, which had previously been predominantly white, suddenly became predominantly black. Since the granting of internal self government to Barbados in the 1950s, it has never had a white premier or prime minister. Nor has there been a white governor general since the retirement of Sir John Stow, the last of the colonial governors, in 1967. The black presence is everywhere. White headteachers and predominantly white priests have given way to blacks; and white heads of departments in the civil service have done the same.[68]

In these circumstances, Barbadian cricket had no choice but to revolutionize itself. It would have been incongruous if the exclusive clubs had remained exclusively white while the political institutions were steadily becoming exclusively black. Thus, by the 1960s, cricket clubs ceased to represent separate strata of the society. The white minority, in fact, withdrew from politics and almost entirely from cricket. All the vibrant new clubs which emerged, like Banks, Maple and St Catherine, were primarily black. Old clubs, such as Pickwick and Wanderers, gradually became primarily black also.

Barbadian cricket is thus no longer distinguished by that pernicious brand of racism by which it had so long been strangled. No longer are there artificial rules prohibiting groundsmen, and lower class blacks generally, from playing. No longer is it necessary to appoint a white captain to lead the national team. The last white captains of Barbadian cricket XIs were John Goddard and Denis Atkinson. Since their retirement, Barbadian teams have been ably led by such black stars as Everton Weekes, Garfield Sobers, David Holford, Vanburn Holder, Carlisle Best, Desmond Haynes, Roland Holder, Courtney Browne and Philo Wallace.[69] These changes have been reflected also in the administrative leadership of the BCA itself, even though Peter Short, a white man from the Wanderers club, held the presidency from 1973 to 1994. Ever since the 1960s, the majority of its executive officers, such as Charles Alleyne, Stanton Gittens, Charles Griffith, Harold Griffith, Peter Lashley, Tony Marshall, Seymour Nurse, Cammie Smith, Everton Weekes and Keith Walcott, have been black.[70]

It is only within the past 40 years or so that the vast majority of Barbadians have finally been able to give full vent to their cricketing genius. Very few of the great black stars of the past were allowed to prosper without restraint. Such an excellent fast bowler as W.T. Burton, for instance, had to emigrate to Demerara in order to play organized cricket at a satisfactory level. Herman Griffith, one of the best fast bowlers in Barbadian history, was kept out of international cricket until he was well past his prime. His first tour to England came in 1928 when he was 35. At his peak, in 1923, he was inexplicably omitted from the West Indian team that toured England. In his stead, George Francis was chosen, in fact hand-picked by H.B.G. Austin, the Barbados and West Indies captain. Francis was expected to be more docile than the notoriously temperamental Herman, who (as was then very well known) resented being ordered around by men whom he regarded as white nincompoops who were manifestly his cricketing inferiors. Poor Francis, of course, as a lower class black, could not then take part in any form of organized cricket in Barbados at all. He had not played in a single first class match when, at the age of 26, he first toured England with the West Indies team. More tragically still, he was selected to represent Barbados on only four occasions throughout his career. He did so against touring teams from England, but (illogically) was considered ineligible for intercolonial competition.[71]

George N. Francis (1897–1942) was selected only four times for Barbados

The Legacy of George Challenor

In this stifling atmosphere, the only true cricket champion produced by Barbados before World War II was George Challenor. Batting with a poise and charm hitherto unseen in the West Indies, he made countless runs for Wanderers in local club cricket, and was one of the mainstays of Barbados' batting for almost 25 years. Test cricket came too late for

George Challenor (1888–1947), the father of modern Barbadian batsmanship

him. He was already 40 years old by 1928, but at least he had an opportunity in 1923 to show the English spectators his worth. He struck six centuries during that tour and scored 1,556 runs at an average of 51.86 per innings. Such was the impression he created upon his hosts that they promptly elected him that year to special MCC membership.[72]

Challenor, needless to say, is a Barbadian legend. He is better remembered than any of the leading scholars, priests or politicians of his era. Even though he played for the most snobbish and élitist of clubs, he yet commanded the respect and admiration of all Barbadians. There was something universal and eternal in the excellence of his batsmanship. When, in 1927, he scored that brilliant 220 against Trinidad, he was defiantly making a Barbadian statement rather than a parochial, racist, or aristocratic one. He was the people's hero, and all Barbadian batsmen, black as well as white, tried slavishly for many years to copy his style and method. His most famous supporter, in fact, was that engaging character, Fred Flannigan, a Wanderers groundsman, who followed the great George everywhere and literally worshipped him.[73]

Challenor's tradition of aggressive strokeplay combined with effective defensive technique has remained the dominant one. It is fortunate for Barbados that it did. The flourishing of modern strokeplay might have been lost had the cricketing community chosen instead to follow the example of Percy H. 'Tim' Tarilton, Challenor's constant opening partner at the intercolonial level throughout the 1920s. Tarilton, who represented Pickwick, was a much more stolid player who tended to stress defence and to attack only the worst deliveries. Here, perhaps, the two batsmen were reflecting their socio-economic origins and backgrounds. While the one could afford to play his strokes with the confidence and panache of a Georgian aristocrat, the other displayed all the sobriety and frugality of a

Victorian *petit bourgeois*. Tarilton was probably more reliable than Challenor, but he was much less stylish and attractive. Even so, it should not be forgotten that, in terms of runs made on behalf of Barbados, he outdid his more flamboyant partner (1,885 to 1,713) and left a local record that would take Clyde Walcott more than 20 years to break.[74]

The Magnificence of the Three Ws

Since the days of George and Tim, Barbados has produced a lengthy sequence of brilliant strokemakers. The dominance of Barbadian cricket for about 30 years after World War II, in fact, was securely based on the quality of its batsmanship. For more than two decades, West Indian cricket was overshadowed by the magnificence of the Ws. None of them batted quite like Challenor but they all seemed somehow to have learnt essential lessons from him, although they were extremely young when the great George played his final games for Wanderers. Worrell was easily the most graceful, the most compelling. He batted with an almost languid charm that left English commentators speaking eloquently, after the famous tour of 1950, about the " right-handed Woolley". Weekes seemed quicker on his feet, more businesslike, more violent. His attack was obviously grounded on sound defensive methods, so that he scored his runs in a brisk, rather Bradmanesque manner, without the suggestion of risk or danger. Walcott, a massive man, simply struck the ball with awesome power and amazing consistency. It was not so much that he lacked style as that, like the immortal W.G. Grace before him, he appeared more interested in the pragmatic accumulation of runs than in the aesthetic manner in which those runs were garnered.

In first-class cricket during the period 1941–64, the Three Ws recorded 115 centuries between them and scored almost 39,000 runs at better than 55 per innings. They amassed 12,113 runs in Test cricket at an average of 54.81 runs per innings.[75] They represented the heart and soul of West Indian batting for a quarter of century. More importantly, they served as role models for the youth. They were literally idolized by thousands of youngsters who deliberately attempted to emulate their styles and mannerisms. They kept alive the Challenor tradition of attractive batting and taught countless disciples never to let the ball assume dominion over the bat.

How well the Ws taught their lessons was quickly seen by the emergence of such batsmen as Robin Bynoe, Teddy Griffith, Conrad Hunte, Peter Lashley, Seymour Nurse, Cammie Smith and Gary Sobers during the

The 'Three Terrible Ws' dominated West Indies cricket from 1945 to 1960

1950s. The influence of Weekes was especially visible in the stance, mannerisms and approach of Hunte and Nurse, who, by no means accidentally, showed flashes of Weekes' genius from early in their career. They cut like him, and drove like him, even though (much later on) Hunte was persuaded to temper his style to suit the needs of a Test match opening batsman. Ironically, the man from Belleplaine who wanted most to bat like George Challenor thus found himself playing the role of Tim Tarilton for the major portion of his Test career.

Flamboyant Openers

Aggressive opening batsmanship became almost the norm after Challenor's retirement. Thus, when Hunte made his memorable first-class début at the Kensington Oval in 1951, his grand assault on the Trinidad fast bowlers was not in itself unusual. This, after all, had been the pattern set by such

Gordon Greenidge, the finest of all Barbadian opening batsmen

disciples of Challenor as George Carew and Charlie Taylor. Roy Marshall, too, was known to be forever in haste to remove the shine as soon as possible from the new ball. This attitude was much in evidence also in the approach of the young Cammie Smith, who delighted in hitting fast bowlers for six whenever the opportunity presented itself. With the possible exception of Merton Robinson, Empire's careful opening batsman during the 1940s, the patient and frugal Tim Tarilton found very few emulators indeed.

The torch so ably carried by Carew, Hunte, Marshall, Nurse, Smith and Taylor was passed on to Carlisle Best, Gordon Greenidge and Desmond Haynes. Here were three gifted batsmen who could open the innings without allowing such a responsibility to inhibit their strokeplay. In this they were obviously copying the methods of George Carew, Roy Marshall and Cammie Smith; and it is Smith, especially, who seems to have provided the inspiration for the young Philo Wallace, who is perhaps the most impetuous of the current crop of Barbadian openers. But the styles of all these batsmen have suggested an emulation of Weekes, even though it is highly unlikely that any of them ever saw the great Everton in action. Greenidge, in particular, appeared to have combined the techniques of Weekes with the savagery of Walcott – especially in his approach to such strokes as the cut and the hook. Even the young Sherwin Campbell, born (in 1970) so long after the three Ws had retired, seems to have inherited the principal elements of his batsmanship from these three famous models.

The Greatest of Them All

The player who learnt most from the Three Ws and eventually surpassed them all was Gary Sobers. His footwork was so swift that he seemed always to have extra time in which to make his final decisions. He moved quickly, but gracefully, across his wicket and invariably finished up playing off the back foot, unless the ball was overpitched. This technique allowed him to play well even on unfriendly pitches, and to improvise strokes beyond the capacity of lesser mortals. In general terms, his driving and cutting were orthodox, but his hooking was not. He tended to swish the ball from off his nose from an upright position with his feet in the wrong place, as purists were often quick to notice. More delightful to watch was his flick through midwicket off the back foot, a stroke impossible for others to play at all and very difficult for spectators to describe. It was neither a drive nor a pull, just a wristy movement of the bat. By dint of such glorious strokes, Sobers succeeded in scoring more than 28,000 runs in first-class cricket, including 8,032 in 93 Tests, at an average of 57.78 per innings.[76] Having played most of his early cricket on unprepared strips in the Bay Land, either on or near the old headquarters of the Wanderers club, Sobers never had too much difficulty coping with pitches which gave the bowlers more help than usual. He seemed, in fact, in his natural element when, with cracks all around him and dust everywhere, he was compiling that remarkable century against England in 1968 at Sabina Park.[77]

Sir Garfield Sobers, the greatest cricketer of them all

Sobers emerged at the time of Independence and seemed to symbolize all that Barbadian blacks had been striving for ever since the days of slavery. At a time when the new nation was searching for heroes, he could readily pose as the new messiah in a way in which no previous Barbadian cricketer had been able to do. Even more clearly than Challenor or Worrell or Weekes, Sobers had become *the* people's champion. He combined his extraordinary batting skills with the ability to field brilliantly in any position and to bowl effectively in several styles. He captured 235 Test wickets and held 109 Test catches. These are enviable statistics indeed, but they fail to do ample justice to his overall contribution to

West Indian cricket. Sobers left a positive impression wherever he performed and has gone down in the cricket history books, quite deservedly, as perhaps the greatest allrounder ever to have played the game. Apart from being the world's greatest batsman of his generation, he was one of its most brilliant fieldsmen and easily its most versatile bowler.

Gary Sobers retired from first-class cricket in 1974 and (like Sir Frank Worrell in 1964) was knighted in the following year for his distinguished services to the game. A testimonial game had been played on his behalf in 1973. In 1994, the fortieth anniversary of his Test début was celebrated in Barbados with a multiplicity of lucrative and exciting events coinciding with the England tour of the West Indies. His magic was still in evidence everywhere, as Barbadians flocked to make a contribution to the Sobers Fund. The University of the West Indies, in conjunction with CLICO international life insurance company and the Centre for Cricket Research (CCR) in Barbados, also sponsored a cricket lecture series in his honour. Ever since his retirement, Barbados has been searching for a successor to assume his mantle. Several great cricket stars have appeared, but no recognizable hero in the Soberian mould.[78]

Of some interest is the curious fact that the most recent Barbadian cricket stars have, in the main, been fast bowlers. Since 1960, Barbados has produced, among a host of others, such notable speedsters as Hartley Alleyne, Gregory Armstrong, Keith Boyce, Sylvester Clarke, Anderson Cummins, Wayne Daniel, Othniel Downes, Vasbert Drakes, Richard Edwards, Ricardo Ellcock, Roddy Estwick, Joel Garner, Ottis Gibson, Charles Griffith, Victor Greene, Wesley Hall, E.S. Hinkson, Vanburn Holder, Mark Lavine, Malcolm Marshall, Dayne Maynard, Ezra Moseley, Hallam Moseley, Anton Norris, George Rock, Sammy Skeete, Gladstone Small, Milton Small, Franklyn Stephenson, Patterson Thompson and Victor Walcott. Five members of this group (Garner, Griffith, Hall, Holder and Marshall) have captured 90 or more wickets in Test cricket and two of them (Garner, 259 and Marshall, 376), with more than 250 Test scalps each, have stamped themselves as among the greatest fast bowlers of all time.[79] This is as fine an array of talent in a single department as anyone can expect to see anywhere. But the Barbadians are dissatisfied. They are unhappy because they have never really identified with fast bowlers in the same way that they have identified with stylish and effective batsmanship. There may well be a message here of some kind. Perhaps this is a subconscious relic of the Victorian habit of glorifying the aristocratic batsman at the expense of the plebeian bowler.[80]

The Fetish for Style

Cricket in Barbados has invariably meant attractive and stylish strokeplay. The Barbadians, in fact, have always had a peculiar fetish for what they simply call 'style' – a word that is richer in meaning there than anywhere else perhaps. It connotes 'class' as well as 'beauty' or 'elegance'. The Barbadians prefer to be mesmerized by the manner in which the strokes are made rather than be overwhelmed by the actual torrent of runs. Hence the enormous popularity of such batting stylists as Harry Ince and Lawson Bartlett in days gone by. Ince was arguably the finest left-handed batsman produced by the West Indies before World War II, while 'Barto' played excellent cricket for Spartan during the years 1925–40.[81] The reputation of these players is considerably more substantial than their statistical records would seem to warrant. Bartlett finished his first-class career with a batting average of less than 25 and the great Ince averaged less than 30 runs per innings in 35 first-class matches.[82] It is largely this obsession with style that explains the Barbadians' undying attachment to Sir Garfield Sobers, who played his cricket with matchless panache and flamboyance.

This fetish for style can explain, too, why Barbadians so quickly relate to certain foreign heroes. They cared not so much for Leonard Hutton, the robot, as for Denis Compton and Tom Graveney, who played what they described as 'West Indian' strokes. They adored Fred Trueman, with his theatrics, rather than Brian Statham, with his proficiency. They idolized Lawrence Rowe, despite his Jamaican roots and his notorious unpredictability, more than they did some of their own Barbadian native players. They preferred the elegant David Gower over Geoffrey Boycott, the perfectionist. And they now are totally devoted to the charismatic Brian Lara of Trinidad, in a way in which they never really cheered for Vivian Richards, the Antiguan 'Master Blaster'. Guyana's enigmatic and inconsistent Carl Hooper is idolized by older Barbadians now because, like Rowe, he reminds them of 'Tae' Worrell in his prime. It does not matter that Hooper's batting average in more than 60 Test matches is less than 35 runs per innings.

Wesley Hall was not, by any stretch of the imagination, a stylish batsman; but he seemed somehow to warm the hearts of all Barbadians by the 'style' of his bowling. He was (and to some extent still is) a genuine folk hero. Big, affable, tremendously strong, and fast as lightning, Hall caught the public imagination in the early 1960s. His obvious enthusiasm and his antics endeared him to the crowds, almost everywhere. He could be as dangerous as a Ray Lindwall or a Frank Tyson, but he somehow lacked

Charles Griffith terrorized batsmen during the 1960s

their transparent malevolence as bowlers. Having emerged after many years of dearth, Hall was warmly welcomed by the Barbadian cricket public.[83] The only Barbadian fast bowlers of real note between the careers of Herman Griffith and Wes Hall had been E.A.V. 'Foffie' Williams and Frank King. Griffith had retired from first-class cricket in 1941; the great 'Mannie' Martindale had played his last first-class cricket match in 1939; and 'Foffie' had last played for Barbados in 1949. Barbados was anxious, by the late 1950s, to welcome any speedster of quality.[84]

The emergence of Hall and Charles Griffith towards the end of the 1950s denoted something else. There were so many fine batsmen in Barbados at that point that the only opportunity for the adventurous youngster was in the area of fast bowling. The West Indies, too, found themselves perennially short of fast bowling talent after World War II. This was a totally unexpected development, since the West Indies had previously boasted such great fast bowlers as Learie Constantine, George Francis, Herman Griffith, George John, Prior Jones, Hines Johnson, 'Mannie' Martindale, Lance Pierre and 'Foffie' Williams. Their strength had rested with their men of speed at a time when their batting was brittle, their spin bowling mediocre, and their fielding (apart from Constantine's and Headley's) generally inept. In the 1950s, the West Indies found themselves entrusting the new ball to such medium pacers as Denis Atkinson, Gerry Gomez and Frank Worrell.[85] It was to fill that vacancy that so many fast bowlers suddenly came forward.

In fact, the absence of really fast bowlers in the West Indies had left the local batsmen, even the much vaunted Three Ws, dangerously vulnerable to effective pace. This weakness had been cruelly exposed against Australia in 1951–52 and against England in 1957. West Indian cricket administrators therefore deliberately began to search for their own nuclear weapons to counter the Lindwalls, Millers, Stathams, Truemans and Tysons by whom they had been so signally humbled. Many Barbadian youngsters, too, noted the depth of the batting chart and tried to make the national team by bowling fast. Hall, for instance, who had played his cricket for Combermere as a wicketkeeper/batsman and could never have represented Barbados in such a capacity, shifted his focus to fast bowling only after joining the staff of Cable & Wireless (now Barbados External Telecommunications or BET) in 1955. Similarly, Charlie Griffith had begun his BCL career as a wicketkeeper/batsman, patterning himself after Clyde Walcott. Mainly because of their size and strength, Hall and Griffith were encouraged by their captains to bowl fast since their respective clubs lacked speedsters. In both cases the experiment produced astonishing early results.[86]

The Age of Fire

Thus was born the 'age of fire'. But the fire seems bent on destroying not only the opposing forces but home-grown batting talent as well. Barbados has spawned perhaps too many terrifying fast bowlers during the past 30 years. They have inhibited the natural strokes of local stylists and left them groping at the crease in the manner of Australians and Englishmen. The pendulum has swung full circle, and even the club matches which once saw the mastery of bat over ball are being dominated now by such fiery men of pace as Cummins, Drakes, Gibson, Lavine, Maynard, Skeete, Thompson and Walcott. A bowling attack, which once consisted of two fast men, one medium and two slow, is not now considered adequate with fewer than four fast bowlers. Just as the West Indies have opted for a four-pronged pace assault, so has Barbados and so too have the individual clubs in the island. Run scoring in the BCA first division competition is not as prolific as it once was. Some knowledgeable critics point to wicket preparation as the essential difference between club cricket now and club cricket in the 1950s.[87] Whereas the groundsmen (with the notable exception of those at Bank Hall) once prepared the strip to favour their batsmen, they now tend to favour their bowlers. The standard of fielding, which was once so uneven, has generally improved to the point where more runs are saved in the field and fewer catches are dropped. Be that as it may, it is highly unlikely that any batsman in the late 1990s can duplicate Cammie Smith's feat of amassing over 300 runs in five hours of excitement on a single Saturday afternoon.[88]

QUO VADIS?

All these matters, however, are cyclical. Barbadian batsmen will doubtless devise an effective strategy to cope with relentless fire. Far more constant, and ultimately more significant, is the Barbadian will to dominate this particular sport. The cricket tradition has been so well established here, especially in and by the academic institutions, that it is hardly likely to be undermined in the near future, either by its own fast bowling or by any one else's. All the Barbadians really have to do is to encourage their youth to continue to play the game with earnestness and desire.

As with all things, the future rests, in the final analysis, with the younger generation, and it is up to the community at large to keep alive the cricket nurseries so that the sport will not languish. The history of Barbadian cricket nurseries is a very rich one indeed – no less so than the actual history of Barbadian cricket itself. Had Combermere, Harrison College and the Lodge School not attached so much importance to this sport above all others, it is unlikely that Barbadian cricket would have prospered as it did during the last 100 years of colonialism. If most of the new academic institutions can recapture even a fraction of the intensity formerly displayed by these three élite schools, Barbadian cricket would definitely continue to flourish.

It is the purpose of the following chapters to emphasize the contribution of the leading nurseries, so that one can understand why, and how, it came to pass that a small nation, despite its lack of manpower and natural resources, could make such a huge impression on the rest of the cricketing world.

NOTES

1 Keith A.P. Sandiford, "Cricket and the Barbadian Society", *Canadian Journal of History* 21 (December 1986): 353–70; Brian Stoddart, "Cricket, Social Formation and Cultural Continuity in Barbados: A Preliminary Ethno-history", *Journal of Sport History* 3 (Winter 1987): 317–40.

2 Keith A.P. Sandiford, *Cricket and the Victorians* (Aldershot, 1994), 144–60.

3 Keith A.P. Sandiford and Brian Stoddart, "The Elite Schools and Cricket in Barbados: A Study in Colonial Continuity", *International Journal of the History of Sport* 4 (December 1987): 333–50.

4 See the *Combermerian* and the *Combermere School Magazine* (1913–64), the *Harrisonian* (1916–65) and the *Lodge School Record* (1911–66).

5 *Barbados Globe*, 20 November 1882; *Harrisonian* (December 1921); 7. BCA, *100 Years of Organised Cricket in Barbados, 1892–1992* (Bridgetown, 1992), 70–71.

6 James A. Mangan, *Athleticism in the Victorian and Edwardian Public School* (Cambridge, 1981), passim; and "Grammar Schools and the Games Ethic in the Victorian and Edwardian Era", *Albion* 15 (Winter 1983): 313–35.

7 Bruce E. Haley, *The Healthy Body and Victorian Culture* (Harvard, 1978), passim.
8 Sandiford, "Cricket and the Barbadian Society", 358.
9 L. Walcott, "The Barbados Cricket League: Forty Years of Service", UWI undergraduate paper, Cave Hill, 1978.
10 Empire Cricket Club, *The Empire Club, 1914–1989* (Bridgetown, 1989) 16–20; Keith A.P. Sandiford, " 'Sons in the Sun': Combermere School and Cricket in Barbados", *Cricket Lore* 2, no 5 (1995): 41–5.
11 See, for example, *Harrisonian* (1975), 7.
12 *Harrisonian* (April 1923), 2–4, 12; Philip Thorn, *Barbados Cricketers 1865–1990* (West Bridgford, 1991), 29; BCA, *100 Years*, 116.
13 *Harrisonian* (July 1934), 5–6; BCA, *100 Years*, 68; Keith A.P. Sandiford and Earle H. Newton, *Combermere School and the Barbadian Society* (Kingston, 1995), 48–55.
14 See the files of the *Harrisonian* (1916–65) and the *Lodge School Record* (1911–65).
15 *Barbados Globe*, 17 April 1876, and 24 April 1876.
16 *Combermere School Magazine*, Third Term 1915–16, 12; Sandiford and Newton, *Combermere School and the Barbadian Society*, 14–15, 22.
17 Sandiford and Newton, *Combermere School and the Barbadian Society*, 41–2.
18 Ibid., 62–4.
19 Ibid., 63; M.T.G. Mahon to A.E. Armstrong, 22 July 1936, Combermere School Records, Waterford.
20 Sandiford, *Cricket and the Victorians*, 162.
21 Bruce Hamilton, *Cricket in Barbados* (Bridgetown, 1947), 5–64.
22 Trevor Marshall, "Race, Class and Cricket in Barbadian Society, 1800–1970", *Manjak*, 11 November 1973; Martin C. Ramsay, "A Critical Examination of Factors affecting the Formation of Major Cricket Clubs in Barbados", UWI undergraduate paper, Cave Hill, 1979; and, especially, Brian Stoddart, "Cricket and Colonialism in the English-speaking Caribbean to 1914: Towards a Cultural Analysis", in *Pleasure, Profit, Proselytism: British Culture and Sport at Home and Abroad 1700–1914*, edited by James A. Mangan (London, 1988), 231–57.
23 Stoddart, "Cricket and Colonialism", 241–42.
24 Wanderers Cricket Club, *Wanderers Cricket Club Centenary 1877–1977* (Bridgetown, 1977), passim.
25 BCA, *100 Years*, 56; Stoddart, "Cricket and Colonialism", 242–43.
26 Hamilton, *Cricket in Barbados*, passim; Stoddart, "Cricket and Colonialism", 244.
27 Hamilton, *Cricket in Barbados*, 44.
28 Ibid., 43; BCA, *100 Years*, 5.
29 BCA, *100 Years*, 5.
30 See "Anti-Discrimination Laws in Barbados", anonymous and undated pamphlet in the Barbados National Archives.

31 F.A. Hoyos, *Grantley Adams and the Social Revolution* (London, 1974), passim.
32 Stoddart, "Cricket and Colonialism", 243–44.
33 Keith A.P. Sandiford, "The Spartan Cricket Club, 1893–1993", *Journal of the Cricket Society* 16, no. 3 (Autumn 1993): 43–6.
34 Stoddart, "Cricket and Colonialism", 244–45.
35 Sandiford and Newton, *Combermere School and the Barbadian Society*, 85.
36 *Barbados Globe*, 28 August 1899 and 16 November 1899.
37 *Barbados Advocate*, 27 October 1900, 5.
38 *Barbados Advocate*, 19 December 1896, 5; *Barbados Globe*, July 1899 to March 1900.
39 *Barbados Agricultural Reporter*, 16 December 1899.
40 *Barbados Advocate*, 15 May 1903, 6.
41 Colonial Annual Reports, Barbados, 1938–39, 2, 5.
42 Stoddart, "Cricket and Colonialism", 245–48.
43 *Barbados Advocate*, 8 February 1897, 7.
44 *Barbados Agricultural Reporter*, 27 March 1899; *Barbados Globe*, 27 March 1899.
45 *Barbados Advocate*, 15 May 1903, 6. See also Hamilton, *Cricket in Barbados*, 75.
46 *Barbados Advocate*, 15 May 1903, 6; 27 May 1903, 5; 3 June 1903, 7; 4 July 1903, 5; 7 July 1903, 7; 11 July 1903, 6; and 30 July 1903, 6.
47 John Wickham, "Herman", *West Indies Cricket Annual 1980*, 12–14.
48 Empire Cricket Club, *Empire Club*, 19.
49 Barbados Cricket Association, *Report and Statement of Accounts, 1st April 1994 to 31st March 1995*, 34.
50 Hamilton, *Cricket in Barbados*, 74.
51 The Scheme of Government was the official instrument which contained the clauses and provisions by which each school was administered in those days.
52 *Combermere School Magazine* (1916–25) and the *Combermerian* (1926–29).
53 *Barbados Advocate*, 15 June 1896, 6.
54 BCA, *100 Years*, 29.
55 Christopher Nicole, *West Indian Cricket* (London, 1957), 19.
56 Peter Wynne-Thomas, *England on Tour* (London, 1982), 66.
57 Michael Manley, *A History of West Indies Cricket* (London, 1988), 21.
58 Hilary McD. Beckles, "The Making of the First 'West Indian' Teams, 1886–1906", in *Liberation Cricket: West Indies Cricket Culture*, edited by Hilary McD. Beckles and Brian Stoddart (Manchester, 1995), 198–202.
59 BCA, *100 Years*, 21–4. L. Walcott, "The Barbados Cricket League"; see also Clyde A. Walcott's short essay on Barbadian cricket in *New World* (1966), 3: 51–3.
60 BCA, *Report and Statement of Accounts from 1st April 1984 to 31st March 1985*, 5; and *1st April 1995 to 31st March 1996*, 34.
61 See all BCA reports from 1949 to the present.
62 BCA, *100 Years*, 27.

63 *The Advocate Year Book and Who's Who 1951* (Bridgetown, 1951), 141.
64 Ibid., 39–44.
65 Keith A.P. Sandiford, *Frank Mortimer Maglinne Worrell: His Record Innings-by-Innings* (West Bridgford, 1997), 14.
66 Keith A.P. Sandiford, *Clyde Leopold Walcott: His Record Innings-by-Innings* (West Bridgford, 1996), 10.
67 Keith A.P. Sandiford, *Everton DeCourcey Weekes: His Record Innings-by-Innings* (West Bridgford, 1995), 6.
68 Keith A.P. Sandiford, "Barbados Then, and Barbados Now", *Banja: A Magazine of Barbadian Life and Culture* (1989/90): 49–53.
69 Sandiford, "Cricket and the Barbadian Society", 364.
70 BCA, *Report and Statement of Accounts, 1st April 1994 to 31st March 1995*, 75–6.
71 BCA, *100 Years*, 73–4; Thorn, *Barbados Cricketers*, 24.
72 BCA, *100 Years*, 64.
73 Stoddart, "Cricket, Social Formation and Cultural Continuity", 337.
74 BCA, *100 Years*, 116–17; see also Sandiford, *Clyde Leopold Walcott*, 20; Thorn, *Barbados Cricketers*, 23, 30.
75 Bridgette Lawrence and Ray Goble, *The Complete Record of West Indian Test Cricketers* (Leicester, 1991), 356–57, 360–61, 369–70. See also Sandiford's trilogy on the Three Ws, published recently by the Association of Cricket Statisticians and Historians.
76 B. Lawrence and R. Goble, *Complete Record of West Indian Test Cricketers*, 346–49.
77 Bertram A. Callender and Keith A.P. Sandiford, "Growing Up in the Bay Land: Sir Garfield Sobers and His Roots", in *The Greatest Cricketer Ever: Sir Garfield Sobers Souvenir Programme* (Bridgetown, 1994), 23–8; reprinted in *Cricket Lore* 2, no. 7 (1996): 27–8; Keith A.P. Sandiford, *Garfield St Aubrun Sobers: His Record Innings-by-Innings* (forthcoming).
78 Keith A.P. Sandiford, "Sir Garfield Sobers: An Appreciation", *Journal of the Cricket Society* 17 no. 1 (Autumn 1994): 28–30. See also Hilary McD. Beckles, ed. *An Area of Conquest: Popular Democracy and West Indies Cricket Supremacy* (Kingston, 1994).
79 *Wisden's Cricketers' Almanack* 1996 (hereinafter *Wisden*), 164.
80 Sandiford, *Cricket and the Victorians*, 133–34.
81 Sandiford, "The Spartan Cricket Club", 45.
82 Thorn, *Barbados Cricketers*, 21, 26.
83 Keith A.P. Sandiford, *Wesley Winfield Hall: His Record Innings-by-Innings* (West Bridgford, forthcoming).
84 BCA, *100 Years*, 84.
85 See *Wisden* (1950–60).
86 Charlie Griffith, *Chucked Around* (London, 1970), 27, 34; Wesley Hall, *Pace Like Fire* (London, 1966), 20–1.
87 Personal observations and interviews.
88 BCA, *100 Years*, 87.

2

The Lodge School

Cradle of Cricket in Barbados

The Lodge School, situated in St John, Barbados, is one of the most important cricket nurseries in the world. Established in 1745 as a residential school for Barbadian whites, it achieved first-grade secondary status as a result of the Education Act of 1878. Thereafter, like Harrison College in Bridgetown, it catered to the sons of the richest families in the island. Because of its boarding facilities, the Lodge also attracted several of the sons of plantocrats from neighbouring colonies. The school therefore played no small part in the growth and development of cricket throughout the Caribbean.[1]

In the history of Barbadian cricket, the Lodge School holds a very special place. It is the oldest of all the extant cricket clubs in the island. Harrison College had to wait until 1873 before acquiring the necessary playing fields and the great Wanderers CC was not established until 1877. The only cricket clubs which survived beyond the nineteenth century and could claim perhaps to have been older than the Lodge were Codrington College, the Garrison and St Ann's. But they have long ceased to operate. As Bruce Hamilton has observed, if the British soldiers, who occupied the garrison on the boundaries of Christ Church and St Michael, can be regarded as the missionaries who brought the sport to the colony, then the Lodge School boys and masters must surely be seen as the real pioneers of cricket in Barbados.[2]

This is all the more remarkable when one considers that there were never very many students at the Lodge during the nineteenth century. When Revd T. Watts and Revd S. Farr were sent out from England to administer the school in 1829, they found only 24 pupils at the Lodge. As late as 1863, when Revd W.T. Webb was the headmaster, there were still only 36 students altogether, including 25 boarders. Almost incredibly, the roll at the Lodge did not consistently exceed 50 until about 1910.

Sometimes, too, the school ran into either financial or other difficulties and had to close its doors. In 1880, for instance, because of dwindling numbers, the trustees thought it necessary to suspend activities. The Lodge was finally rescued by the legislature which voted to provide it, as a government-aided first-grade secondary school, with substantial annual grants from 1881 onwards. Even so, the pupils played cricket extremely well — largely because all of the early headmasters regarded it as a compulsory feature of the curriculum.[3]

THE CRICKET TRADITION ESTABLISHED AT THE LODGE

This tradition was continued during the 1880s and 1890s under such headmasters as Charles Tracey and William Burslem. A graduate of Oxford, Tracey was himself a keen and excellent cricketer and the game prospered at the Lodge while he was there (1881–93). Burslem, who administered the Lodge from 1893 to 1895, eventually took up an appointment at the Queen's Royal College (QRC) in Trinidad.[4] He, too, was a cricketer who struck the ball with enviable ferocity. As a very old former Lodge Boy, Richard Henry Smith, recalled in his late years, the school selected two elevens during Tracey's tenure, even though only two masters were cricketers and the school roll was so small. Smith, who had himself represented Barbados in two games in 1894, described Tracey as a fair bowler and a hard hitter and Eustace Bowen as a good bat. Practice was then compulsory at least twice per week and absenteeism meant a fine of 6d, which was by no means a light penalty in those days. The captains of the Lodge in his time there were Elliot Skeete, Clifford Goodman, Howard Smith and R.H. Smith himself. It is interesting to note that, as the school could not then afford to hire a groundsman, the boys had to prepare the pitch themselves.[5]

Lodge Boys as Cricket Pioneers

Given this approach on the part of its administrators and the pupils, the Lodge was always in the vanguard of early cricket in Barbados. In fact the oldest surviving complete Barbadian cricket scorecard involves the match between St Michaels and the Lodge in 1861, which the schoolboys lost by the narrowest of margins. Four of the Lodge boys who participated in that historic game (Ernest King, Richard Parris, Lyall Speed and Augustus Smith) represented Barbados against Demerara in the very first West Indian intercolonial match which took place in 1865.[6]

When Barbados met Demerara again in 1871, the team consisted almost entirely of Lodge boys past and present. This was not surprising. The Lodge was then the only well-organized cricket club in the island. During the 1860s most of the important cricket matches played in Barbados involved the Lodge and the Garrison, composed entirely of British soldiers stationed temporarily there. At that time, the Lodge was ably supported by such fine players as G.R. Challenor, N. Deane, the Skeetes (John Brathwaite and Torrence Seymour), and the two Smiths (Frederick Bonham and Augustus Elder), who virtually defeated Demerara by themselves in 1865. Challenor was the father of the great George who would later make Harrison College competitive in Barbados at the turn of the century and Barbados virtually unbeatable in the Caribbean in the generation bisected by World War I.[7]

The Ascendancy of the Lodge

During the 1870s the Lodge remained by far the strongest club in the colony and was powerful enough in 1874 to defeat 'Eleven Gentlemen of the Island' rather easily. The Lodge was at that time producing able players such as W.N. Alleyne, Flavius Goodman, Herbert Greaves, Malcolm Greenidge, John Hutson, Walter Outram, T. Parris, Randall Phillips, Stephen Phillips, John Frere Pilgrim, the two Rowe brothers, Beresford Seale, Ernest Skeete and Arthur Speed. These cricketers formed the nucleus of the teams which represented Barbados at the beginning of intercolonial cricket in the Caribbean. The boys were also joined regularly by such masters as Revd Thomas Clarke and Revd T. Lyall Speed, both of whom were good enough themselves to earn selection to early Barbadian teams.[8]

Revd Speed is of special interest because he not only helped to make the Lodge a powerful cricket force in Barbados for several years, but he took his skills to Harrison College (where he taught briefly during the 1870s) and then to Combermere School, where he served as headmaster from 1879 to 1896. There he stressed the virtues of cricket, even though the school did not have a playing field of its own. One of his prize pupils was George Learmond, a native of Demerara, who became the first captain of the Spartan CC in 1893. A sound right-handed batsman and wicketkeeper, 'Learie' went on to become the first cricketer to represent three territories in the Caribbean. He was also a member of the first West Indies team to England in 1900. On that tour he became a firm friend of Lebrun Constantine who named his famous son after him.[9]

During the 1880s, even when Pickwick and Wanderers were emerging as very good cricket clubs, Harrison College and the Lodge were still the dominant forces in Barbadian cricket mainly because their headmasters attached so much importance to the game. At this time it was generally believed throughout the British Empire that cricket could transform rambunctious lads into constructive and law-abiding citizens. The British educators who transported this notion to Barbados made cricket an almost compulsory feature of secondary education. Headmasters of the Lodge, consistently after 1860, treated cricket virtually as a religion. This was especially true in the days of Revd W.H. Prideaux, a graduate of Oxford, who administered the Lodge during the 1870s.[10] As this doctrine was readily accepted by many generations of scholar-athletes, it is not surprising therefore that two of the later headmasters, Oliver DeCourcey Emtage (1898–1931) and W.A. Farmer (1947–53), produced sons who eventually achieved first-class status as cricketers. Farmer's grandson did the same.[11] This devotion to cricket drew fulsome praise from a sports reporter for the *Barbados Herald*, who was once moved to declare: "It was indeed a sight dear to the hearts of all true lovers of the game to see an Eleven composed chiefly of boys and most of them little boys, stand up so manfully and confidently against the swift and usually damaging bowling of the Wanderers."[12] A potent Wanderers XI had been reduced by the youngsters to a 'dishonourable draw' on 16 October 1886 although two of their opponents had not yet reached the age of 13.

Clifford Goodman (1869–1911), one of world's best bowlers in the 1890s

THE GOODMANS FROM ST PHILIP

The Lodge also owed its success during the 1880s to that veritable pride of Goodmans, all five of whom would ultimately play key roles in the development of cricket in Barbados, and four of whom were trained at the Lodge. Clifford emerged eventually as the greatest of the early West Indian bowlers. Lord Hawke, one of the most important personalities in Victorian cricket, had no hesitation in calling Goodman the finest bowler in the Caribbean in 1897.[13] He mesmerized two visiting English teams during the 1890s and managed to claim no fewer than 126 wickets (av: 10.70) in a first-class career that spanned only six years and involved only 15 games. In 14 games for Barbados he captured 117 wickets at 10.45 runs each and this tally remained a Barbadian record for 80 years. In fact, it was not approached until Vanburn Holder (134 wickets) and David Holford (130 wickets) were winding up their careers in the late 1970s at a time when opportunities for first-class competition were much more plentiful. Along with George Hirst of Yorkshire, Clifford Goodman was one of the leading pioneers of the swerve and, at his peak, was universally regarded as one of the most dangerous bowlers in the world. When Arthur Priestley's team visited Barbados in January 1897, the great A.E. Stoddart was completely bamboozled by Clifford who claimed his wicket on six of eight opportunities, clean bowling him three times. The high quality of Goodman's bowling during that tournament was underlined by the fact that Stoddart, who could achieve so little in Barbados, still enjoyed otherwise a very successful tour of the West Indies, hitting centuries in Antigua, Jamaica, St Kitts and Trinidad.[14]

In addition to Clifford and Flavius, the Goodman brotherhood included Aubrey, who was educated at Harrison College and would later captain Pickwick with conspicuous success; Evan, who would emerge as a fine all-rounder for Barbados and then Demerara, capable not only of fielding brilliantly, batting aggressively and bowling very fast, but also of keeping wicket competently; and Percy, the youngest, who was destined to develop into the finest of all West Indian batsmen before the advent of George Challenor. Four of these five brothers played 49 matches between them for Barbados during 1891–1913. Flavius, the eldest, would certainly also have played several times for Barbados had there been regular intercolonial cricket in the West Indies when he was in his prime. The Goodmans made the Lodge a very powerful team before they joined the new Pickwick club, which they also made virtually unbeatable in Barbados for an unconscionably long time.[15]

Percy Goodman (1874–1935), the first great Barbadian batting hero

Thanks largely to the Goodmans, Pickwick won the

first division crown on the first three occasions after the inception of the Challenge Cup competition in Barbados in 1892–93. It proceeded to win no fewer than 10 championships during the first 14 years of the competition and 12 of the first 17 championships. Much of Pickwick's success depended on the consistently excellent all-round form of Percy Goodman who remained its best player for over 20 years. He was also an intercolonial star for a very long time. In 1891, Percy was not yet 17 when he made his début for Barbados. In 28 matches for the island, he scored 1,170 runs (av: 30.78) and claimed 77 wickets (av: 12.20). He also held 31 catches. His first-class career record reads: 1,824 runs (av: 30.91), 88 wickets (av: 13.58), and 47 catches. These are excellent statistics for a player of that generation. Percy also toured England with the West Indies teams in 1900 and 1906, heading his side's batting average on the second occasion with 607 runs (av: 31.94) from 22 innings (3 times not out). He struck two fine centuries (against Northamptonshire and Yorkshire) and captured 8 wickets from rather limited bowling opportunities.[17] He thus confirmed the promise he had shown in England in 1900 when, in matches illogically classified by the MCC as not first class, he had registered four centuries and averaged 28.15 per innings.[18] Percy Goodman, in short, was the finest batsman produced by the West Indies up to his own time. After his retirement as an active player, he continued to make a contribution to the game by taking the cricket gospel to Foundation Boys' School in Christ Church which he served as headmaster for many years.[19]

While at the Lodge, the Goodmans found able support from the three Cox brothers – Alan Pile, Hampden Tudor and Percy Ince – all of whom gained selection to Barbadian teams. A.P. was destined to die tragically young. He was a useful cricketer who made a valuable contribution to the Wanderers cause during the 1890s and played for Barbados in one match in 1896 (just before his death). The best of the Coxes was P.I., a right-handed allrounder, who played for Barbados on eight occasions and toured England with the first West Indies team in 1900. Inexplicably, even the matches against the strongest counties that summer were not considered first class. But Cox scored 755 runs and averaged more than 30. His elegant style elicited much favourable comment especially when he made a superb 142 against Surrey at the Oval, sharing with C.A. Ollivierre of St Vincent in a fine opening stand of 208. For Barbados, during 1895–1900, Percy Cox scored 256 runs (av: 21.33) and claimed 10 wickets (av: 7.50). He then migrated to Trinidad and represented that island on several occasions.[20]

EDWARDIAN HEROES

At the turn of the century, among the great Lodge School heroes were C.E. Blades, Mikey Mayers, B.H.V. Outram, L.O. Wood, Aubrey Worme and L.T. Yearwood. Charlie Blades was a left-handed allrounder of great promise. In a memorable match for Barbados at Kensington Oval in January 1906, he helped to defeat Trinidad by 16 runs in a low-scoring game by capturing 3 wickets for 9 runs after having scored a defiant 40 on a tricky pitch. He shortly migrated to the United States of America (USA) where he died in 1914 at the tender age of 31.[21]

Lear Wood is almost a legend in the history of cricket in Barbados. He played the game with unusual verve for what seemed an eternity. He was only 13 when he was first selected to represent the Lodge in 1898. After rendering long and faithful service to Pickwick, he joined Leeward. He later threw in his lot with Central and played for that club until he was 67 years old. There was considerable mourning throughout the island when he finally died, on 31 December 1977, at the advanced age of 92. Apart from his own contribution to Barbadian cricket, Lear Wood also fathered a superior player, Gerald, who kept wicket extremely well for Harrison, Pickwick and Barbados in the next generation.[22]

Blades and Yearwood, like Wood, went on to play with some distinction for Pickwick and to gain selection to Barbadian teams. Yearwood made his greatest contribution to Barbadian and West Indies cricket as an administrator. One of the driving forces behind the Challenge Cup Committee, he also became a founding member of the West Indies Cricket Board of Control (WICBC, now simply West Indies Cricket Board) in 1927.[23] The other Lodge School cricket stars of those days, who also played for Barbados, became staunch supporters of Wanderers. Worme was one of the finest bowlers for a few years in the Challenge Cup competition. It was as a batsman, however, that he distinguished himself at the intercolonial level when, in 1900, he once batted for over an hour at No. 11, making 2 invaluable runs at one end while Percy Cox was scoring 70 at the other to help Barbados defeat Demerara.[24]

A much greater Worme appeared in Lodge School cricket very early in the twentieth century. He was Stanley Mills, Aubrey's younger brother, who developed into the best right-arm fast bowler in Barbados in the period just before World War I. He played nine matches for the island between 1908 and 1913, claiming 36 wickets at 20.69 runs apiece.[25] Stanley Worme, who is still regarded as one of the most promising fast bowlers ever produced by his school, would undoubtedly have represented the West Indies in Test cricket had there been that opportunity then.

The Legendary 'Tim'

In those days, however, the real Lodge School cricket champion was Percy Hamilton Tarilton, simply known throughout Barbados as 'Tim'. He made his début for the Lodge during the 1896–97 season when he was only 11 years old (a long-standing Barbadian first division record which he now shares with Clyde Walcott) and was the mainstay of the school team for the next seven years. When still only a little 'mite', at the age of 12 in 1897, he showed extraordinary courage and patience in an innings against Spartan at Belleville that lasted almost an hour and produced 10 runs in a losing cause.[26] His batting technique was impeccable though many contemporaries expected him to develop into a superior bowler. He really came into his own as a prolific right-handed opening bat after he joined Pickwick in 1903. Thereafter, he was one of the most difficult batsmen in the Caribbean to dislodge. He had a good repertoire of stylish strokes but he was a most patient player who proved himself the perfect foil for the more assertive George Challenor with whom (until the arrival of Gordon Greenidge and Desmond Haynes) he formed the most famous opening partnership in Barbadian cricket history. From 1905 to 1930, George and Tim remained the most feared opening partnership in the West Indies and laid many a promising foundation for a Barbadian innings.[27]

'Tim Tarilton' (1885–1953) held the Barbadian record (1,885 runs) for many years

With the possible exception of Roy Marshall, Tim Tarilton is the best opening batsmen ever produced by the Lodge. His achievement of maintaining a batting average in excess of 50 over 25 years of intercolonial competition was an extraordinary one for that period. He represented Barbados in 28 matches, scoring 1,885 runs and averaging 53.85 per innings.[28] His seven centuries included a mammoth 304 not out against Trinidad at Bridgetown, in 1920. That score stood as a Barbadian record in first-class cricket for the next 24 years. It was the first triple century ever achieved by a West Indian in first-class cricket. It was finally surpassed by Frank Worrell in 1944. Tarilton had been the author of another important record in 1911 when he struck 210 not out for Pickwick against Spartan. That was then the highest score achieved in West Indian first division club cricket.[29] It lasted only four years before being broken by Eric Collymore, a precocious Harrisonian. Much longer lasting was his 1,885 record aggregate on behalf of Barbados. That mark survived for 21 years before being surpassed by Clyde Walcott in 1951. In his solitary tour of England, with the West Indies in 1923 at the advanced age of 38, he could muster only 554 runs (av: 21.30) but Tarilton yet finished with 2,777 runs (av: 38.56) in a first-class career that encompassed 51 games.[30]

YEARS OF ECLIPSE

After Tarilton's departure, the Lodge experienced a lengthy eclipse. The school team became so weak that it was demoted to the second division for many years and did not regain first division status until the 1920s. Its cricket captain, writing in the *Lodge School Record* in 1918, lamented that "in a small school such as ours, . . . it is always difficult to raise more than four or five First XI players; whereas Harrison's can always boast some 150 or more pupils from whom to pick". At first, however, the Lodge School, proved a trifle too powerful for the junior ranks. It won the second division championship outright in 1909–10, when it went through the season unbeaten (winning 10 matches and drawing 2); successfully defended its title in 1910–11, when it proved itself one of the best fielding teams in the island; and lost by a single point to Pickwick II in 1911–12. The school team also toured St Lucia in the summer of 1913 with gratifying results.[31] Consistent play in the junior division, despite its limited student body, eventually persuaded the cricket committee to restore the school to the first division competition in 1926.

The gradual regeneration of the Lodge in the first decades of the twentieth century was due almost entirely to the zeal of its most famous headmaster, O. DeC. 'Bill' Emtage (1898–1931), who brought with him from Deighton's Harrison College the general idea that a good secondary school should be patterned along the lines of the leading Victorian public schools. He therefore introduced the house and prefect systems and set up a model boarding establishment. He stressed the importance of games, which he himself personally supervised, and encouraged the senior pupils to sit on the games committee which he created. He maintained a very keen interest in cricket and firmly believed in its character-building powers. For many years he used the *Lodge School Record* to address the students in his 'Headmaster's Letter', alluding almost always to the value of games and invariably exhorting his wards to practise more assiduously.[32] The headmaster's emphasis on the role of cricket in preparing his charges for adulthood could hardly fail to produce an impact. The Lodge consequently spawned a number of promising athletes in Emtage's time, when the roll grew from a mere handful of students at the end of the nineteenth century to 115 by 1925.[33]

One of the principal Lodge School stars in those days was W.A. Farmer, an extraordinary scholar–athlete. From 1907 to 1911 he was by far the dominant force in Barbadian athletics. He led the Lodge to victory in four successive inter-school athletic championships and, in 1911, became the first Barbadian schoolboy to long jump in excess of 20 ft. At the Lodge School sports in 1912, he established a long jump record of 21 ft 8½ in. that survived for more than 50 years. It was still standing triumphantly when Farmer himself died in 1957. Farmer was also a quarter-mile sprinter, a half-mile champion and a high jumper of note. The 440-yard record of 55 seconds, which he set at the Lodge in 1911, was not equalled until 1943 (by R. Von Glatz). His half-mile record of 2 mins 10 secs, established at the inter-school sports in 1911, also endured for over 20 years. When Owen Alexander 'Graffie' Pilgrim, also of the Lodge, set the Barbadian high jump record of 5 ft 7½ in. in 1912, he defeated Farmer by a single inch.[34]

W.A. Farmer is one of the most significant names in the history of cricket and athletics at the Lodge. He played a key role in the many triumphs achieved by the school in the second division cricket competition during 1907–26. He was a hard-hitting batsman and a steady right-arm off-break bowler. Following his departure from school in 1912, he studied classics at Codrington College, taught briefly at Harrison College and then returned to teach at his alma mater from 1917 until his retirement in 1953. He thus enjoyed an almost unbroken connection with the Lodge for nearly half a century and served as its headmaster during his last six years there. He played excellent cricket for the Lodge for more than 20 years. In the 1924–25 season, he captured 63 wickets and scored 298 runs and then headed the school's bowling and batting averages in the next year. He was still the school's best cricketer when it was readmitted to the first division in 1926–27 and he continued to take valuable wickets in the senior competition until 1936. In his final years as an active cricketer, Farmer had the satisfaction of playing on the First XI with his son, Wilfred, who was then a very promising fast bowler. W.A. Farmer was not only a source of inspiration to his son and grandson but to countless other students of the Lodge.[35]

Apart from Farmer, the best cricketers produced by the Lodge during its second division days were T.W. Alleyne, R.A.J. Boyack, J. St F. Dare, James Bernard Emtage, C.W.F. Laurie, Joseph Evelyn Phillips, O.A. 'Graffie' Pilgrim and H.E. Skeete. Alleyne was a good enough player to gain selection for the Barbados Colts XV against the MCC in January 1926.[36] Dare eventually played for his native British Guiana in the late 1920s.[37] Laurie was a quintessential scholar–athlete. A brilliant mathematician, he won the Barbados Scholarship in 1922 and proceeded to Oxford University before joining the Harrison College staff. Not only was he the Lodge's cricket captain and best cricketer in 1920, he was also its hockey captain in addition to being a second lieutenant in the cadets.[38] He never achieved first-class status as a cricketer but did show enormous promise in his youth.

R.A.J. Boyack, who was selected to play for his native Trinidad immediately following his departure from school in 1925, was one of the best cricketers ever to represent the Lodge. The editor of the *Lodge School Record* thought it "safe to describe him as unquestionably one of the finest batsmen the School has ever produced". In his last year at school, Boyack established a second division record by scoring 710 runs. He also took 70 wickets during that 1924–25 season. He was easily the most consistent performer for the school during the early 1920s.[39] But his first-class career proved disappointing.

Other disappointments at the first-class level were Bernard Emtage, J.E. Phillips and H.E. Skeete, who represented Barbados at various points between 1919 and 1929. Phillips was the school's cricket captain before studying medicine at the University of Edinburgh.[40] When he came back to Barbados just after World War I, he was still promising enough as a right-arm medium-fast bowler to gain selection for the island against Trinidad in January 1920. But he took only one wicket in his two matches for Barbados. Dr Phillips soon emigrated to Scotland and played two games for that country in 1923. Altogether, in four first-class matches, he mustered only 52 runs (av: 8.66) and captured only 2 wickets (av: 59.00).[41] Slightly more successful was Dr Harold Skeete, a right-arm fast bowler, who represented Barbados twice. His finest moment came on a bad Kensington wicket in January 1925 when he did most, with 5 wickets for 33, to rout Jamaica for 80. He was a consistently good player for Wanderers during that decade.[42]

Bernard Emtage, the headmaster's scholarly and athletic son, was a tower of strength for his school both as a student and as a teacher. In addition to being a promising cricketer, he was an excellent long jumper, whose Division III record of 15 ft $7^1/_2$ in., set in 1915, remained intact at the Lodge until 1938.[43] In 1922, he went off to Oxford, where he scored two centuries and averaged almost 70 runs per innings for Magdalen College in 1926, but yet failed to win his 'blue'.[44] A sound right-handed batsman, he was also a steady right-arm bowler of medium pace. He and W.A. Farmer dominated the school's batting and bowling averages in the first division competition during the late 1920s. But in his solitary innings for Barbados in 1922 he scored only 2. His single wicket in that match also cost him 52 runs. Emtage eventually emigrated to England in 1931 and was lost to Barbadian cricket thereafter.[45]

RETURNING TO THE FIRST DIVISION

Shortly after the Lodge was readmitted to the senior competition, it appeared to have discovered a new superstar in A.G.F. Seale, a promising bowler with exceptional talent. He took 16 wickets in his first season (1929–30) and then captured 40 in the following campaign when he dismissed 10 good Empire batsmen in a single match. He joined Wanderers in 1932 but then seemed to have disappeared.[46] His place in the school team was partly filled by the arrival of A.R.V. Newsam, an Old Harrisonian, who joined the staff in 1931, served as games master periodically during the next two decades and then succeeded Farmer as headmaster in 1954. Newsam was an excellent scholar–athlete, who played soccer brilliantly and was a very steady allround cricketer.[47]

Perhaps the Lodge's best player between the retirement of Tarilton and the arrival of John Goddard was 'Graffie' Pilgrim, a lanky medium-fast right-arm bowler, who was capable of swinging the ball both ways and, because of his great height, of achieving unusual pace and bounce off the pitch. He made a substantial contribution to Lodge School cricket not only during its early years in the second division, but in the 1921–22 season when he taught there. He played on four occasions for Barbados during 1919–26, capturing 15 wickets at 23.93 runs each. His greatest performance came during the Goodwill tournament of 1920 when, against Trinidad at Kensington Oval, he captured 5 wickets for 21 runs in 15 overs and did most to dismiss the visitors for 197 in their first innings. Barbados won that game largely on the strength of Pilgrim's match figures of 9 for 105.[48] In a later age, when Test cricket opportunities had become much more plentiful, a player of his quality would unquestionably have gained selection to the West Indies team. 'Graffie' ranks with Clifford Goodman, Richard Edwards and Stanley Worme among the very best bowlers ever produced by the Lodge.

'Graffie' Pilgrim represented Spartan after he left school and then made his greatest contribution to Barbadian cricket by encouraging (and regularly playing with) the boys at Combermere School where he taught mathematics from 1926 to 1950. He had a great deal to do with the development of such first-class cricketers as George Carew, C.O'B. Crick, John Lucas, N.S. 'Brickie' Lucas, E.A. 'Mannie' Martindale, J.E.D. Sealy, C.D. 'Pampie' Spooner, F.G. 'Fluffie' Thomas, E.A.V. 'Foffie' Williams and Frank Worrell. 'Graffie' always regarded Worrell as his special protégé and was among the first to predict that 'Tae' Worrell would reach exceptional heights as a batsman even when the youngster was playing for Combermere mainly as a left-arm spin bowler.[49]

The Influence of 'Bessie' Walcott

Cricket at the Lodge received an enormous boost when Leslie Arthur 'Bessie' Walcott was appointed games master there in 1932. In that capacity he served the school until 1947 while remaining on the staff until 1953. Those 21 years witnessed a steady but remarkable transformation of the Lodge. What had been an essentially white school of roughly 120 pupils in 1932 became an integrated one of three times that number by the time of Walcott's departure. This social revolution was signalized by the appointment of Sam Headley, a bright and promising black scholar–athlete, as school captain in 1946 to the everlasting chagrin of many conservative families in the parish of St John. The games master helped enormously in this process of integration, endearing himself to white and black students

Leslie Arthur 'Bessie' Walcott (1894–1984), easily the most famous of all Barbadian cricket masters

alike. He began the system of awarding separate ties for athletics, cricket, football and hockey and furnishing both the senior and junior cricket teams with caps. He kindled the boys' enthusiasm for all sports and left an abiding impression on every student who attended the Lodge in his time.[50]

Walcott, who had himself attended Combermere and Harrison College in his youth, was a fine allrounder who played eleven matches for Barbados and one Test for the West Indies. For more than 40 years, he rendered yeoman service to Harrison, the Lodge and (occasionally) Pickwick. He served as games master at Harrison College for 11 years before defecting to the Lodge. At both schools he left an indelible imprint. He continued to play with the Lodge School team in the second division until he was well past 50 years old. A very capable right-handed batsman, he scored 515 runs for Barbados at an average of 30.29. He played some very good innings for the colony, most notably his 73 not out against MCC in 1929, his 62 against Trinidad in 1927, and 53 against Trinidad in 1936. He was also a good enough right-arm offbreak bowler to take 16 first-class wickets at 29.50 runs apiece. He was already 36 when he was invited in January 1930 to represent the West Indies in the Bridgetown Test against England. He acquitted himself reasonably well in that encounter, scoring 24 and 16 not out in his two innings and taking 1 wicket (George Gunn's) for 32 runs in 8 overs. In 1933, when almost 40, he was paid the compliment of being selected captain of the Barbados team which toured Trinidad. As late as 1941, when he was 47 years old, he finished fifth in the first division batting averages of the BCA. An entire nation mourned when the beloved 'Bessie' died at the great age of 90 on 28 February 1984. He had for some years been the oldest surviving West Indian Test player.[51]

While at the Lodge, Walcott coached such gifted cricketers as Wilfred Farmer, Michael Frederick, John Goddard, Ken Goddard, Roy Marshall, Tony Skinner, A.M. 'Charlie' Taylor and Rupert Wood, all of whom gained selection to Barbadian teams. Three other Lodge School cricketers who profited from Walcott's coaching and showed great promise during the 1940s were Sam Headley, Hubert Laurence Johnson and Torrey Pilgrim, who were extremely unlucky not to have been selected to play for Barbados. Johnson and Pilgrim were superb batsmen and Headley was a very good allrounder, who was impressive enough as an aggressive right-handed batsman and right-arm medium-fast bowler to be invited several times to the trials. After graduating with a classics degree from Codrington College, Headley eventually taught for several years at Harrison College, making a very good contribution to that school's cadets, cricket and football. His son, Sam A.E. Headley, also played fine cricket for the Lodge and was good enough to earn selection on the Barbados Schoolboys XI against the English Young Cricketers in 1976.[52]

Laurie Johnson, who was invited to the BCA trials in January 1945, failed to make the Trinidad tour. One year later, he did make the trip to Trinidad with the Barbados team but was not given an opportunity to play. On returning to Barbados that year, he began the new season with centuries against Combermere, Spartan and Wanderers.[53] Eventually Johnson migrated to England, turned professional in 1951 and scored more than 14,000 runs for the Derbyshire County Cricket Club during 1949–66. He exceeded 1,000 runs in six seasons and registered more than 1,872 (av: 37.44) when at his peak in 1960.[54] Pilgrim, one of 'Graffie's' nephews, also migrated, and played good cricket for Grenada, St Kitts and the Windward Islands in official tournaments between 1949 and 1953.

John Douglas Claude Goddard

The great Lodge School athletic star of the 1930s was John Goddard, a brilliant sprinter, superb footballer and excellent thrower of the cricket ball. In 1936, when only 17, he was selected to both the Barbadian cricket and soccer teams. As a cricketer, Goddard was a magnificent fieldsman, an attacking left-handed batsman with a wonderful range of scoring strokes, and a steady right-arm medium-paced bowler, whose offcutters were virtually unplayable on a turning pitch. In his last year at the Lodge (1936–37), he struck a blistering 200 not out against St Ann's and became only the fourth Barbadian schoolboy to achieve a double century in first division cricket. Goddard was the most consistent of the Caribbean batsmen during the war years when he scored five centuries against British Guiana and Trinidad in three goodwill tours. On one of these occasions, he scored 218 not out in what was then a world record fourth wicket partnership of 502 runs with Frank Worrell.

John Goddard (1919–87), the outstanding Lodge School athlete of the 1930s.

Altogether, in 32 games for Barbados, Goddard amassed 2,102 runs (av: 52.55), took 51 wickets (av: 26.98) and held 27 catches. One of the most successful of all West Indian allrounders, his Test record was also very creditable. In 27 matches for the West Indies, he scored 859 runs (av: 30.67), captured 33 wickets (av: 31.81) and took 22 catches. He participated altogether in 111 first-class matches, recording 3,769 runs (av: 33.35), 146 wickets (av: 26.33), and 94 catches. Goddard is now best remembered as the captain of the first West Indies team to defeat England in England (1950). He was also captain of the first West Indies team to defeat India in India (1948–49) and New Zealand in New Zealand (1952). As a captain of Barbados, he lost only 1 of 13 matches, and this in a very close tussle (by one wicket) to the MCC in 1953–54. That solitary loss he almost transformed into a victory by some magnificent bowling on the last day when he took 5/43 from 27 of the most searching overs. Not once, under him (between 1946 and 1956), did Barbados lose a match in regional competition. At home, Goddard was for several years one of Pickwick's major stars both on and off the field. From 1952 to 1965 he also served on the board of management of the BCA and was vice president during six of those years. After his retirement as an active player, he helped to select teams to represent both Barbados and the West Indies in the early 1960s. John Goddard died at 68 in 1987 but is still remembered as one of the most important among Barbadian cricket heroes. He was honoured with an OBE in 1951 and by the BCA in April 1986 when it erected the John Goddard Gates at the Kensington Oval. The BCA also honoured him posthumously during its centenary celebrations in 1992.[55]

'Charlie' Taylor, one of the most generous of the Lodge's benefactors

Joining Goddard at Pickwick was the effervescent A.M. 'Charlie' Taylor, one of the most remarkable athletes in Barbados during the 1940s and 1950s. Charlie was an aggressive opening batsman, a fleet and brilliant outfielder and a competent wicketkeeper. He also played soccer and field-hockey extremely well. As a cricketer, he confirmed his early promise at the Lodge by scoring a fine 110 against British Guiana at Georgetown in 1945 and a sparkling 161 against the MCC at

Bridgetown in 1948. In January 1949, against Trinidad at the Kensington Oval, he totally dominated an opening partnership of 278 which he shared with the young Roy Marshall. That was the occasion on which he achieved his highest first-class score of 168. Altogether Taylor played 16 matches for Barbados, scoring 860 runs and averaging 34.40 per innings.[56] His contribution to cricket in his native island was considerable. Not only did he represent Barbados with much success on a number of occasions, but he gave excellent support to Pickwick for over 20 years. He also donated money to his alma mater to allow the Lodge to erect a new scoreboard and hire cricket coaches during the 1950s and 1960s. On the strength of Charlie's largesse, such eminent cricketers as Charlie Griffith, Seymour Nurse and Everton Weekes were invited to instruct the youngsters. Taylor also produced a son, Alfred Maurice, who represented Barbados as a wicket-keeper/batsman in the late 1960s.[57]

Other outstanding Lodge School players in Goddard's time were A.F.G. Austin, R.G. Blackman, H.B. Bourne, Wilfred Farmer and A. O'N. Skinner. Frankie Austin, a nephew of the great Sir Harold B.G. Austin, showed sufficient promise as an opening batsman to be invited to the trials in 1935 and 1936 and was most unfortunate never to have won a Barbadian cap. He and Skinner once scored centuries in a huge first-wicket stand

The Lodge School XI, 1936–37. *Standing*: J. Barrera, A. Skinner, J. Shand, H. Webster, W. Farmer; *seated*: Mr L. A. Walcott, H. Bourne (capt.), J. Goddard, Mr A.R.V. Newsam; *front*: F.G. Austin, C.R. Packer

for the Lodge against Pickwick at Kensington.[58] He was lost to Barbadian cricket after proceeding to Cambridge University during the war years. He played some fine cricket there, winning his 'blue' in 1943.[59] Hilary Bourne, a brilliant batsman, would certainly have made the island team in January 1937 had he not been injured. He captained the Lodge to its most successful first division season in his final year (1936–37). The school won three games, drew three, lost only two, and finished second to Spartan in the BCA competition. Bourne was then the Lodge's leading batsman with 389 runs at an average of 48.6 per innings. As a schoolboy batsman, he was very highly regarded by cricket pundits in Barbados and was confidently expected to achieve Test match status. But he soon departed to study medicine at McGill University and was lost to first-class cricket after that.[60] Tony Skinner did eventually play two games for Barbados and lead Wanderers to a BCA championship in 1948 but his first-class career, thanks mainly to pressure of business, was all too short for a stylish right-handed batsman of his potential.[61]

Roger Blackman was a magnificent athlete who almost single-handedly led the Lodge to the inter-school athletic championships in 1934. He was easily the best footballer in the island at that time. He was an excellent right-handed batsman who averaged more than 50 runs per innings in his four matches for Barbados during 1940–42. He emigrated to Trinidad shortly thereafter and was lost to first-class cricket for ever. Blackman is one of the few athletes who can claim allegiance to all three of the Barbadian élite cricket schools. He attended Combermere for a short time before enrolling in Harrison College. He then spent his last schooldays at the Lodge. During the late 1930s, he also made a significant contribution to the Spartan cause and was one of that club's most successful players on its tour of Trinidad early in 1938.[62]

A Second and Mightier Farmer in the Field

A big and powerful lad, Wilfred Farmer was one of the hardest hitters that the game has known. He delighted in hitting huge sixes and it was his determination to slog at most of the deliveries he received which generally impaired his effectiveness. Even so, his technique was sound enough when he was in the right mood and he finished up with a first-class average in excess of 50 runs per innings. In nine games for Barbados between 1946 and 1959, he accumulated 663 runs (av: 51.00). At his peak in 1951–52, Farmer amassed well over 500 of these in five innings against British Guiana and Jamaica. His greatest batting performance was a glorious 275

The Lodge School XI, 1944–45. *Standing*: D. Evelyn, H. Mendez, D. Tudor, S. Headley, T. Pilgrim, L. Crichlow; *seated*: J. Hutson, P.D. Short, M. Frederick (capt.), H.L. Johnson, H. Massiah

at Jamaica's expense in January 1952. Perhaps had he not emerged at the same time as the Three Ws, he might well have gained a berth on a West Indies Test XI or two. In his youth, before his back broke down, Farmer was also a formidable fast bowler. Between 1935 and 1937, many pundits thought him potentially as good and as fast as any of the famous Empire quartet of speedsters (Herman Griffith, 'Mannie' Martindale, 'Pampie' Spooner and 'Foffie' Williams). Wilfred Farmer's main claim to fame, however, is the well-known fact that, as Commissioner of Police in Barbados, he befriended the young Gary Sobers in the early 1950s, encouraged the lad to join the Police Boys' Club and found a place for him on the regular Police XI in the first division competition of the BCA. That proved to be the turning point in Gary's career. Captain Wilfred, himself the son of a famous scholar–athlete, made another contribution to cricket by fathering Stephen Farmer who became a regular member of the Barbados team during the 1970s. Farmer is also known to have offered considerable encouragement and support to such young policemen as Cecil Bradshaw and Carl Mullins, who played for Barbados briefly during the 1950s.[63]

In the years between the departure of John Goddard and the arrival of Roy Marshall, three interesting cricketers appeared at the Lodge. They did not eventually represent Barbados but they left their mark nevertheless on the history of the growth and development of the sport in the island. One was Ronald G. Hughes, a scholar–athlete, who played cricket and soccer for the school with perhaps more enthusiasm than skill. He eventually graduated from the University of Toronto with an honours degree in history and returned to teach at Combermere where he served as cricket master from 1952 to 1958. It was there that he left a lasting imprint on the game, coaching such first-class cricketers as Rawle Brancker, Wes Hall, Peter Lashley and Lionel Williams. Ronnie did much to make Combermere a force in BCA cricket during the 1950s.[64]

One of Ronnie's younger contemporaries at the Lodge was P.D.B. Short who made a major contribution to the life of the school in his senior years. By 1945, he had become vice captain of cricket, vice captain of football, captain of boxing, a sergeant in the Lodge School cadet corps, vice president of the debating society and a school prefect. Like Hughes, a grand nephew of the great Harry Ince, Peter Short eventually threw in his lot with Wanderers, the club to which his father and grandfather had also sworn allegiance. His claim to fame, however, is based less on his performance on the cricket field than his administrative role off it. Short, who was elected president of the WICBC in 1994, was for 21 years president of the BCA, serving in that capacity for a longer spell than anyone before him. He had also been the secretary of the WICBC during the late 1960s.[65]

One of Short's contemporaries at the Lodge in the late 1930s and early 1940s was Colin Deane who became an Empire stalwart after leaving school and made a name for himself as one of the leading cricket scorers in the island. He has been an official scorer for Empire, Barbados and the West Indies for many years and was deservedly honoured for his contribution to the game when the BCA celebrated its 100th anniversary in 1992.[66]

ROY EDWIN MARSHALL AND THE STARS OF THE 1940S

The great Lodge School star of the 1940s was Roy Edwin Marshall who developed into one of the finest opening batsmen in the world during the 1950s and 1960s. Roy was a thrilling player of all the strokes and delighted in carrying the attack to the fast bowlers. He played only four Tests for the West Indies but had the satisfaction of contributing enormously to Hampshire's cause for 20 years (1953–72) and of helping that county to its very first championship in 1961. Marshall ended his career with 35,725 runs (av: 35.94) in first-class cricket. He was the first West Indian to achieve more than 50 centuries and wound up his career with 68 altogether. Most of these were scored outside of the Caribbean, but

Roy Edwin Marshall (1930–92), the Lodge School star of the 1940s

Roy is still fondly remembered in Barbados where many pundits consider him one of the best batsmen ever produced by the island and terribly unlucky not to have played many more Tests. For Barbados, Marshall's personal record was quite exceptional. In eight games he scored 695 runs, and averaged 57.91 per innings. When he made his début against Trinidad at Port-of-Spain in January 1946, he was only 15 years, 276 days old. He therefore remains the youngest player ever to represent Barbados. Marshall's 191 against British Guiana in 1950 is still considered one of the great innings played at the Kensington Oval in Bridgetown.[67]

Apart from Johnson, Headley, Marshall and Pilgrim, the Lodge produced such fine cricketers in the 1940s as B.K. Bowen, E.W. Cave, M.C. Frederick, and W.G. Patterson, among whom only Michael Frederick achieved first-class status. He played for Barbados, Jamaica and Derbyshire between 1944 and 1954. A sound (rather than flashy) right-handed opening batsman, he also played one Test for the West Indies, scoring 0 and 30 against England at Sabina Park in 1954.[68] In this he was much more fortunate than Keith Bowen who was, for so many years, one of the leading spin bowlers in Barbados. It is still difficult to believe that he was never awarded a cap for his native island. In the 1947–48 season, he took 43 wickets at 16.77 runs each in BCA first division competition but was "rather surprisingly overlooked", to quote the *Lodge School Record* which expressed dismay at the fact that Bowen was not even invited to the trials.[69] He was destined to suffer many a similar fate while bowling impressively for Spartan for several years. Cave, who once struck a glorious century against Carlton to save the Lodge from certain defeat, never really fulfilled the expectations of his supporters.[70] 'Billy' Patterson, who promised so much as a 15-year-old allrounder during the 1948–49 season, died tragically young in the very next year.[71]

Lodge School Stars of the Fifties

It was in the 1950s that the social revolution, begun in the previous two decades, was completed. The Lodge gradually became a predominantly black school, with its intake eventually reaching 400 in 1956. This meant that it had doubled its student roll within 15 years and the 'day boys' now easily outnumbered the residential students. While Sam Headley's elevation to the school captaincy had caused a great furore, leading indeed to the resignation of the headmaster, T.L. Evans, in 1946, no such excitement attended the appointment of Oscar W. Jordan, another black scholar-athlete, in 1957. In that year, in fact, Jordan was head prefect, house captain, president of the School Guild, editor of the *Lodge School Record*, cricket captain and a cadet officer. He was also one of the brightest boys in the school, winning a much coveted Barbados Scholarship in 1958.[72] The Lodge School stars of this decade consequently came from various strata in the Barbadian society and, for the first time, included more blacks than whites.

The biggest names in Lodge School cricket during the 1950s belonged to David Allan, Arthur Bethell, V.H.C. Brookes, Richard Edwards, John Evelyn, Owen Estwick, Patrick Frost, Stephen Hinkson, G. St C. Hutchinson, Oscar Jordan, A.C. Mayers, T.L. Mayers, Eddie Perkins, C.C. Smith, A.L. Walker and N.G. Wilkie. Not all of them, however, did ample justice to the great potential they had shown as schoolboy cricketers. 'Nobbie' Estwick, who was more famous for his lack of inches than his fluency of stroke, showed sufficient leadership skills to be appointed captain of the Second XI in 1953. He made his mark on Barbadian cricket later on by rendering yeoman service both to the BCA and the BCL.[73]

John Evelyn and Eddie Perkins showed great promise as bowlers, the former fast, the latter slow. But neither made it beyond the trials. Perkins was an interesting spinner who had previously bowled well for Harrison College, but both he and Evelyn lacked consistency. The same could not be said of Gray Wilkie, a very steady off-break bowler, who made an invaluable contribution to cricket at Wanderers after leaving the Lodge though he failed to achieve first-class status. Unfortunately, slow bowlers like Bowen, Perkins and Wilkie had to compete throughout their careers with such spinners as Adzil Holder, Horace King, Gary Sobers and C.B. 'Boogles' Williams for a berth on the Barbados team.

Vere Brookes, Anthony Mayers, Chris Smith and Audley Walker were all members of the Combined Schools XI which opposed the E.W. Swanton XI at the Kensington Oval in 1956.[74] Brookes, a fine left-arm

The Lodge School XI, 1956–57. *Standing*; A. deV. Browne, W.B. Hadley, Mr E.W. Glasgow, C.P. Brathwaite; *seated*: A. Bethell, P.D. Frost, O.W. Jordan (capt.), T.L. Mayers; *front:* D.A. Simmons, A. Cozier

spinner, played for Empire afterwards. Walker was a clever right-arm medium-fast bowler who failed to fulfil his early promise. Smith, a stylish left-handed batsman, proceeded to Edinburgh University which he represented on the cricket field for a few years.[75] Mayers, one of the fastest bowlers in Barbados at his peak, was twice selected to represent the island. He also played successfully for Spartan for many years and captained that club briefly when Cammie Smith was touring Australia with the West Indies team in 1960–61. His first-class career, however, was suddenly curtailed by the meteoric rise of Charles Griffith and Wes Hall in the late 1950s.[76]

Patrick Frost, Oscar Jordan and Trevor Mayers, three very promising young batsmen, were all invited to the trials in preparation for the Pakistan tour of 1957–58.[77] Mayers, who was also a left-arm spinner, was again invited to the trials one year later. But he never did gain his Barbados cap. Jordan, the team's captain in 1957 when he struck an attractive century against Pickwick, was an elegant, right-handed strokeplayer with enormous potential. Three years previously he had, with Anthony Mayers, been selected to play for the Combined Schools' XI against a Barbados team at the Kensington Oval. But his cricket progress, like that of so many others, was impeded by his studies. After winning a Barbados Scholarship in 1958, he proceeded to Edinburgh University where he qualified himself as a doctor. While there, he served as captain of the university cricket team during the early 1960s.[78] After returning to practise medicine in Barbados, however, he made little impact as a cricketer.

The Legacy of Frost

Much more significant historically was Patrick Douglas Frost, who not only played very well as a schoolboy, captaining the Lodge intelligently during his final year there, but returned to teach at his alma mater and continued to represent the school with much distinction on the cricket field. In 1959, just before departing for Oxford University, he presented the school with the P.D. Frost Cup to be awarded annually to its most outstanding fieldsman. At Oxford, Frost became one of the very few West Indians to represent this university, but played (in 1961) in only one first-class match.[79] During the 1960s, he remained one of the best players in the Lodge's First XI, doing much to inspire a whole new generation of schoolboy cricketers. He devoted countless hours to coaching at the school during the 1970s. As late as 1976 he led the school's batting averages by scoring 547 runs. Frost, who finally retired from the Lodge School staff in 1996, is perhaps best remembered as a cricketer for his role in the record sixth wicket stand of 276 runs which he shared with Stephen Farmer against a strong Spartan club in 1969. His role in the development of cricket at his old school is quite substantial indeed.[80]

Geoffrey Hutchinson was the youngest of several brothers who contributed enormously to the growth of the Carlton Club. He began his cricket career at Harrison College but defected to the Lodge in the late 1940s. He was a stylish right-handed batsman who played twice for Barbados during 1955–56 (scoring 63 runs in 3 innings) at a time when the island was exceptionally strong in middle-order batting.[81] His son, Gregory, was also destined to play for the Lodge. Both of them participated in the Past vs Present Lodge cricket match in 1974, top-scoring for their respective sides when Geoffrey retired after hitting 68, and Gregory made 63 not out.[82] Stephen Hinkson was a good right-arm fast bowler who eventually toiled manfully for Carlton, which he captained most efficiently during the 1970s, but his first-class career involved but a single game, against Guyana in 1974, when (at 32) he was probably past his peak.[83]

Arthur Bethell was an attractive left-handed batsman and a left-arm bowler at a brisk medium pace. He created a very favourable impression as an allrounder both at the Lodge and at Pickwick. He eventually earned 16 caps for Barbados between 1963 and 1970 but scored fewer than 500 runs in first-class cricket and averaged only 26.10. His 10 first-class wickets also cost 391 runs. These are very disappointing statistics for so fine a player, especially when his superb 157 for the Barbados Colts against the Australians in 1965 is recalled. On that occasion he put the tourists to the sword, hitting 3 sixes and 23 fours while sharing a fifth wicket stand of 196 with the veteran, Everton Weekes.[84] As Pickwick's captain in 1963, Bethell also had the distinction of performing the double: 50 wickets and 500 runs in BCA first division competition. That is a very rare feat in BCA history.[85]

Two Lodge Men Who Reached the Pinnacle

David Allan and Richard Edwards did considerably better. The former developed into one of the finest of all West Indian wicketkeepers, only to be eclipsed in the end, after playing five Tests, by the great Deryck Murray of Trinidad. Allan showed such promise as a schoolboy wicketkeeper that he was invited to play for Barbados against E.W. Swanton's XI in 1956 when he was only 18 years old. He remained a regular fixture on the island team for the next 10 years, scoring 268 runs (av: 14.88) and effecting 39 dismissals in his 19 appearances for Barbados. He made two tours with West Indian teams to England, performing creditably in both. In 54 first-class matches altogether, he took 117 catches and stumped 24 batsmen. This tally of 141 dismissals remains one of the highest for any Barbadian wicketkeeper. Allan is still the greatest wicketkeeper ever produced by the Lodge and the finest yet to have played for Wanderers. He had excellent hands and was equally competent with both spin and pace. But he simply had the misfortune to have emerged at the wrong time and to have become injured at too critical a stage of the 1963 tour.[86]

David Allan, the finest wicketkeeper thus far produced by the Lodge

'Prof' Edwards, who was clearly one of the best fast bowlers ever produced by the

Lodge, even though he never played for its first division team, became one of the liveliest bowlers in the West Indies after the retirement of Wes Hall and Charlie Griffith in the late 1960s. Had it not been for those two famous speedsters, 'Prof' might well have gained a few more Test caps than the five which he did. In those games, he took 18 wickets for the West Indies and was particularly impressive against New Zealand at Wellington in March 1969 when he took seven wickets in the match, including 5 for 84 runs in the first innings. In 20 matches for Barbados between 1961 and 1970, he captured 42 wickets (av: 33.21). In 35 first-class games altogether, Edwards scored 389 runs (av: 11.78), took 15 catches and claimed 78 wickets (av: 36.29). He enjoyed his most successful afternoon in February 1967 when he captured 6/45 to help Barbados defeat the Leeward Islands at Basseterre, St Kitts. After his retirement from first-class cricket, Edwards continued for many years to represent Wanderers, before becoming a very popular and penetrating cricket commentator. 'Prof' has made another important kind of contribution to Caribbean cricket by overseeing the preparation of the pitch at the Kensington Oval. His wickets there have become deservedly famous for their ability to produce conclusive results. They are lively enough to encourage the best fast bowlers without discouraging the best strokeplayers. In fact, Kensington Oval has established a remarkable world record by producing not a single drawn Test for more than 20 years.[87]

One of the products of the Lodge at this time was Tony Cozier who batted and played soccer fairly well for his school but was destined to make his mark in cricket not as a player but, like Edwards, as a commentator. After playing First XI cricket for the Lodge between 1955 and 1957, Tony proceeded to study journalism at Carleton University in Ottawa, Canada. He returned to Barbados in 1961 to assume the post of sports editor of the *Barbados Daily News*. Since 1965, he has been covering West Indies Test cricket for a variety of newspapers in England and the Caribbean. Cozier is universally recognized as the greatest cricket commentator thus far produced by the West Indies and his voice is well known to radio and television audiences everywhere. His contribution to Caribbean cricket literature is immense. Not only has he written one book and countless articles on West Indies cricket, but he persevered to edit and publish the *West Indies Cricket Annual* almost single-handedly for more than 20 years (1970–91). He is now trying his utmost to keep alive the very useful *Red Stripe Caribbean Cricket Quarterly*. Quite deservedly, he was honoured by the BCA during its centenary celebrations in 1992 for his contributions to the game.[88]

A Kind of Cricketing Renaissance

When E.W. Swanton led another squad to Barbados in 1960, he managed to arrange a very interesting match against a Lodge School XIII, composed of pupils past and present. This Lodge team, inevitably captained by John Goddard, included David Allan, Arthur Bethell, Richard Edwards, Randall Goddard, Geoffrey Hutchinson, Anthony Mayers, Trevor Mayers and Charlie Taylor. Colin Blades, Leonard Brathwaite, Philip Headley and Alfred Taylor, four of the most promising among the present boys, were then added to the squad.[89] While Headley, Sam's younger brother, migrated to Canada shortly after leaving school, the others generally fulfilled their early promise as cricketers. Brathwaite and Taylor were invited to the Barbadian trials at the end of the 1959–60 season. Blades, Brathwaite and Taylor (along with T. Peirce) were selected to the Combined Schools' cricket team which toured Jamaica in 1961. The four Lodge School representatives acquitted themselves extremely well on that trip.[90]

This was a period, in fact, when the Lodge appeared to be enjoying a cricket renaissance, thanks in large part to the efforts of A.G. Sumpter, who had joined Graham Wilkes as assistant games master in 1953. He himself was an aggressive batsman and a brilliant fielder who had played inter-state cricket in New Zealand. Under his tutelage, the Lodge won the second division championship in 1956 (for the first time since 1911), finished fourth in the intermediate division in 1958, won the Ronald Tree Cup (for which the three élite schools were then competing) in 1960 and 1961, and placed third in the first division in 1961 and 1963.[91] The Lodge also seemed to have profited immensely from the coaching of Everton Weekes, which the *Lodge School Record* described in 1963 as "invaluable".[92]

This was the period, too, when the young and incredibly talented Colin F. Blades flashed like some proverbial comet across the sky of Barbadian sport. At the Lodge School sports in 1962, he finally eclipsed W.A. Farmer's 53-year-old long jump record by achieving 22 ft 0¼ in. That same year, he scored 518 runs in the BCA competition while taking 37 wickets with his accurate leg-breaks and occasional googlies.[93] He followed this up with 796 runs in the 1962–63 season, after which he was selected to represent Barbados against British Guiana.[94] But at the first-class level, Blades never quite did justice to his exceptional talents. In 12 matches for Barbados between 1963 and 1970, he scored fewer than 500 runs and averaged only 18.45 per innings. Always a brilliant fielder, he held 11 catches in these games. For a player who was considered by many to have been one of the very best schoolboy cricketers ever seen in Barbados, these are not very impressive statistics.[95]

Leonard Brathwaite and Alfred Taylor were among the best of Colin's teammates at the Lodge. Brathwaite was unfortunate never to have been chosen to play for Barbados, especially since he was a member of the final thirteen in 1963. He continued to receive several invitations to trial matches at the Kensington Oval when he played for Empire. He also represented that club at soccer.

Alfred Taylor, Charlie's son, was a right-handed wicketkeeper/batsman like his father. He was only 16 when first invited to the trials in 1960.[96] Eventually he played four matches for Barbados in the first year of the Shell Shield competition (1966–67). He only scored 79 runs in those games, but they included one fine innings of 46. He also took 11 catches.[97] Alfred, again like his father, made a valuable contribution to Pickwick's cause after leaving the Lodge.

A Period of Slump

During the last 30 years or so the Lodge School, like Harrison College and Combermere, became noticeably less productive of promising cricketing stars. Whereas it had spawned most of the Barbadian representatives up to World War I, the Lodge is now less important as a cricket factory. Not only have many more secondary schools emerged but the BCA has been less snobbish in its approach to players without secondary education. Whereas it used to be very difficult for working class cricketers to gain selection, the process since the 1960s has become much more progressive. The result is that only three Lodge boys of the 1960s — Colin Blades, Stephen Farmer and Alfred Taylor — eventually achieved first-class status. Thereafter the pickings became even slimmer and the only Lodge School alumni to represent Barbados during the 1970s and 1980s were Teddy Foster, Michael Inniss and Clinton St Hill, none of whom ultimately reached great heights.[98] Two others, Hugh Gore and Shane Julien, achieved first-class status when they played for their native territories in the Shell Shield competition following their departure from school. Gore (an Antiguan) represented the Combined Islands during the 1970s, and Julien (a native of Grenada) made his débût for the Windward Islands in 1982.[99]

The measure of the Lodge's decline as a cricket nursery since Independence (1966) can best be appreciated by noting that, prior to Floyd Reifer's selection in 1997, the last Lodge alumnus to play for the West Indies was Edwards in 1969. The best Lodge players since then have been

Stephen Farmer, Teddy Foster and Floyd Reifer. Farmer was one of the most consistent performers in the BCA first division competition from 1970 to 1985. As captain of the Lodge in 1969, he struck a defiant 203 against Spartan in a match-saving innings that spanned all three days. After his team had been bowled out cheaply on a difficult strip on the first day, Spartan quickly declared after securing a first innings lead. Farmer survived in the second innings on the same day before combining with Frost to put Spartan to the sword on the second Saturday. He was still unbeaten on the third afternoon when the Lodge innings ended. He had thus become the sixth (and last) schoolboy to score a double century in BCA first division competition.[100] An attacking right-handed batsman and penetrative medium-paced bowler, he was the mainstay of Wanderers for a very long time and earned 17 caps for Barbados between 1969 and 1977. But his first-class record, 551 runs (av: 23.95) and 16 wickets (av: 48.06), is not in keeping with his enviable reputation as a club cricketer.[101] Foster, a left-handed allrounder who eventually made a fine contribution to Spartan's cause, represented Barbados on 11 occasions between 1975 and 1981 and also played professionally in Holland. But he too left an undistinguished first-class record: 276 runs (av: 21.23) and 13 wickets (av: 38.53).

More promising thus far has been the young Reifer, a left-handed wicket-keeper/batsman, who has retained a regular berth on the Barbados squad over the past five years. In 13 first-class matches up to 1996, he had scored 661 runs at an average of almost 35 per innings and had struck a fine 126 against Guyana at Albion in 1992 when only 20 years old.[102] He finally forced his way into the West Indies team by establishing a new record of 756 runs during the 1996–97 Red Stripe season. It is a pity, however, that he failed to make a more lasting impression on the selectors. He managed to compile only 48 runs against Sri Lanka in his first four Test innings.

AN ASSESSMENT OF THE LODGE'S CONTRIBUTIONS

If the Lodge has generally been eclipsed by other nurseries in the production of famous Test players since 1960, it has made a notable contribution of another sort by producing able administrators. Such Lodge School Old Boys as Theodore Alleyne, Arthur Bethell, Owen Estwick, John Goddard, O.A. Pilgrim, P.D.B. Short and Tim Tarilton have rendered yeoman service to the BCA. Peter Short, the President of the BCA from 1973 to 1994, led it through its most difficult (and in many ways its most successful) phase.[103] He has also made a fine contribution to West Indies cricket as its delegate to the International Cricket Council (ICC). He served as president of the WICBC during 1994–96. In addition to his long and valued service as a member of the BCA board of management, 'Nobbie' Estwick presided over the affairs of the BCL for many years.

Even though the Lodge failed to maintain its early reputation as a cricket nursery, its overall contribution to cricket in Barbados is almost incalculable. Not only did it produce a large number of excellent players who strengthened the ranks of Pickwick and Wanderers, making those two cricket clubs among the most famous in the West Indies, but some of its alumni, like 'Graffie' Pilgrim and Revd Lyall Speed at Combermere, Sam Headley at Harrison College and Percy Goodman at the Foundation Boys' School, did much to disseminate the cricket gospel throughout the island. While the Goodmans played a key role in the establishment of Pickwick in one century, Wilfred Farmer had an equally vital part to play in the establishment of Police in the next. The Leeward and Windward cricket clubs were largely sustained in their earlier days by old Lodge boys; while Geoffrey Hutchinson gave staunch support to Carlton during the 1950s and 1960s as Stephen Hinkson was to do one decade later.

Philip Thorn, in *Barbados Cricketers 1865–1990*, has identified 324 players who represented the island during its first 125 years of first-class competition. Of these, at least 58 (i.e. about 18 percent) are known to have learnt their cricketing skills at the Lodge. Among them, David Allan, Percy Cox, Richard Edwards, Michael Frederick, John Goddard, Percy Goodman, Roy Marshall and Tim Tarilton also gained selection to West Indian touring teams and five of them played in international Tests. In more concrete and mundane terms, six Lodge School Old Boys in 44 Tests recorded 1,220 runs (av: 22.59), 51 wickets (av: 33.15), and 43 dismissals, including 3 stumpings. This arithmetic would have looked much more impressive had the Lodge not reached its cricketing peak prior to the inception of Test cricket in the West Indies. Five of its greatest stars – Cox, Clifford and Percy Goodman, Pilgrim and Tarilton, for instance – had all retired by 1930. Marshall, too, would have made a much more substantial contribution to the West Indian cause, had he not decided to emigrate while at his peak. He could well have been a fixture on the West Indies Test XI after the retirement of Alan Rae and Jeffrey Stollmeyer at a time when Conrad Hunte so constantly lacked a regular opening partner.

A Lodge Team For All Seasons

It is often possible to measure the overall contribution of an institution to a particular sport by selecting a team to represent it over the years. This provides the reader with a most useful index of the institution's quality. The batting order of an all-time Lodge School cricket XI might well be: Tim Tarilton, Roy Marshall, Wilfred Farmer, Percy Goodman, Percy Cox, John Goddard (captain), Clifford Goodman, David Allan (wicketkeeper), Richard Edwards, Stanley Worme and Owen Pilgrim.

This team is a good reflection of cricket at the Lodge over the years. Its main strength lies in the depth and quality of its allrounders and its batsmen. Few schools anywhere can boast of having produced batsmen to match the skills of Arthur Bethell, Roger Blackman, Hilary Bourne, Percy Cox, Wilfred Farmer, Michael Frederick, John Goddard, Percy Goodman, Laurie Johnson, Roy Marshall, Floyd Reifer, Tim Tarilton and Charlie Taylor. Bethell, Goddard, Percy Goodman and Stephen Farmer were also excellent allrounders. For an institution that catered for so long to the sons of the Barbadian aristocracy, it is surprising to observe that it still established a very good fast bowling tradition. The Lodge can point with pride to the first-class careers of such alumni as Richard Edwards, Clifford Goodman, Anthony Mayers, 'Graffie' Pilgrim and Stanley Worme. This may perhaps have been due to the fact that the Lodge was never wealthy enough to hire a ground staff whose assignments included bowling fast to patrician batsmen. In fact, at the turn of the last century, the school was in such dire straits that, as we have seen, it was the pupils who prepared the wickets!

On the surface it would appear that the Lodge was never really noted for the quality of its spin bowlers since only a few of its alumni achieved first-class status in this capacity. But such fine spinners as Keith Bowen, Eddie Perkins and Gray Wilkie may well have been invited to represent Barbados had they not arrived at inopportune times. The school's major area of weakness has perhaps been behind the stumps. Even so, it produced, in David Allan and Alfred Taylor, two wicketkeepers of outstanding ability. Its dream team, in the final analysis, would present an enormous challenge to that of most grammar and public schools in the cricket-playing world.

NOTES

1 The only general history of this institution is still the brief, but useful F.A. Hoyos, *Two Hundred Years: A History of the Lodge School* (Bridgetown, 1945).

See also Keith A.P. Sandiford, " 'Sons in the Sun': The Cricket Story of the Lodge School of Barbados", *Cricket Lore* 2, no. 3 (1995): 34–7.

2 Bruce Hamilton, *Cricket in Barbados* (Bridgetown, 1947), 18–23.

3 *Lodge School Record* (1911), 8–12.

4 *Lodge School Record* (1912), 1–4.

5 *Lodge School Record* (1968), 100–101.

6 Hamilton, *Cricket in Barbados*, 9–10.

7 Ibid., 18–22.

8 Ibid., 20–1; Philip Thorn, *Barbados Cricketers, 1865–1990* (West Bridgford, 1991), 10, 18.

9 BCA, *100 Years of Organised Cricket in Barbados, 1892–1992* (Bridgetown, 1992), 98; Keith A.P. Sandiford and Earle H. Newton, *Combermere School and the Barbadian Society* (Kingston, 1995), 14–15, 22.

10 *Lodge School Record* (1931–32), 45.

11 BCA, *100 Years*, 72–3; *Lodge School Record* (1927), 1; Thorn, *Barbados Cricketers*, 11, 24.

12 *Barbados Herald*, 21 October 1886.

13 *Barbados Advocate*, 21 May 1897, 6.

14 Hamilton, *Cricket in Barbados*, 53–4; Peter Wynne-Thomas, *England on Tour* (London, 1982), 41–2.

15 Thorn, *Barbados Cricketers*, 12, 24.

16 BCA, *Report and Statement and Accounts 1st April 1994 to 31st March 1995*, 34.

17 Gerry Wolstenholme, *The West Indian Tour of England 1906* (Blackpool, 1992), 40.

18 Ibid., 7.

19 BCA, *100 Years*, 78; Gerry Cotter, *England versus West Indies* (London, 1991), 22; Hamilton, *Cricket in Barbados*, 67, 81–2.

20 Hamilton, *Cricket in Barbados*, 67; Thorn, *Barbados Cricketers*, 10, 23.

21 Hamilton, *Cricket in Barbados*, 80; Thorn, *Barbados Cricketers*, 8.

22 *Lodge School Record* (1977), 104.

23 See notes on the foundation of the WICBC by Peter D.B. Short, in BCA, *Report and Statement of Accounts 1st April 1970 to 31st March 1971*, 24–5.

24 Hamilton, *Cricket in Barbados*, 60.

25 Thorn, *Barbados Cricketers*, 30.

26 *Barbados Bulletin*, 18 October 1897.

27 BCA, *100 Years*, 116–17.

28 Thorn, *Barbados Cricketers*, 30.

29 *Lodge School Record* (1912), 32.

30 Keith A.P. Sandiford, *Clyde Leopold Walcott: His Record Innings-by-Innings* (West Bridgford, 1996), 21.

31 *Lodge School Record* (1911), 14, 25; *Lodge School Record* (1912), 32. *Lodge School Record* (1914), 21–3.

32 Keith A.P. Sandiford and Brian Stoddart, "The Elite Schools and Cricket in Barbados: A Study in Colonial Continuity", *International Journal of the History*

of Sport (December 1987), 4: 336–37. See also the files of the *Lodge School Record* for the years of Emtage's tenure.

33 *Lodge School Record* (1927), 4.

34 *Lodge School Record* (1911), 13–15, 21; and *Lodge School Record* (1912), 7.

35 *Lodge School Record* (1911–58).

36 *Lodge School Record* (1927), 17.

37 Ibid., 38.

38 *Lodge School Record* (1922), 3, 9, 41; *Lodge School Record* (1927), 39.

39 *Lodge School Record* (1926), 7, 10, 21.

40 *Lodge School Record* (1912), 32.

41 Philip Bailey, Philip Thorn and Peter Wynne-Thomas, *Who's Who of Cricketers* (London, 1984), 802.

42 Hamilton, *Cricket in Barbados*, 110.

43 *Lodge School Record* (1938), 36.

44 *Lodge School Record* (1927), 1, 38.

45 *Lodge School Record* (1931–32), 1. Thorn, *Barbados Cricketers*, 24.

46 *Lodge School Record* (1929–30), 18; *Lodge School Record* (1930–31), 16; *Lodge School Record* (1931–32), 43.

47 *Advocate Year Book and Who's Who 1951* (Bridgetown, 1951), 221; *Lodge School Record* (1947–48), 19; *Lodge School Record* (1954), 5.

48 Hamilton, *Cricket in Barbados*, 101–2.

49 BCA, *100 Years*, 108–9.

50 Sandiford and Stoddart, "The Elite Schools", 343–34; *Lodge School Record* (1953), 4–5.

51 BCA *100 Years*, 124; *Wisden* 1985, 1203. See also *Harrisonian* (1916–31); *Lodge School Record* (1932–54).

52 *Lodge School Record* (1976), 8.

53 *Lodge School Record* (1945–46), 41.

54 Bailey, Thorn and Wynne-Thomas, *Who's Who of Cricketers*, 550.

55 BCA, *100 Years*, 77; Thorn, *Barbados Cricketers*, 24; Keith A.P. Sandiford, *John Douglas Claude Goddard: His Record Innings-by-Innings* (West Bridgford, forthcoming).

56 BCA, *100 Years*, 117; Thorn, *Barbados Cricketers*, 30.

57 *Lodge School Record* (1954), 9; *Lodge School Record* (1955), 21.

58 *Lodge School Record*, 1935, 40; *Lodge School Record*, 1936, 46. See also Hamilton, *Cricket in Barbados*, 143.

59 *Lodge School Record* (1943), 15.

60 *Lodge School Record* (1936), 8, 23, 46; *Lodge School Record*, 1940, 51.

61 Thorn, *Barbados Cricketers*, 29.

62 Ibid., 8, 22. Keith A.P. Sandiford, "The Spartan Cricket Club 1893–1993", *Journal of the Cricket Society* 16, no. 3 (Autumn 1993): 45.

63 BCA, *100 Years*, 73.

64 Ibid., 91; Sandiford and Newton, *Combermere School and the Barbadian Society*, 85–6.

65 *Lodge School Record* (1944–45), 146–47. BCA, 100 Years, 111.
66 BCA, *100 Years*, 45.
67 BCA, 100 *Years*, 103. See also Roy Marshall, *Test Outcast* (London, 1970); and Victor Isaacs and Philip Thorn, *Hampshire Cricketers 1800–1982* (Retford, 1983), 34.
68 Bailey, Thorn and Wynne-Thomas, *Who's Who of Cricketers*, 363.
69 *Lodge School Record* (1947–48), 37.
70 *Lodge School Record* (1948–49), 25.
71 *Lodge School Record* (1949–50), 6.
72 *Lodge School Record* (1958), 10
73 *Lodge School Record* (1953), 21; BCA, *100 Years*, 24; BCA, *Report and Statement of Accounts, 1st April 1994 to 31st March 1995*, 76.
74 *Lodge School Record* (1956), 33.
75 *Lodge School Record* (1958), 19–20.
76 *Lodge School Record* (1961), 23.
77 *Lodge School Record* (1958), 51.
78 *Lodge School Record* (1962), 26.
79 Bailey, Thorn and Wynne-Thomas, *Who's Who of Cricketers*, 366. See also *Wisden* 1962, 695.
80 *Lodge School Record* (1957–78).
81 Thorn, *Barbados Cricketers*, 13, 26.
82 *Lodge School Record* (1975), 85.
83 Thorn, *Barbados Cricketers*, 25; *Lodge School Record* (1975), 4.
84 Thorn, *Barbados Cricketers*, 21; *Wisden* 1966, 828.
85 *Lodge School Record* (1963), 24.
86 BCA, *100 Years*, 53.
87 Ibid., 72. See also Bill Frindall, ed., *The Wisden Book of Test Cricket 1877–1994*, 2 vols. (London, 1995). The last Test at Bridgetown to end in a draw was West Indies vs Pakistan in February 1977.
88 BCA, *100 Years*, 68–9.
89 *Lodge School Record* (1960), 14.
90 *Lodge School Record* (1961), 15.
91 *Lodge School Record* (1956), 3; *Lodge School Record* (1958), 52; *Lodge School Record* (1960), 19; *Lodge School Record* (1961), 44.
92 *Lodge School Record* (1963), 53.
93 *Lodge School Record* (1962), 9, 43.
94 *Lodge School Record* (1963), 53.
95 Thorn, *Barbados Cricketers*, 22.
96 *Lodge School Record* (1960), 19.
97 Thorn, *Barbados Cricketers*, 30.
98 Ibid., 24, 26, 29.
99 *West Indies Cricket Annual 1979*, 84; *West Indies Cricket Annual 1982*, 87.
100 *Lodge School Record* (1969), 7.

101 BCA, *100 Years*, 73.
102 Thorn, *Barbados Cricketers*, 24. See also *Barclays West Indies Players' Guide 1996*, 3.
103 BCA, *Report and Statement of Accounts, 1st April 1994 to 31st March 1995*, 75–6.

3

The Overwhelming Influence of Harrison College

Few schools anywhere can possibly be as significant as Harrison College in the development of modern cricket. Established in 1733, it steadily grew into one of the leading schools in Barbados and was accorded first-grade secondary status in 1878.[1] Catering thereafter to the élite, it consistently attracted the sons of the wealthiest families in the Caribbean. Pelham Warner, for instance, was sent to Harrison as a lad by his father, Charles William Warner, who had for many years been the attorney general of Trinidad.[2]

Young 'Plum' spent three years at Harrison before his mother took him and his brother to England following his father's death in 1887. He readily admitted that his cricketing skills were honed during his early days on the playing fields of Harrison. He was only 13 when he gained selection to the first XI in 1886. He must have shown exceptional promise for the school then boasted one of the strongest sides in the colony.[3] Warner was fortunate in attending Harrison during the administration of the famous Horace Deighton, its headmaster from 1872 to 1905. It was Deighton, himself a fine cricketer and an Oxford graduate, who transformed Harrison into a veritable cricket nursery. Firmly believing that cricket possessed certain magical qualities that could transform rambunctious boys into honourable citizens, Deighton encouraged all of his pupils to play the game and instituted two matches that became annual classics in due course: the Masters vs the Boys and Past vs Present Harrisonians. Deighton also did much to establish the BCCC which administered the sport in Barbados prior to the advent of the BCA in 1933.[4] His enviable reputation as an educator was such that the Harrison College student body increased from 67 at the time of his advent to 138 before his departure.[5]

During Deighton's regime, Harrison participated in regular matches even before Barbadian cricket became organized on a more structured basis.

It thus naturally became one of the seven founding clubs (with Belleville, Codrington College, the Garrison, the Lodge School, Pickwick and Wanderers) when the first division competition was inaugurated in 1892–93. For the next 70 years Harrison remained a competitor in the island's élite league. To its everlasting credit, although it was often overmatched by the adult clubs, the college won the first division competition twice, and placed second on a number of occasions.

Harrison's role in the development of cricket in Barbados cannot adequately be measured solely by results achieved on the field. It is true that the school trained dozens of cricketers who later went on to represent Barbados. It is also true that, over the years, Old Harrisonians played leading roles in the success of such clubs as Carlton, Pickwick, Spartan and Wanderers. But it is much more important to note that most Barbadian teachers were trained by Deighton and his apostles after 1870 and it was they who took the cricketing cult with them to the other academic institutions. Such headmasters of Combermere, for instance, as Revd Arthur Evelyn Armstrong, G.B.R. Burton and 'Gussie' Cox had been scholar–athletes at Harrison in Deighton's time. The same is true of O. DeC. 'Bill' Emtage (1898–1931) and Harry Beaujon Gooding (1932–41), who became headmasters of the Lodge. It is clear therefore that Harrison had a good deal to do with the early growth of cricket in Barbados and with that game's ultimate rise to dominance as a Barbadian national symbol.

Deighton was, in many respects, continuing the work already begun by the energetic Revd Charles Clarke, his famous predecessor as Harrison's headmaster. Reminiscing in the *Harrisonian* of March 1903, C.P. Bowen recalled that Clarke was deeply mourned when he died in 1872 and described him as a "perfect martinet in the matter of making boys take part in Cricket and games of every nature". He was obviously a firm believer in the doctrine that boys should play, as well as work, with all their might.[6] Some of Clarke's and Deighton's assistant masters also took the sport beyond the boundaries of Barbados. William Burslem, for example, eventually became a celebrated headmaster of Queen's Royal College (QRC) in Trinidad where, at the beginning of the twentieth century, he left an abiding impression on the young C.L.R. James, who was destined to become one of the pioneers of modern cricket sociology. G.F. Franks also became a legend as a teacher in British Guiana.[7]

THE STRONGEST ELEVEN IN THE COLONY

Already by the end of the 1870s, under Deighton's guidance, Harrison was playing very good cricket and fielding arguably the most powerful eleven in the West Indies, despite the fact that it catered to fewer than 100 students. In 1877, it was strong enough to beat a Wanderers team and two years later it was able to make a successful tour of St Kitts and Antigua, defeating the best of the local clubs. The early Harrisonian heroes were P.B. Austin, the Brownes (Alfred, Clement and Robert), Theodore G. Clarke, Gilbert and Greenidge Elliott, Edward Evelyn, Aubrey Goodman, William Howell, E.C. Jackman and H.B. Stokes. Most of their names would reappear in Barbadian elevens during the early intercolonial competitions. This was true of the three brothers Browne who eventually contributed enormously to the establishment of Pickwick in the 1880s. The Elliott brothers both reached first-class status as Greenidge played for Barbados in 1883–84 while Gilbert went to Britain to study medicine and returned with Priestley's team to the Caribbean in 1896–97.[8] Clarke was perhaps the best allrounder in the West Indies during the 1880s. Not only was he a superb batsman and a fine bowler but he was an excellent wicket-keeper who, it is said, "could stand up to fast bowling and stump off it". He served for some years as an inspirational captain of Wanderers before migrating to the USA and performing splendidly for a cricket club in New Jersey.[9]

Harrison remained one of the strongest cricket teams in Barbados throughout the 1880s and was almost invincible during the last years of that decade when it boasted such stars as John Gardiner Austin (H.B.G.'s brother), E.L. Challenor (George's brother), Howell Clarke (Theodore's nephew), 'Gussie' Cox, C. Harris, Ernest Hinkson and Stephen Rudder. With the exception of Harris, they were all destined to gain selection for Barbados. Harris combined with Rudder to make Spartan, founded in 1893 as the first non-white club in Barbados, competitive in its infancy.[10] Harrison was so powerful that it could easily defeat a touring St Vincent team by an innings and 133 runs in 1888.[11]

Masters on the Field

One of the strengths of the college at the turn of the century came from Deighton's deliberate policy of encouraging masters to play with the boys (acting perhaps more as sources of inspiration than as formal coaches). Thus the Harrison XI often included as many as four teachers. One of the latter, H.J. Tiffen, served for many years as the manager and treasurer of the school's cricket club before he departed in 1903, just after capturing 30 wickets and heading Harrison's bowling average in his final season. Such good cricketers as Revd F.G. Ambridge, Revd E.A. Cutting, and Messrs

Arthur Somers Cocks (1870–1923), a source of inspiraton to hundreds of Harrisonians

Walter Boyce, Andrew Low, R.H. Smith and Winter also turned out regularly for the school.[12]

This policy was continued with the arrival of Arthur Somers Cocks from Oxford in 1892 and the return of G.B.Y. Cox to teach at his alma mater after graduating from Codrington College with a classics degree and teaching briefly in Antigua. 'Gussie' Cox and Somers Cocks were two enormously talented players who made Harrison a force to be reckoned with during the early days of the cup competition. Two of the best cricketers in the Caribbean during the 1890s, they inspired dozens of young Harrisonians to play cricket and left an indelible mark on the school as athletes and teachers. Somers Cocks, who married one of Deighton's daughters and produced a son who also taught at Harrison, served briefly as this school's headmaster before his early death in 1923. He was for many years one of Harrison's best cricketers and footballers. For Barbados, Somers Cocks played 10 matches during 1894–1902, scored 200 runs (including a memorable 62 not out at the expense of Slade Lucas's XI in 1895) and captured 53 wickets at just under 19 runs apiece. He was one of the finest fast bowlers of his generation and perhaps second only to Clifford Goodman in those days as a pace bowler in the Caribbean. At his peak, during 1895–1909, he took over 550 wickets at a little over 11 runs each in Barbadian first division cricket. Somers Cocks left a profound impression upon students and colleagues alike and many of his contemporaries sincerely believed that the school would have been much better off had he (rather than Dr H.A. Dalton) been chosen to succeed Deighton immediately as headmaster in 1905.[13]

The name of 'Gussie' Cox is almost inseparable from that of Arthur Somers Cocks. They played cricket and soccer together for what seemed like an eternity. Between them, they represented Barbados on 25 occasions and Cox had the unique distinction, in 1897, of scoring the first century in intercolonial cricket at Kensington Oval. In a fine first-class career that involved 18 matches altogether between 1893 and 1905, Cox held 16 catches and scored 767 runs (av: 27.39). He continued to play regularly for Harrison even during the 1920s. At the age of 53, he was still good enough to make 18 and 33 in two vital innings against a powerful Empire club during the 1923–24 season.[14] Cox is one of the most important names in the history of Harrison College cricket. He also left his mark on Combermere which he served as headmaster from 1926 to 1934 and for which he played second division cricket as late as 1927 when he was already 56 years old.[15]

Ernest Hinkson, a right-handed batsman who captained Harrison in the late 1880s when the school team was so powerful, was destined to play only two games for Barbados; but he proved himself a tower of strength for Wanderers, which he also captained in the 1890s, over a long period.[16]. Stephen Rudder enjoyed much greater success at the first-class level. In nine matches altogether during 1896–1902, he captured 37 wickets at an average cost of less than 12 runs apiece and scored 183 runs at an average of 15.25 per innings. His finest hour occurred on 9 September 1897 when he achieved the extraordinary bowling analysis of 14–10–5–5 to dismiss Trinidad for 92 runs at the Kensington Oval. Rudder was a penetrative right-arm bowler of fast-medium pace and an aggressive right-handed batsman, good enough to score a plucky 53 for a composite West Indian XI against Arthur Priestley's team in 1897 (when he and L.S. D'Ade added 101 for the tenth wicket). He was one of the major players for the Spartan cricket club during the first 15 years of its existence.[17]

During the 1890s, when Cox and Somers Cocks were dominant, good cricket was also being played by such pupils as Hallam Cole and Julian St C. Cumberbatch, who eventually achieved first-class status. Not surprisingly, the school ran a very close second to Pickwick during the 1893–94 season.[18] A careful right-handed batsman with a good range of scoring strokes, Cole was one of the steadiest batsmen in Barbados for almost two decades. He became a prolific scorer for Pickwick and helped to make that club the strongest cricket side in the island for many years. In 22 matches for Barbados between 1894 and 1908, he scored 909 runs at an average of just over 25 runs per innings. [19]At his peak in 1900, Cole was good enough to earn selection on the first West Indies touring team to England but had to decline for business reasons.[20] Cumberbatch was a promising wicketkeeper/batsman in his youth, but gained only one selection for Barbados even though, like Rudder, he was one of main bulwarks of the Spartan Cricket Club during its fledgling stage. He made a contribution of another sort by producing a fine cricketing son, Chester St Clair Cumberbatch, who also achieved first-class status.[21]

TURN OF THE CENTURY

Sir H.B.G. Austin (1877–1943), the father of West Indies cricket

At the turn of the century, in addition to Cox and Somers Cocks, Harrison was profiting from the services of the young H.B.G. Austin, who was destined to become one of the greatest names in the history of Caribbean cricket. He became a long-serving captain of Wanderers, Barbados and the West Indies. When his playing days were over, Harold Austin continued to serve as the leading cricket administrator in the region. In 1927, he was the driving spirit behind the establishment of the WICBC and served as its first president. He captained the West Indies teams to England in 1906 and 1923. His contribution to Wanderers was incalculable. He not only provided that club with leadership on and off the field for over 30 years but he often spent his own money to defray its debts. As a cricketer, he was a stylish batsman, a competent wicketkeeper and a useful bowler. For Barbados, he appeared 30 times between 1894 and 1926, scoring over 1,300 runs and averaging more than 32. Although he took only 15 wickets in first-class cricket, he once bowled Wanderers to a championship (during the 1896–97 season) when he claimed 38 wickets for less than 5 runs each. His 30 appearances for Barbados remained a record until it was broken by John Goddard in 1958. In 65 first-class matches, he accumulated 2,643 runs (av: 28.42). An energetic public servant in his later years, Sir Harold Austin was the first native Barbadian cricketer to be honoured with a knighthood.[22]

After Austin's departure from Harrison, Thomas Webb Roberts emerged as its leading schoolboy cricketer. He showed enormous promise as a batsman in the mid 1890s and played four matches for Barbados before entering Oxford University, where his colour militated against his gaining a cricket 'blue'. The very first black student to win a Barbados Scholarship, Roberts qualified himself as a barrister, joined the imperial civil service and ended up as a famous jurist in Ceylon (now known as Sri Lanka). One of the very few black pupils who attended Harrison College during the nineteenth century, Roberts became a well-known cricket administrator in Ceylon and did much to advance the cause of cricket in his adopted country. He often played extremely well for it against touring teams from Australia and England. He is best remembered for striking a glorious 70 in 70 minutes in 1908 against an English team returning from Australia. He died in London in 1976 at the ripe age of 96. His two sons, T.F.C. and G.C. Roberts, both played fine cricket for Harrison in the early 1920s before returning to join him in Ceylon.[23]

F.W.G. Austin, C.K. Bancroft and Kenneth Mason were three other Harrisonians of unusual merit between Harold Austin's exit in 1894 and George Challenor's arrival in 1901. Francis Austin, H.B.G.'s youngest brother, became a very fine left-arm medium-fast bowler for Wanderers, Barbados and British Guiana (where he spent a number of years in his adulthood).[24] Keith Bancroft is often described as the best wicketkeeper to attend Cambridge without receiving his 'blue'. He played twice for Barbados in 1905 and kept wicket "with high distinction" for the 1906 West Indies team in England.[25] He was a good enough batsman to topscore with a courageous 53 in a losing cause against Kent on that tour.[26] Bancroft ultimately migrated to Canada, where he succumbed to the influenza epidemic on 12 January 1919 at the tender age of 33.[27]

For over 30 years Kenneth Mason was the most consistent bowler in Barbados, taking countless wickets for Wanderers. He was also an attacking right-handed batsman who scored a brilliant century against Trinidad in 1920, sharing with C.F. Browne in a Barbadian seventh wicket record partnership of 224 runs which is still standing after more than 75 years. Mason captured 50 wickets (av: 28.04) with his right-arm off-spinners in 17 matches for Barbados. Had he emerged somewhat later, he would undoubtedly have represented the West Indies. He shone as one of the brightest stars in the Barbadian cricket firmament for a very long time. One of the best spin bowlers produced by Harrison College and one of the best ever to play for Wanderers, he was one of the leading allrounders in the Barbados Challenge Cup Competition between 1895 and 1930.[28]

The Advent of George Challenor

If, in some respects, Deighton was merely building on the platform erected by Clarke, his own work was continued by his English successor, Dr Herbert Dalton, an Oxford graduate, who sought a warmer climate after having served as a successful headmaster of St Edward's School as well as Felsted. Under him, Harrison College simply prospered during 1905–22, increasing its roll from 137 students to more than 200.[29] It became known throughout the British Empire as one of the most famous secondary schools, especially for its production of brilliant mathematicians and classical scholars. It was Dalton who introduced the Oxford and Cambridge certificates as well as the house and prefect systems. He encouraged every pupil to take part in sports and started the system whereby each boy paid a subscription to the games fund every term. The house matches became great events in the life of the school and served as useful trials for the selection of Harrisonian teams. It was universally agreed that while Deighton had made Harrison a good secondary school, it was Dalton who had made it comparable with the best public schools in England.[30] The main difference between Deighton and Dalton was that the latter preferred to see the school represented in cricket and soccer by boys (rather than masters) and he did his best to make Harrison resemble Winchester College where he himself had taught during the 1880s. The age of Dalton is not therefore much unlike that of his predecessor and it had the good fortune to witness the blossoming of George Challenor, one of Harrison's most celebrated alumni.

George Challenor was the greatest West Indian batsman before the advent of George Headley. Only 13 years old when he first gained selection to the Harrison team, he made his début for Barbados in 1906. On a treacherous pitch, Challenor made 20 in a first innings total of 122 and 34 (out of 157) in the second.[31] His technique seemed so impeccable that Austin gambled on taking him to England with the West Indies team later that year. He showed extraordinary promise for a boy of 18 and enjoyed his best day at Trent Bridge in early August when he scored 108 off a Notts attack that included John Gunn, A.W. Hallam and Tom Wass.[32] In 24 first-class matches that summer the young prodigy registered 684 magisterial runs (av: 28.50) and left a very positive impression on the immortal Dr W.G. Grace, who prophesied that he would go far as a cricketer.[33]

This tour was the turning-point in the great George's career. He batted with supreme confidence thereafter, scoring bushels of runs for Wanderers and, with his opening partner Tim Tarilton, dominating intercolonial competitions in the Caribbean for the next 20 years. It was his majestic batting in the 1923 tour of England, as much as anything else, which persuaded the MCC to accord the West Indies Test match status. That summer he struck six centuries while amassing 1,556 runs (av: 51.86) and finishing third in the overall batting averages to Patsy Hendren and Philip Mead. Such was the impression Challenor created on the English pundits that they were willing to rank him among the very best batsmen in the world. He is still regarded, rightly, as the father of modern West Indian batting. In 24 matches for Barbados, he recorded 1,713 runs (av: 55.25), 45 wickets (av: 21.20) and 10 catches. In 95 first-class matches, he established a long-standing record for a Barbadian, of 5,822 runs (av: 38.55), that would eventually take Frank Worrell more than 20 years to eclipse. His record of eight centuries on behalf of Barbados lasted until 1964 when it was finally equalled by Everton Weekes.[34]

George was the youngest of four Old Harrisonian brothers who played cricket brilliantly and eventually achieved first-class status. The eldest, Brig. Gen. Edward Lacy Challenor, distinguished himself in the imperial army and served many years in England, India and South Africa. He was therefore able to play 29 first-class games for Barbados, Leicestershire, MCC, Natal and Western Province in a career that lasted from 1894 to 1914 and produced 1,106 runs (av: 21.68). Like all of his brothers, he was an aggressive right-handed batsman.[35] Robert L. Challenor, best remembered as 'Laddie', was a wicketkeeper/batsman who represented Barbados on 11 occasions between 1904 and 1925. He played 13 first-class matches in all, scoring 413 runs (av: 21.73) and effecting 19 dismissals. Vicary Clive was the least known among the cricketing Challenors. But he registered 239 runs (av: 26.55) in his five matches for Barbados during 1901–4.[36]

While George Challenor remained at Harrison, the school was extremely competitive because of the presence also of such gifted cricketers as Herbert Bailey, H.W. Barnes and William C. Hoad. Bailey became a fine allrounder for Pickwick and played three matches for Barbados between 1908 and 1911. Barnes was a superb batsman who represented Barbados in 4 games during 1903–5. Hoad was a member of a well-known Pickwick family. He was a good legbreak spin bowler who took 11 wickets in six first-class matches.[37]

The Brothers Browne

The vacuum left at Harrison after Bailey, Barnes, the Challenors and Hoad had gone was filled by the famous Browne Brothers, 'John' and 'Snuffie'. They played excellent cricket for their school during Dalton's tenure before entering the Spartan ranks and making that club one of the most powerful in the island. Both were destined to play for Barbados. 'John' (Chester Allan) was one of the best batsmen in the Caribbean for an exceptionally long time. His first-class career spanned 22 years (1908–30) and in 20 matches for Barbados, he scored 816 runs (av: 35.47), including one century.[38] The more famous 'Snuffie' (Cyril Rutherford) was easily the greatest of all West Indian allrounders until the emergence of Learie Constantine. He played seven games for Barbados before migrating to British Guiana, which he led to two intercolonial championships. He made two tours to England in the 1920s and represented the West Indies in their first Test series when he was almost 38. He was an attacking batsman and an aggressive right-arm bowler of leg-breaks and googlies at an almost lively medium pace. In 74 first-class matches during 1908–39, he recorded 2,077 runs (av: 19.97), 278 wickets (av: 22.40) and 59 catches.[39]

'Snuffie' Browne (1890–1964), one of the leading West Indian cricketers during the 1920s

Reflecting, in 1933, on the influence of Harrison College as a cricket nursery in Barbados, 'Snuffie' made a number of interesting observations in an issue of the *Harrisonian*. He considered the period 1904–10, roughly coincident with his own attendance at Harrison, as pivotal in the development of Barbadian cricket. Not only was a second division just introduced to provide increased opportunities for organized play, but the Challenge Cup committee took the important step of extending first division games to three days in 1909. This compelled batsmen to focus more sharply on defense and therefore brought about a marked improvement in Barbadian cricket technique.[40]

Now that Harrison had the privilege of selecting two elevens, it could prepare its students more thoroughly for the senior ranks and 'Snuffie' was not surprised to see that Harrison was able to produce so many first-class players during that short span. He identified Keith Bancroft, Howell Barnes, Ritchie Batson, Allan Browne, George Challenor, Freddie Clairmonte, Allan Collymore, William Murray Howell, Lionel Hutson, Harry Ince, Freddie Packer and Harold Skeete as among the finest cricketers ever produced by the college and most of them had represented Barbados between the ages of 16 and 18, while still at school. In those six years, Snuffie observed, Harrison had provided the West Indies with their best wicketkeeper, their greatest batsman and some of their best bowlers. This would not have been possible, he concluded, had it not been for the influence and inspiration of Arthur Somers Cocks and Gussie Cox, who were then in their prime, and the good bowling in the nets of such 'professionals' as Joe Benn, Oliver Layne, William Shepherd and Joe Worme.[41]

Richard Batson, Allan Collymore, Harry Ince and Courtenay Reece attended Harrison just when the Brownes were leaving. Batson was a stylish batsman who dazzled the local crowds for about three years before departing to study medicine in Scotland. He played four times for Barbados, leaving an indelible mark with a century against Trinidad in 1912 on a Bridgetown pitch described as 'doubtful'. At his peak in 1911–12, Batson averaged 124 in first division matches, hitting two brilliant centuries for Wanderers against Pickwick and another against Spartan. But his medical career seemed to have brought an end to his first-class cricket even though, as a student at the University of Edinburgh, he twice represented Scotland in the early 1920s.[42]

A steady right-handed batsman with considerable gifts, Collymore was a much less flamboyant stroke-player than either Batson or Ince. He did manage to score a blistering 212 for Wanderers against Harrison in 1923, but generally he failed to live up to the promise he had displayed as a schoolboy cricketer. He was invited to play only once for Barbados and although he rendered good service to Wanderers, he is best remembered now as one of the leading administrators of the BCA in the period 1932 to 1958 and as an outstanding public servant who was eventually honoured with a knighthood.[43]

Harry Ince remained an active and productive cricketer for a much longer time. He was a magnificent left-handed batsman with a extraordinary range of attractive strokes which persuaded some experts to compare him with the immortal Frank Woolley of Kent and England. He was a failure during the 1923 West Indies tour to England, but his record in 15 matches for Barbados (during 1912–30) was very good indeed: 754 runs (av: 47.12). His greatest innings perhaps was the sparkling 167 he struck at Port-of-Spain for a West Indian XI against the touring MCC squad in February 1913 when he was not yet 20 years old. Ince was the greatest left-handed batsman produced by Barbados before the advent of John Goddard. Even as late as 1928, at the age of 35, he was still good enough to average almost 65 runs an innings in first division cricket.[44]

Courtenay Reece was a promising right-arm medium-fast bowler who was noted for his uncanny ability to swing the ball very late in the air. He was almost good enough to win his cricket 'blue' at Oxford University where he studied law in the early 1920s. As a barrister, he returned to Barbados to render yeoman service to Spartan, which he captained with much success during the 1930s. It was he who led the Spartan team on its tour of Trinidad in 1938 and is reported to have left a very positive impression on Roger Blackman at a time in his life when the younger man needed firm handling. Reece represented Barbados on three occasions between 1926 and 1930, taking 10 wickets for 354 runs. His most memorable first-class performance was 4/72 against British Guiana at Kensington in 1927. Shortly before the outbreak of World War II, Reece left Barbados to serve in the imperial bureaucracy and eventually died in Hong Kong in 1984 in his 85th year.[45]

THE INFLUENCE OF 'BESSIE' WALCOTT

Just before World War I Harrison spawned another cricketer of remarkable gifts. He was L.A. 'Bessie' Walcott who played for many years for Harrison, Pickwick and the Lodge (where he served as games master from 1932 to 1947). A sound batsman and a steady off-break bowler, he represented Barbados on 11 occasions and gained selection on the West Indies Test team against England at Bridgetown in 1930. 'Bessie' left his mark not only as a cricketer but as a coach. At Harrison where he taught from 1921 to 1931, he exerted a profound influence upon such pupils as Lawson Bartlett, Lionel Birkett, Chester Cumberbatch, J.R. 'Bunny' Edwards, Stanton Gittens, the Inniss Brothers (Bruce and Clifford) and Lionel Stuart. At Lodge, where his influence was even more profound, his protégés included Wilfred Farmer, Michael Frederick, John Goddard, Sam Headley, Laurie John-

The Harrison College XI, 1930–31 first division champions. Bruce Inniss and Mr L.A. Walcott flank the trophy

son and Roy Marshall. In short, 'Bessie' made two distinct kinds of contribution to Barbadian cricket. For the island he scored 515 runs (av: 30.29), captured 15 wickets (av: 29.33) and held 8 catches. Not only did Walcott serve as a player and as an effective captain of the team which toured Trinidad in 1933, but he was the most influential of all Barbadian cricket masters.[46]

During the war years, cricket at Harrison was almost dwarfed by the incredible exploits of young Eric Collymore who is still considered by old Barbadians as one of the greatest schoolboy batsmen of any era. Bruce Hamilton, in *Cricket in Barbados*, described him as a "spectacular batsman, a beautiful off driver and in general a very strong off side player, and as sound and reliable as he was brilliant." In the 1914–15 season, he dazzled Barbadian cricket fans with innings of 124, 15, 83 and 0 in the two games against Pickwick; 77, 50 and 124 against Spartan; and 49, 144, 17 and 62 not out against Wanderers. He headed the island's batting average with 82.67. In the next season, he headed the averages again with 63.6, registering two more centuries – including a mammoth 215 not out against Wanderers at the Bay, which remained a Harrison record for 17 years. That was then the highest score ever made by any schoolboy in Barbadian first division cricket and has since been exceeded only once. In Collymore's last season, just before the cup competition in Barbados was discontinued for three years, he averaged only 38.88 runs per innings and managed only three 50s.[47]

That proved to be the end of an amazing, yet enigmatic career. Collymore was also a bowler of some distinction, capturing 33 wickets very cheaply during his final two years at Harrison.[48] He, quite simply, was the outstanding allrounder in Barbados during World War I. When the regular competition resumed, however, he had already faded into oblivion. Eric Collymore was undoubtedly the greatest batsman never to have played for Barbados. He was the first of only six schoolboys who have struck double centuries in first division competition in this island.[49]

Collymore's captain and most successful comrade-in-arms at Harrison was W.H.L. 'Golly' Medford, a talented scholar–athlete, who eventually returned to teach at his alma mater after graduating from Cambridge with a classics degree. He then served for many years as an inspirational cricket master during the 1930s and 1940s and is one of the most important names in the history of Harrison cricket. Hamilton considered him "perhaps the finest utility cricketer who has never had the opportunity of playing for Barbados".[50] Lisle Medford was a steady bowler and a sound batsman. In 1914–15 he scored 119 against Wanderers while also heading the school's bowling averages. In the 1915–16 season, he scored another century against Pickwick and achieved the fine batting average of 35.9.[51]

Eric Collymore and Lisle Medford would certainly have taken Harrison to its first cup triumph had the school's bowling been more penetrative at that time. Apart from these two allrounders, however, Harrison could depend only on H.F.K. Greaves, a slow left-arm bowler, who took 27 wickets at 16.7 runs each during the 1915–16 season. But the school lacked an opening bowler of real pace or quality. Greaves, who became a valuable performer for Pickwick, was destined to represent Barbados on eight occasions between 1923 and 1930.[52]

Thanks largely to 'Bessie' Walcott's encouragement, Bartlett and Birkett emerged as very promising Harrisonian batsmen in the early 1920s. Bartlett was an unusually elegant stroke player who is still regarded as a legend by older Barbadians, despite his modest first-class record. In 42 matches he scored only 1,581 runs (av: 23.25) and struck but a single century. Apart from an impressive 84 at Adelaide in December 1930, he did little in his five Tests for the West Indies. In 17 matches for Barbados, he registered 639 runs at an average of less than 22. At the club cricket level, however, he was Spartan's leading batsman for many years. A dapper little man, 'Barto' brought a touch of class to everything he did. His stylishness made him a special favourite with Barbadian crowds.[53]

Lionel Sydney Birkett became one of the very few players to represent three West Indian territories. In a first-class career that lasted from 1925 to 1944, he played for British Guiana and Trinidad as well as Barbados. He earned selection on four West Indian Test teams and remained one of the best batsmen in the Caribbean throughout the 1930s. Having begun his cricket career at Combermere School, Birkett is one of those students who is claimed by at least two academic institutions. In 26 first-class matches altogether, he scored 1,295 runs (av: 33.20), captured 9 wickets (av: 56.00) and held 22 catches. As vice captain of the West Indies team which toured Australia in 1930–31, he performed extremely well in the first ever Test between these two countries, scoring 27 and 64 in the two innings at Adelaide.[54]

Another prominent member of the Harrison XI at that time was Arthur Ralph Vernon Newsam, a remarkable scholar–athlete, who performed consistently well both in the classroom and on the playing field. He was a talented cricketer and footballer, who took his skills for a while to Jamaica where he taught briefly at Cornwall College. He was good enough as a soccer player to represent Jamaica in that sport during the late 1920s (at a time when the standard of Jamaican soccer was much higher than that in

Barbados). Newsam returned to his native island in 1931 to make a more lasting impression on the Lodge School. As an assistant master there, he continued to play cricket and soccer and served occasionally as games master before assuming the headship in 1954. He was a source of inspiration to three or four generations of students at the Lodge.[55]

Two First Division Cups

Harrison College enjoyed its greatest triumphs during 'Bessie' Walcott's last days as its games master. Year after year, throughout the 1920s, he was a virtual tower of strength in both batting and bowling. In 1925, for instance, he scored 424 runs (av: 32.5) and claimed 28 wickets (av: 12.5).[56] Thanks in no small measure to his achievements on the field, the school became one of the strongest teams in the island, winning the championship in 1927–28 and in 1930–31. During the 1927–28 season, when Harrison won its first cup, it played unbeaten while achieving outright victories twice over St Ann's and the Lodge.[57] Among its stars in 1927–28 were J.R. Edwards, Clifford Inniss and Lionel Stuart. 'Bunny' Edwards, a fine batsman and a useful legbreak bowler who later played very well for Wanderers, was selected to the Barbadian XI on five occasions and captained the team against Trinidad in January 1937.[58]

Inniss and Stuart formed perhaps the most famous schoolboy opening partnership in the history of Barbadian cricket. They repeatedly got their team off to a solid start and once achieved an opening stand of 207 against St Ann's with Inniss proceeding to score 120 not out. During the 1927–28 campaign, Inniss amassed 577 runs (av: 81.43) and Stuart 338 (av: 37.56). Inniss also took 23 wickets at 13 runs apiece and Stuart 12 at 15.[59] But neither of these outstanding schoolboy stalwarts fulfilled his early promise. Not once was Lionel Stuart ever invited to represent Barbados. He studied medicine in Britain after leaving Harrison and showed flashes of his old form at Edinburgh University where he was awarded his 'blue' in 1929 after heading his team's batting averages and also bowling well.[60] But his practice as a doctor left him too little time for cricket when he returned to Barbados. Clifford Inniss, too, played only seven matches for Barbados with chequered results: 351 runs (av: 27.00) and 1 wicket for 50 runs.[61] However, it is interesting to note that, while he was a student at Oxford, he twice represented the West Indies during the 1933 tour of England. He shared a third wicket partnership of 149 with George Headley in a memorable victory over the MCC. In ten first-class matches during 1927–38, he scored 474 runs (av: 27.88). He might have gone much further in the game had he been able to devote more energy to it after leaving Oxford; but Inniss became a famous jurist, serving in Africa and Belize, and was rewarded with a knighthood.[62]

When Harrison won the championship in 1930–31, Walcott was ably supported by Chester Cumberbatch (Julian's son), Frankie Field, S. O'C. Gittens, G.B. Hunte and Bruce Inniss (Clifford's younger brother). The last-named shared with Walcott in a long-standing third wicket record partnership of 303 runs against Wanderers.[63] Inniss developed into a fine allrounder, but he was selected only once for Barbados, scoring 33 in his lone first-class innings against Trinidad in 1942. For many years, Field and the two Innisses served as bulwarks of Pickwick, and Bruce played a notable part also as a member of the BCA board of management. Cumberbatch captained Harrison after Bruce Inniss's departure in 1931 when he began the season in truly rare form, scoring 219 not out against the Lodge, 94 against Police and 102 vs Pickwick. His double century was then a Harrison record, eclipsing the mark of 215 previously established by Eric Collymore. It remains the highest score ever achieved by a schoolboy in Barbadian first division cricket.[65] Cumberbatch went on to play regularly for Spartan and represented Barbados on five occasions, scoring 170 runs (av: 21.25) and taking 3 catches. Field never participated in a first-class match, but he did have the honour of leading a Barbados XI to victory over Trinidad in an exhibition match in 1939.[67]

Stanton Gittens had the unique distinction of participating in all three of the first division championships won by Barbadian schools. Not only was he a member of the two victorious Harrison squads, but he represented Combermere as one of its masters when it triumphed in 1940–41. He also played a key role in the championships won by Empire in 1932, 1934, 1935 and 1941. Gittens was a patient opening batsman whose finest moment came in January 1937 when he scored 105 for Barbados (in a total of 242) against Trinidad at Port-of-Spain. At his peak, he was also one of the best wicketkeepers in the Caribbean. In 11 matches for Barbados, he effected 20 dismissals which remained a local record for several years. After his retirement from the game, Gittens served regularly as a BCA administrator until 1973. He also served during 1961–71 as the first black headmaster of Combermere and left a solid imprint there.[68]

HARRISONIAN STARS OF THE 1930s

During the 1930s, among several very good cricketers, Harrison produced Theodore Birkett (Lionel's brother), Bertie Clarke, M.I.C. Clarke, W.M.

Foster, Shirley Gill, L.F. 'Shell' Harris, Eric D. Inniss, H.B. DeC. Jordan, Harold Jordan, Harold Kidney, C.G. Manning and Tom Peirce. Kidney, whose father (Jack) had represented Barbados and managed West Indian touring teams, never made it to the first-class ranks himself but he played effectively for Pickwick in his adulthood and left his mark on the game as one of the island's leading radio commentators. When he worked briefly in Trinidad during the 1940s, he was still good enough to gain selection for the South against the North in the annual Beaumont Cup competition. At the time of his death in 1981 at the age of 64, he was serving as president of Pickwick.[69] 'Cortez' Jordan, who captained the Second XI while at Harrison, eventually emerged as one of the most famous of all Barbadian umpires. He stood in 22 Test matches and became the first West Indian to officiate at that level on every Test venue in the Caribbean. He was, in fact, the first West Indian umpire to officiate in a Test match outside of his own island when, in 1955, he served with Eric Lee Kow at the Queen's Park Oval in Port-of-Spain.[70] 'Charlie' Manning was a stylish batsman whose career, like that of so many others, was interrupted by medical studies abroad. Invited to the trials in 1936, he scored a delightful century but was still not selected for Barbados against Trinidad.[71] He departed shortly after that for McGill University. He returned to play briefly for Wanderers during the 1940s but never rediscovered his schoolboy form or confidence.

Bertie Clarke studied medicine also but not before leaving a more telling mark on West Indian cricket. An extremely good right-arm spin bowler whose pace was almost medium fast, he made Spartan the strongest club in the island during the late 1930s. In the 1937–38 season he took 53 wickets for an incredible average of just over 5 runs each.[72] Playing for the 1939 West Indies team in England, he claimed 87 wickets and would assuredly have exceeded 100 had that tour not been curtailed by the advent of World War II. He captured 6 wickets in his three Tests for the West Indies that summer. He captained the British Empire XI in England during the war, and settled down there permanently afterwards. Bertie eventually played 49 times for Northamptonshire and 18 times for Essex. Altogether, in 97 matches, he claimed 333 wickets (av: 26.37) in first-class cricket, playing his final game at that level for the MCC in 1961 when he was 43. But his major claim to fame as a cricketer perhaps lies in the fact that he participated enthusiastically in BBC Sunday matches until he was 70 years old and was still good enough to win the First XI Bowling Cup in his final season. In 1983, Dr Clarke was awarded the OBE for his community service among West Indians in the London area. He eventually died in Putney in 1993. Although Clarke played only three matches for Barbados (capturing 12/362) before migrating to Britain, he is still fondly remembered as one of the greatest spin bowlers ever produced by his native country.[73]

Theodore Birkett, M.I.C. Clarke, Foster, Gill, Harris, Harold Jordan and Peirce all played for Barbados with varying degrees of success. Birkett remained a prolific scorer for Pickwick until he was almost 40. He was unlucky to have been allowed only two first-class innings. In one of these he scored a useful 57 against Trinidad in 1956 when, at 38, he was already beyond his peak.[74] He had the misfortune to emerge at a time when Barbados was extremely strong in batting. 'Micey' Clarke was, for many years, a useful right-handed allrounder for Wanderers. He was selected only twice to play for Barbados, but in one of these matches he struck a spectacular 151 against Trinidad at the Queen's Park Oval in 1941.[75] Foster, who became one of the pillars of the young YMPC club, played once for Barbados against Trinidad in the goodwill tour of 1942.[76] Gill played briefly for Empire during the early 1940s before emigrating, like so many of his contemporaries, to Trinidad. 'Shell' Harris, another Empire supporter, was a clever right-arm bowler of medium pace and a very steady right-handed batsman who took over the captaincy of his school team after Bertie Clarke's departure. But his fielding often left much to be desired. He returned to teach briefly at his alma mater during the 1950s and played a few more seasons for them. 'Shell' also played occasionally for Spartan. In his five games for Barbados during 1942–45, he took 12 wickets at a cost of just over 26 runs each.[77] He served sometimes as a sports commentator when his playing career was over. Jordan, a slow left-arm spinner, who toiled so valiantly for Pickwick throughout the 1940s, was invited only once to play for the island though his performance in that game (3 for 95) was eminently satisfactory.[78]

Thomas Noel Peirce (1916–88), a great Barbadian captain and administrator

Thomas Noel Peirce, who captained Wanderers successfully from 1940 to 1950, also provided Barbados with inspirational leadership for more than a decade. Taking over the reins at a time when Barbadian confidence was low, he led his island to some memorable victories over Trinidad and British Guiana in the famous goodwill series. His selection as captain raised several eyebrows, since many pundits did not think that he merited a place in the Barbados XI on the strength of his cricketing ability alone. But, highly respected and very much liked by his players, Tom proved himself one of the most successful of all Barbadian cricket captains. Nor was his individual contribution at all shabby. In 16 matches for Barbados, he scored 261 runs (av: 15.35), captured 29 wickets (av: 37.75) and held 16 catches. He was a very slow right-arm spinner of leg-breaks and a brilliant fielder close to the wicket. Against Trinidad in 1942, he established a Barbadian first-class record by taking seven catches in a single match. Peirce was only 23 when, in 1939, he was first elected to the BCA board of management, which he served for 20 years before assuming the presidency in 1959. He gave up that post in 1964 when elected president of the WICBC. A most efficient administrator, he was awarded the CBE in 1967 for his services to cricket.[79]

Destined also to become a famous administrator was Eric Inniss who succeeded Peirce as president of the BCA in 1965 and remained in that post until his sudden death on 21 April 1972. For nearly 30 years he was a member of the BCA board of management and was elected vice president in 1956. He was also a representative on the WICBC during the last 10 years of his life. Inniss, who had played both cricket and football for Harrison in the early 1930s, did the same afterwards for Spartan and captained that club at cricket in the early 1940s. Quite deservedly, the Eric Inniss Stand was erected in his honour at the Kensington Oval in 1986.[80]

During the late 1930s, Harrison received noteworthy contributions from D. DaC. Marshall, its cricket master, Carlisle A. Burton, a promising wicketkeeper/batsman, and Val McComie, a useful right-handed allrounder. Marshall had been the school's cricket captain in 1926 and a member of the first Harrison XI to win the Challenge Cup. Except for the three years (1928–31) when he studied for his classics degree at Codrington College, his association with Harrison went back unbroken to 1919, since he joined its teaching staff immediately after his graduation. In 1932, he succeeded Leslie Walcott as games master and held that post until his untimely death in 1938. Marshall never reached first-class status as a cricketer but his influence on Harrison cricket was most significant. He inspired several generations of Harrisonians to play the game.[81] Burton, too, taught at his alma mater during the 1940s and offered valuable guidance to the younger players in his quiet, unassuming and inimitable way. A grandson of W.T.

Burton, one of the greatest West Indian fast bowlers at the turn of the century, Carlisle Burton was later knighted for his work as a civil servant. McComie took his abundant skills to the Lodge School, where he taught for many years before becoming an important diplomat. He was a fine hard-hitting batsman and a penetrative medium-fast bowler. He had the ability to swing the ball both ways off the seam and was often compared to India's great fast bowler, Dattu Phadkar.

Keith and Clyde

As was the case at the Lodge School, Harrison College began to change its social and racial composition during the inter-war years. A first-grade secondary school deliberately intended by the Education Act of 1878 to serve the interests of the white élite, it gradually became an integrated institution as the sons of middle class blacks, well-to-do enough to afford the fees or bright enough to win first-grade scholarships and exhibitions, could not be excluded. By the end of the 1930s therefore there was a sizeable contingent of black students on the Harrison College roll. Among this group were the two famous Walcott brothers, Clyde and Keith. While the former was destined to reach more dazzling heights as a cricketer, it was his elder brother who showed the greater promise at first. Keith was only 15 when, in 1939, he put Pickwick and Spartan to the sword, scoring dazzling centuries against them in consecutive matches. He remained one of the hardest hitters of the ball and one of the game's finest fielders until his premature retirement from first-class cricket. In 15 matches for Barbados during 1941–52, he scored 536 runs and averaged 26.80 per innings. He also held 11 catches. Had it not been for failing eyesight, he must surely have played more often for Barbados and perhaps even for the West Indies. Keith is best remembered now as a cricket administrator and as a pillar of Spartan. He served the BCA most capably from 1959 to 1991.[82]

While Keith Walcott was a schoolboy prodigy, Harrison was one of the most formidable clubs in Barbados. He found considerable support from his younger brother, who was only 16 when he made his début for Barbados in 1942. When the school was inexplicably demoted to the second division in 1941, Clyde headed the batting averages with 491 runs at 81.33 per innings and was third in bowling.[83] He continued to score centuries against the senior clubs when Harrison was restored to the first division. Clyde Walcott developed into one of the world's greatest batsmen, scoring 15 Test centuries for the West Indies, for whom he also kept wicket and sometimes bowled. His batting average of 56.68 remains one of the best in international cricket. In 146 first-class matches, he recorded 11,838 runs (av: 56.64), including 40 centuries. For Barbados, he became the very first batsman to score 2,000 runs after breaking Tim Tarilton's long-standing record of 1,885 in 1951. His new mark of 2,328 was eventually surpassed by Everton Weekes in 1963. One amazing record which has yet to be approached, however, is the 11 stumpings which Walcott achieved in only 16 Tests for the West Indies. His 64 dismissals in Test cricket remained a West Indian record until the emergence of Deryck Murray in the 1960s.[84]

After his retirement as an active player, Clyde Walcott served for many years as a BCA administrator before being elected president of the WICBC. On 1 October 1993 he was appointed the first non-British chairman of the ICC and in 1994 was knighted for his services to the sport. His dedicated service to cricket has brought him a number of honours and distinctions. His name is one of those which adorn the 'Three Ws Stand' at the Kensington Oval in Bridgetown. From the government of Guyana he was awarded the Arrow of Achievement (AA) after having been honoured with an OBE. Walcott also received the Gold Crown of Merit (GCM) in the Barbados Order of St Andrew and was made an honorary life member of the MCC and of the Surrey County Cricket Club, where one of the hospitality boxes has been named after him by the Cable & Wireless, one of the sponsors of West Indies cricket. Among his numerous contributions to Caribbean cricket was a son, Michael Alex Clyde Walcott, who represented Barbados briefly in 1975. Working in British Guiana during the 1950s, Sir Clyde also helped to develop the skills of such promising batsmen as Basil Butcher, Rohan Kanhai and Joseph Solomon while promoting the claims of Port Mourant's disadvantaged players. Doing his utmost to break down the complex racial barriers that had traditionally separated Guyanese blacks, browns and whites, Walcott earned the everlasting gratitude even of that crusty old warhorse, Ivan Madray, the promising leg-spinner, with whom the West Indies selectors had dealt rather shabbily some 40 years before.[85]

Also in the Harrison XI in those days were such future Barbadian players as H.L.V. Griffith, and C.B. 'Boogles' Williams. Harold Griffith was the eldest son of Herman, the celebrated West Indian fast bowler of the 1920s and 1930s. His first-class statistics are not impressive, 347 runs (av: 24.78) and 3 wickets (av: 79.66), but his role as an allrounder was crucial to many Empire successes during the 1940s.[86] He became an important leader of his club before serving as an influential BCA administrator. An immensely talented player, 'Boogles' was most unfortunate not to have gained selection on a West Indian Test team. He was the best spin bowler in Barbados throughout the 1940s and seemed headed for a Test career against England in 1950 when he was suddenly eclipsed by the meteoric rise of Sonny Ramadhin and Alfred Valentine. His record for Barbados remains one of the best. In 16 matches between 1947 and 1957, he scored 788 runs (av: 41.47) and took 43 wickets (av: 29.95). A fine spinner of legbreaks and googlies, he was also a brilliant fieldsman and a stylish batsman. As captain of the Barbados XI which opposed E.W. Swanton's touring team in March 1956, he scored a majestic 133 against an attack that included Gamini Goonesena, Robin Marlar and Frank Tyson. Williams made a great contribution to the rise to prominence of a new Barbadian cricket club, Carlton, in the period immediately following World War II. He also served in later years as a BCA administrator.[87]

STARS OF THE 1940s

During the 1940s, Harrison College continued to field fairly competitive teams and to produce some outstanding individual cricketers who eventually achieved first-class status. Harold Noad Haskell, its headmaster since 1923, had finally convinced the school's governing body to supply his boys with additional classroom space and playing fields to cater to the needs of a student body that had expanded to 405 by 1942.[88] The improvement in the school's athletics became quite pronounced almost at once, as did the level of its cricket and soccer. The most successful Harrisonian cricketers of the decade were E.L.G. Hoad, Jnr. (W.C.'s nephew), Horace King, Gordon Proverbs and Gerald Wood (Lear's son). Teddy Hoad, who went on to play several years for Pickwick, was a wily legspinner who captured 15 wickets in nine matches for Barbados in a first-class career that lasted from 1945 to 1954. He was also good enough as a batsman to score a defiant 74 against Jamaica at Sabina Park in 1946.[89] King, an Empire stalwart in his later years, was a fine left-arm spinner who would certainly have played many more than three games for Barbados had it not been for the emergence of Adzil Holder and Gary Sobers in the 1950s. He bowled extremely well for Harrison during the 1947–48 season, when he captured 37 wickets at a cost 10.86 runs each.[90] Proverbs was a tenacious batsman who played only six games for his island but remained for many seasons a prolific scorer for Wanderers in BCA first division competition.[91] Wood was an outstanding wicketkeeper who made 15 dismissals in his seven matches for Barbados and spent his adult years playing extremely well for Pickwick.[92] It is nowadays generally acknowledged that Wood would have gone much further in the game had he not emerged at a time when Barbadian and West Indian selectors were choosing batsmen who could keep wicket rather than wicketkeeping specialists.

Several other promising players made invaluable contributions to Harrison cricket in that decade. Bertie Callender, a clever right-arm medium fast bowler, later played fine cricket in Jamaica for the University College of the West Indies. The three Lawless brothers, C.B., D.I. and R.A., were excellent batsmen who were expected to go much further in the game than they eventually did. David was particularly impressive and once hit a glorious century for Harrison against Spartan in 1947.[93] Fred D. 'Washer' Phillips, an enthusiastic fast bowler, with 23 wickets (av: 12.26) in 1948, was another. Harold A. Marshall, a sharp breaker of the ball with his left-arm slows, showed enormous potential also. A really attractive stroke-player with exceptional skills was Oliver Browne. Two of 'Boogles's' younger brothers, Denys and James Williams, were very good medium-fast swingers of the new ball. James was especially unfortunate never to have played for Barbados or Jamaica (where he spent a number of years). And one of the finest fast bowlers ever to play for Harrison without being invited to represent Barbados was George H.C. Griffith, Harold's younger brother. George, who captained the school's cricket team in his last days

The Harrison College XI, 1946–47. *Standing*: N. Edwards, D.A. Williams, D.M. Browne, K.H.C. Griffith, J.A. Williams, B.A. Callender; *seated*: H.A. King, H.D. Wilson, G.H.C. Griffith (capt.), V.O. Smith, H.A. Marshall

there, proceeded to Cambridge University which he represented with rather disappointing results during 1949–51.[94]

GOOD CRICKET IN THE 1950s

During the early 1950s, when Harrison had finally become a largely black school taught mainly by black masters, it continued its production of first-class cricketers and was particularly competitive in the BCA first division seasons of 1950–51 and 1954–55. Geoffrey Foster, E.H.C. Griffith, Albert Hassell, Bobby Morris, Eddie Perkins, Erskine Sandiford, and C.W. Smith all played with distinction while still at school. Neither Morris, Perkins nor Sandiford reached first-class status; but they came close. In the early 1950s, Bobby Morris was simply one of the best fieldsmen in the West Indies. Perkins, who later attended the Lodge, was a prodigious spinner of the ball and might have been selected to play for Barbados had he not once been cruelly maltreated by Everton Weekes and other senior batsmen in an unforgettable trial game at Kensington Oval in 1952. Sandiford, who was destined to become the fourth prime minister of Barbados, was a violent striker of the ball and once scored a sparkling century against Pickwick before departing for the University College of the West Indies, in whose cricket team he served as vice captain in 1958–59.[95] He thereafter allowed his studies, and then politics, to impede his progress as a cricketer.

Geoffrey Foster and 'Runty' Hassell earned Barbadian caps. The former was a left-handed allrounder who played six times for the island between 1958 and 1962. A very steady spinner of the ball, he claimed 14 wickets (av: 31.57) in these matches.[96] Hassell was a promising wicketkeeper, who might have enjoyed a more distinguished career had it not been for the presence of David Allan, his most dangerous and talented rival. His lone first-class opportunity came against E.W. Swanton's XI in 1956 when he effected three dismissals.[97] Ominously, he was replaced by Allan in the very next game, even though he had enjoyed a reasonably good match.

Teddy Griffith was the youngest and the most talented of Herman's four sons. An excellent allrounder, he made his début for Barbados in 1954 just before his 18th birthday. Migrating to Jamaica quite soon thereafter, he remained a tower of strength for his adopted country until 1967. He amassed almost 1,700 runs with an average of 35.95 in first-class cricket.[98] He was an aggressive left-handed batsman with a good enough defence to open the innings several times for Jamaica. He was a magnificent fieldsman and a steady medium-fast right-arm bowler capable of swinging the new ball both ways. Perhaps had Teddy not emerged at the same time as

Gary Sobers he might well have represented the West Indies in a number of Test matches. At his peak during 1955–65, he was one of the leading allrounders in the Caribbean. Griffith was also a marvellous footballer who represented Barbados against British Guiana when he was only 18 years old. After a lengthy stay in Jamaica, he has returned to Barbados and has served both the BCA and the WICBC (now the WICB) in an advisory capacity.[99]

'Cammie' Smith who once struck a whirlwind 300 against Police

Cameron Wilberforce Smith is much better known to cricket fans overseas. He was a punishing right-handed opening batsman who delighted in carrying the attack to the new-ball bowlers. He hit a dazzling 300 in a few hours one Saturday afternoon for Spartan against Police. He scored 1,434 runs in 20 games for Barbados (av: 47.80) during 1951–63, but is perhaps best remembered for his cavalier assault on a startled Alan Davidson and Ian Meckiff in a Test match at Sydney in January 1961. Cammie Smith was also a competent wicketkeeper and would undoubtedly have played more than five Tests for the West Indies had he shown greater discipline as a batsman. In 37 first-class matches altogether he registered 2,277 runs (av: 37.32) and 35 dismissals. He eventually served very effectively on the BCA board of management from 1969 to 1994 and as president of the BCA from 1994 to 1996.[100]

During the late 1950s Harrison was well represented by such promising players as T.E. Bethell, Robin Bynoe, David Holford, Tony King, Al Knight and Rudi Webster. Bethell was good enough to be selected to the Combined School's team which played against E.W. Swanton's XI in 1956 but he emerged at a time when Barbados could boast a galaxy of excellent batsmen. In his day, Knight was the finest schoolboy wicketkeeper in the island. In 1958, along with Holford, he represented Barbados Colts against Pakistan and British Guiana. For the same reason as that which impeded Hassell's career, he never achieved first-class status but he did make a useful contribution to Barbados cricket by serving on the BCA board of management during the 1980s.[101]

Rudi Valentine Webster was a tall, gangling right-arm fast medium bowler who gave batsmen all kinds of trouble because of the unusual height from which he delivered the ball. In his final season for Harrison he looked particularly dangerous when taking 34 wickets in the first division competition.[102] Webster never gained a Barbados cap, but he did represent Scotland in the early 1960s while studying medicine at the University of Edinburgh. He then played for Warwickshire in the English county competition from 1962 to 1966 and for Otago in New Zealand during 1966–68. His first-class career altogether involved 70 matches, in which he scored 867 runs (av: 13.76) and took 272 wickets (av: 19.44).[103] His stint in Warwickshire was a very successful one. In 60 matches for that county he claimed 234 wickets at less than 20 runs each.[104] Against Cambridge University in 1966, he created quite a stir by capturing 8 for 19 and dismissing the undergraduates for 36 in their first innings.[105] Dr Rudi Webster, quite simply, was one of the best fast bowlers ever produced by Harrison College.

Robin Bynoe was a very sound opening batsman and an excellent slip-fielder who made his first-class début before he was 17. In his first innings for Barbados, he shared an opening stand of 123 with Conrad Hunte against Pakistan. For the island he eventually played 37 matches, scoring six centuries and accumulating 2,676 runs (av: 45.35). For Harrison, Wanderers and Barbados, Bynoe batted and fielded brilliantly in a long and illustrious career. It thus remains a mystery why he was selected to only four West Indian Test teams before joining the ranks of BCA administrators.[106] Among a host of other pundits, Sir Garfield Sobers has consistently maintained that Bynoe ought to have been selected to tour England with the West Indian squad in 1966.[107]

Robin Bynoe should have played more often for the West Indies

David Holford, to date the most successful of all Barbadian captains

Holford will always be remembered for his match-saving partnership in the 1966 Lord's Test with his famous cousin, Gary Sobers. For Barbados, he became the first player to score 1,000 runs and take 100 wickets in the Shell Shield competition. In 46 such matches he captured 130 wickets (av: 28.33) and amassed 1,993 runs (av: 36.23). He also held 46 catches. His Test returns are not quite as impressive, but there are still creditable: 768 runs (av: 22.58), 51 wickets (av: 39.39) and 18 catches in 24 games. Altogether, his first-class career (during 1960–79) produced 3,821 runs (av: 31.31), 253 wickets (av: 32.00) and 83 catches in 99 games. Holford was a steady right-arm legspinner, a resourceful right-handed batsman and a brilliant field. He was also the most successful Barbadian captain, losing only 2 and winning 13 of his 25 matches. As an administrator in his later years he rendered invaluable service to Spartan, the BCA and WICBC and served for a long time as one of the West Indian Test selectors.[108]

Tony King, Horace's younger brother, is generally considered one of the best schoolboy batsmen ever seen in Barbados. In his first match for Harrison, at the age of 14, he hit a century against Carlton. During an outstanding school career, he scored 5 hundreds altogether, including a double, a brilliant 201 not out against Police at the age of 17. King fulfilled some of this early promise when he made his débût for Barbados against Trinidad at Port-of-Spain in 1961. Not yet 18, he scored 80 not out in the second innings and helped to save his team from certain defeat. One year later he scored 89 for Barbados against India. Abandoning cricket prematurely, King did not really give himself a chance to realize his full potential as a first-class player. He represented Barbados on only nine occasions between 1961 and 1971, scoring 360 runs at an average of 27.69 per innings. But he amply compensated by managing Barbados teams at home and abroad, serving as a trustee for Empire and spending several years as a member of the BCA board of management.[109]

AN EVERLASTING SLUMP

While Harrison had remained competitive in the first division for most of the period up to the early 1960s, its teams have never again been able to reach such heights. In fact, all the school teams became so weak that the BCA decided to demote them permanently. A Combined Schools' XI was later admitted to the first division in 1978. Almost inexplicably, the number of Combermere, Harrison and Lodge School alumni appearing in the first-class cricket ranks has decreased dramatically in the last 30 years. It can perhaps be argued that cricket became a much less exclusive sport in Barbados from the 1960s onwards. Teams sprang up everywhere and could not indefinitely be omitted from BCA competition. Whereas in 1951 there were only 17 clubs playing in all three divisions (with the major schools and clubs each fielding more than one eleven), that number grew to more than 70 within the next 40 years and a significant number of their members were drawn from the elementary schools. As late as 1965, too, the three élite schools provided the bulk of BCA players and, with Foundation, they then formed the only four vibrant cricket schools in the island. By 1995 as many as 24 secondary schools had become affiliated with the BCA.[110] In 1950, the three leading secondary schools in Barbados accounted altogether for about 1,400 students. Many of the new secondary schools nowadays accommodate more than 600 students each. This means, therefore, there has emerged a much larger and more varied talent pool even when adequate allowance has been made for the fairly even distribution of the sexes in the major schools and colleges.

Even when all of these factors have been considered, however, it is still astonishing to discover that, since Tony King's departure from Harrison in 1962, only one cricketer of any note has been produced by that school. The only Harrisonians who have gained selection to Barbadian teams since then have been Peter Alleyne, William Bourne, Chetwyn Burnham, Trevor Campbell, Geoffrey Greenidge and Michael Walcott. The first four and the last of these between them played for Barbados on a grand total of seven occasions all told, mustering 101 runs as batsmen and 2 wickets (both by Bourne) as bowlers.[111] In English county cricket, however, Bill Bourne performed much better. A medium fast right-arm bowler and hard-hitting lower order right-handed batsman, he took 126 wickets and scored 1,300 runs for Warwickshire between 1973 and 1977. He will long be remembered at Edgbaston for a whirlwind 107 against Sussex in June 1976 when he and Geoffrey Humpage, the wicketkeeper, added 203 in an astonishing eighth-wicket partnership, just 25 short of the county's record.[112]

Only Geoffrey Greenidge, among recent Harrisonians, has managed to carry on the school's noble tradition. Clearly one of the finest of all Harrisonian openers, he made his début for Barbados in February 1967 when, at 18, he scored 39 against the Leeward Islands. One month later, he hit a magnificent 205 against Jamaica at Bridgetown. Greenidge gained selection to 22 Barbadian teams, accumulating 1,237 runs (av: 36.38). He also played five Tests for the West Indies before his eclipse by such superior opening batsmen as Gordon Greenidge and Desmond Haynes. The bulk of his first-class cricket was played in England where he amassed 7,629 runs for Sussex between 1966 and 1975.[113]

THE BALANCE SHEETS

Despite Harrison's failure to produce a significant number of first-class cricketers in the last quarter of a century, it is still nevertheless clear that that institution was one of the most important in the critical early years of the Challenge Cup and BCA competitions. Equally significant is the fact that the vast majority of Barbadian cricket administrators over the years have been Old Harrisonians. Since its inception in 1933, there have so far been seven presidents of the BCA. Five of them – Sir Alan Collymore, Eric Inniss, Tony Marshall, Tom Peirce and Cammie Smith – were Old Harrisonians. The same is true of such vice presidents as Austin, Challenor, F.A.C. Clairmonte, Stanton Gittens, and the Walcott brothers. Cricket in Barbados, in short, has almost always been administered by Old Harrisonians.

The number of Harrisonians who have represented Barbados in first-class cricket is phenomenal. Of the 324 listed by Philip Thorn in *Barbados Cricketers 1865–1990*, at least 83 (26 percent) can positively be identified as Old Harrisonians. Excluding Roger Blackman (Lodge), Darnley DaCosta (Harrow), John Goddard (Lodge), E.L.G. Hoad, Snr (Combermere), Geoffrey Hutchinson (Lodge) and Pelham Warner (Rugby) who owed a greater loyalty to a second academic institution, the roll of ex-Harrisonian cricketers who achieved first-class status is still mind-boggling. One index of the significance of an institution in the history of any sport is the number of its individual members who have reached the pinnacle. It is interesting therefore to consider the list of Harrisonians who eventually played cricket at the Test match level. It is most unusual for any one school to be able to claim as many as ten international stars. Harrison College, however, can boast of the following: Lawson Bartlett, Lionel Birkett, 'Snuffie' Browne, Robin Bynoe, George Challenor, Bertie Clarke, Geoffrey Greenidge, David

Holford, Cammie Smith, Clyde Walcott and Leslie Walcott.

In concrete terms, 11 Old Harrisonians played 102 Tests for the West Indies. They batted a total of 174 innings (19 times not out), scored 5,695 runs (including 16 centuries), and averaged 36.74. Between them they captured 77 wickets for 3,149 runs (av: 40.89), caught 89 opposing batsmen and stumped 12 others. On the whole, except for the bowling, these are eminently creditable statistics. They show that Harrison was famous for the production of gifted batsmen but generally lacked bowlers of exceptional quality. Even so, had 'Boogles' Williams not been superseded very suddenly by meteors named Sonny Ramadhin and Alfred Valentine in 1950, he might well have taken as many Test wickets as Holford (51) was later destined to do. He was also a good enough batsman to have exceeded 1,000 runs in Test cricket. In addition, Austin, Bancroft, Ince, Inniss and Williams played for West Indian touring teams in England. Pelham Warner, of course, also represented England in 15 Tests and captained that country in matches against Australia and South Africa.[114] It is a pity, moreover, that Test cricket came to the West Indies only after Austin, Bancroft, the Brownes, Challenor, Ince, Mason and others had passed their prime or had retired. Challenor and Ince between them must, in a different age, have been worth about 5,000 runs in Test cricket.

Harrison's Dream

Another useful index is the so-called dream team, which often reflects the power of an institution over time. The batting order of such a Harrison XI might well be: George Challenor, Robin Bynoe, Cammie Smith, Lawson Bartlett, Clyde Walcott (wicketkeeper), Lionel Birkett, Teddy Griffith, 'Boogles' Williams, 'Snuffie' Browne, David Holford (captain) and Rudi Webster. This is a truly formidable batting line-up, with the first ten players each capable of scoring a century at the highest level. The bowling can be done by Webster and Griffith with the new ball, followed by Browne, Holford and Williams, three of the best spinners produced by Barbados. Challenor, who took 54 wickets in first-class cricket with his right-arm medium-pacers, and Walcott who claimed 35 in a similar fashion, are also capable of holding their own with the ball. Cammie Smith could also serve, if necessary, as the team's wicketkeeper.

But the obvious problem here is that, while Harrison has produced a surplus of spin bowlers, opening batsmen and wicketkeepers, it has not provided Barbados with any bowler who was genuinely fast. Apart from Webster, Harrison's best fast bowlers over the years perhaps were Francis

Austin, George Griffith and 'Washer' Phillips. On the other hand, it is odd that such excellent opening batsmen as Bynoe, Challenor, Gittens, Greenidge and Smith should all have come from the same school; and that a single institution could have produced such first-class wicketkeepers as Grantley Adams, Bancroft, T.G. Clarke, Gittens, Hassell, Smith, Walcott and Wood. It is also unlikely that any other school can boast of having produced as many spinners of such high quality as 'Snuffie' Browne, Bertie Clarke, Teddy Hoad, David Holford, Harold Jordan, Horace King, Kenneth Mason, Tom Pierce and 'Boogles' Williams. Nor is it possible to conceive of any academic institution failing to find a place on its All-Time XI for cricketers of such quality as Harold Austin, Bertie Clarke, Harry Ince and Leslie Walcott.

It is by bandying about such names as these, both as administrators and as players, that one begins to understand the enormity of the Harrison legacy to the game of cricket. It must surely be a very difficult one for any other school to match.

NOTES

1 There is no general history of Harrison College. The best sources still are *The Harrisonian 250th Anniversary Issue* (Bridgetown, 1983) and the *J.M.G.M. Adams Memorial Issue* (Bridgetown, 1986). See also Keith A.P. Sandiford, " 'Sons in the Sun': The Cricket Story of Harrison College of Barbados'", *Cricket Lore* 2, no. 4 (1995): 38–43.

2 Sir Pelham Warner, *Long Innings: An Autobiography* (London, 1951), 11–16.

3 Bruce Hamilton, *Cricket in Barbados* (Bridgetown, 1947), 35.

4 BCA, *100 Years of Organised Cricket in Barbados, 1892–1992* (Bridgetown, 1992), 70–1.

5 *Harrisonian* (March 1903), 5–6; *Barbados Blue Book 1903–04*, U24.

6 *Harrisonian* (March 1903), 7.

7 C.L.R. James, *Beyond a Boundary* (Sportsmans Book Club, 1964), 38. See also *Harrisonian* (December 1929), 12.

8 Hamilton, *Cricket in Barbados*, 53.

9 Ibid., 35–6.

10 Keith A.P. Sandiford, "The Spartan Cricket Club 1893–1993", *Journal of the Cricket Society* 16, no. 3 (Autumn 1993): 44.

11 Hamilton, *Cricket in Barbados*, 34.

12 Ibid., 36; *Harrisonian* (October 1903), 2. See also *Barbados Herald*, 12 May 1881.

13 BCA, *100 Years*, 116.

14 Ibid., 68; *Harrisonian* (April 1924), 39.

15 *Combermerian* (1926–27), 61.

16 Hamilton, *Cricket in Barbados*, 34, 35, 68.
17 *Barbados Agricultural Reporter*, 11 September 1897. See also Hamilton, *Cricket in Barbados*, 35, 48, 49, 54, 59, 60, 71.
18 Hamilton, *Cricket in Barbados*, 45.
19 Philip Thorn, *Barbados Cricketers,1865–1990* (West Bridgford, 1991), 23.
20 Hamilton, *Cricket in Barbados*, 65.
21 Thorn, *Barbados Cricketers*, 10, 23.
22 BCA, *100 Years*, 56; Hamilton, *Cricket in Barbados*, 57.
23 BCA, *100 Years*, 109; *Harrisonian* (December 1925), 35; Hamilton, *Cricket in Barbados*, 55, 57.
24 Hamilton, *Cricket in Barbados*, 82, 88, 90, 92;Thorn, *Barbados Cricketers*, 7, 21.
25 Christopher Nicole, *West Indian Cricket* (London, 1957), 51.
26 Gerry Wolstenholme, *West Indian Tour of England 1906* (Blackpool, 1992), 36.
27 *Harrisonian* (April 1919), 66; Hamilton, *Cricket in Barbados*, 81; Thorn, *Barbados Cricketers*, 7, 21.
28 BCA, *100 Years*, 104.
29 *Harrisonian* (December 1929), 11–13.
30 *Harrisonian* (July 1922), 44–5; (July 1928), 2–3; (December 1948), 15–18.
31 Hamilton, *Cricket in Barbados*, 71, 79.
32 Nicole, *West Indian Cricket*, 50.
33 Wolstenholme, *West Indian Tour of England 1906*, 38.
34 Michael Manley, *A History of West Indies Cricket* (London, 1989), 24–6. Keith A.P. Sandiford, *Everton DeCourcey Weekes: His Record Innings-by-Innings* (West Bridgford, 1995), 45; Keith A.P. Sandiford, *Frank Mortimer Maglinne Worrell: His Record Innings-by-Innings* (West Bridgford, 1997) 22–4.
35 Philip Bailey, Philip Thorn and Peter Wynne-Thomas, *Who's Who of Cricketers* (London, 1984), 192.
36 Thorn, *Barbados Cricketers*, 9, 23.
37 Hamilton, *Cricket in Barbados*, 73, 74, 77, 85–8, 92, 97; Thorn, *Barbados Cricketers*, 7, 13, 21, 25.
38 BCA, *100 Years*, 60.
39 Ibid., 62. See also Bailey, Thorn and Wynne-Thomas, *Who's Who of Cricketers*, 151.
40 *Harrisonian* (July 1933), 45.
41 Ibid., 45–6.
42 Hamilton, *Cricket in Barbados*, 87, 89, 93; Bailey, Thorn and Wynne-Thomas, *Who's Who of Cricketers*, 81.
43 Hamilton, *Cricket in Barbados*, 109; BCA, *Report and Statement of Accounts 1st April 1994 to 31st March 1995*, 75.
44 BCA, *100 Years*, 93.
45 Hamilton, *Cricket in Barbados*, 112, 118–19, 144; Thorn, *Barbados Cricketers*, 16, 28.
46 BCA, *100 Years*, 124.

47 BCA, *100 Years*, 10; Hamilton, *Cricket in Barbados*, 96–8.
48 *Harrisonian* (December 1916), 22–3; *Harrisonian* (March 1917), 76–7.
49 BCA, *100 Years*, 10.
50 Hamilton, *Cricket in Barbados*, 96–7.
51 *Harrisonian* (December 1916), 21–3.
52 Hamilton, *Cricket in Barbados*, 109–10; Thorn, *Barbados Cricketers*, 12, 25.
53 BCA, *100 Years*, 56.
54 Ibid., 58. At 92, Birkett, who was born in Strathclyde on 14 April 1905, is now (so far as I can ascertain) the oldest surviving Test cricketer.
55 *Advocate Year Book and Who's Who 1951* (Bridgetown, 1951), 221; *Lodge School Record* (1947–48), 19.
56 *Harrisonian* (December 1925), 30–1.
57 *Harrisonian* (April 1928), 10.
58 Hamilton, *Cricket in Barbados*, 141.
59 *Harrisonian* (December 1927), 28; *Harrisonian* (April 1928), 65.
60 *Harrisonian* (July 1929), 21.
61 Thorn, *Barbados Cricketers*, 26.
62 Hamilton, *Cricket in Barbados*, 134; Keith A.P. Sandiford and Brian Stoddart, "The Elite Schools and Cricket in Barbados: A Study in Colonial Continuity", *International Journal of the History of Sport* 4 (December 1987): 349.
63 *Harrisonian* (December 1930), 23.
64 BCA, *Report and Statement of Accounts 1st April 1994 to 31st March 1995*, 75. Hamilton, *Cricket in Barbados*, 138, 141.
65 *Harrisonian* (July 1932), 5; BCA, *100 Years*, 10.
66 Thorn, *Barbados Cricketers*, 23.
67 Hamilton, *Cricket in Barbados*, 148.
68 BCA, *100 Years*, 75–6.
69 *West Indies Cricket Annual 1982*, 88.
70 *West Indies Cricket Annual 1983*, 88.
71 *Harrisonian* (April 1936), 8, 11.
72 Hamilton, *Cricket in Barbados*, 144.
73 *Wisden* 1994, 1337–38; Bailey, Thorn and Wynne-Thomas, *Who's Who of Cricketers*, 205.
74 Jimmy Richards and Mervyn Wong, *Statistics of West Indies Cricket 1865–1989* (Kingston, 1990), 70.
75 Hamilton, *Cricket in Barbados*, 149.
76 Ibid., 152.
77 Thorn, *Barbados Cricketers*, 25.
78 Ibid., 26.
79 BCA, *100 Years*, 108.
80 *West Indies Cricket Annual 1973*, 82; BCA, *100 Years*, 18.
81 *Harrisonian* (July 1938), 34–5.
82 BCA, *100 Years*, 123–24.
83 *Harrisonian* (December 1941), 8.

84 Sandiford, *Clyde Leopold Walcott: His Record Innings-by-Innings* (West Bridgford, 1996), 8, 46.
85 BCA, *100 Years*, 118–20. Sandiford, *Clyde Leopold Walcott*. See also Frank Birbalsingh and Clem Shiwcharan, *Indo–Westindian* [sic] *Cricket* (London, 1988), 115.
86 Empire Cricket Club, *The Empire Club 1914–1989* (Bridgetown, 1989), 26–30.
87 BCA, *100 Years*, 127.
88 *Harrisonian* (April 1942), 5; (December 1942), 3.
89 Hamilton, *Cricket in Barbados*, 167. Thorn, *Barbados Cricketers*, 25.
90 *Harrisonian* (December 1948), 51.
91 Thorn, *Barbados Cricketers*, 28.
92 Ibid., 30.
93 *Harrisonian* (December 1947), 55.
94 Bailey, Thorn and Wynne-Thomas, *Who's Who of Cricketers*, 413.
95 *The Pelican 1959* (Kingston, 1959), 64.
96 Thorn, *Barbados Cricketers*, 24.
97 *Wisden 1957*, 882–83.
98 Thorn, *Barbados Cricketers*, 25.
99 *Harrisonian* (1953–54), 31.
100 BCA, *100 Years*, 113.
101 *Harrisonian* (1958) 25.
102 Ibid., 24.
103 Bailey, Thorn and Wynne-Thomas, *Who's Who of Cricketers*, 1078.
104 Leslie Duckworth, *The Story of Warwickshire Cricket* (London), 645.
105 *Wisden 1967*, 683–84.
106 BCA, *100 Years*, 62–3.
107 Sir Garfield Sobers, *Twenty Years at the Top* (London, 1988), 117.
108 BCA, *100 Years*, 88–9; Thorn, *Barbados Cricketers*, 26.
109 BCA, *100 Years*, 10, 94.
110 BCA, *Report and Statement of Accounts 1st April 1994 to 31st March 1995*, 23.
111 Thorn, *Barbados Cricketers*, 21–30.
112 *Wisden 1977*, 595.
113 BCA, *100 Years*, 79–8; Philip Bailey and Philip Thorn, *Sussex Cricketers 1815–1990* (West Bridgford, 1991), 31.
114 Christopher Martin-Jenkins, *The Complete Who's Who of Test Cricketers* (London, 1980), 158.

4

The Role of Combermere School

Established in Bridgetown in 1695, Combermere School has the distinction of being one of the oldest academic institutions in the British Commonwealth and of being perhaps the first school anywhere to offer secondary education to black children. By the Barbados Education Act of 1878, it was declared a second-grade secondary school and thereafter became comparable to most of the leading grammar schools in Britain. For years the school catered traditionally to the children of lower-middle income families, while the wealthier planters and landowners sent their sons to Harrison College or to the Lodge School, where higher admission fees were paid. Combermere gradually became a predominantly black school and came to serve as a symbol of black excellence in a largely black society. Its emphasis on patient teaching and a more practical curriculum also stood it in good stead over the years.[1]

During the first 75 years of its existence as a second-grade secondary school, Combermere provided the Barbadian community with the vast bulk of its business leaders and civil servants. In the age of independence, when the invidious distinction between first-grade and second-grade secondary education was finally abandoned, Old Combermerians continued to assume a disproportionate importance in the areas of Barba-dian commerce, education, law and politics. In the early 1990s, for instance, the Democratic Labour Party cabinet included such Old Combermerians as Carl Clarke, Warwick Franklyn, Wesley Hall, Harcourt Lewis, Keith Simmons, Brantford Taitt, David Thompson and Cyril Walker.[2] In the field of cricket, too, Combermere has produced more than its fair share of cricketers and administrators.

Like Harrison and the Lodge, Combermere served as one of the most important nurseries of Barbadian cricket for most of the period up to independence. The society was so snobbish for so long that it was extremely difficult for cricketers who had not been trained at the secondary schools to gain selection to Barbadian teams. The number of players who had achieved first-class status by way of the BCL, rather than the élite schools, was negligible prior to 1950. The Alleyne, Coleridge, Foundation and Parry schools had also been totally unproductive. Philip Thorn, in his carefully researched *Barbados Cricketers 1865–1990*, could identify not a single cricketer produced by these four schools during the colonial era.[3] Combermere's role in all of this is most surprising since that school did not receive permission to establish an Advanced Level sixth form until the 1950s. This meant that most of its students had to leave school by the age of 17, while pupils could remain at Harrison and the Lodge up to 19. This gave the two first-grade schools a significant advantage over Combermere, but the latter nevertheless remained very competitive in the field of athletics throughout the twentieth century.

What made Combermere's early contribution to Barbadian cricket all the more astonishing is the fact that the school did not have its own playing fields for a very long time and most of its early matches had to be played at the small Belleville ground on George Street before it gained permission to use the field at Queen's Park. This lack of suitable playing fields was not remedied until the school moved to the spacious Weymouth grounds in 1944 and, even then, Combermere was not provided with a pavilion. In the meantime, the boys had to practice and play their house matches in the confined area near the famous 'marl hole' on Constitution Hill, which was derisively called 'The Tub'. Even after the headmaster, Revd A.E. Armstrong, had cleared away some of the debris from the area to find more playing space for his boys during the 1930s, 'The Tub' remained totally inadequate.[4]

ENTERING THE SECOND DIVISION

Combermere's main disadvantage, then, sprang from its inability to practice properly in the early days. This was duly recognized by the BCCC when it allowed the school to enter a team in the second division competition in 1903. Combermere thus took no part in the senior contests until the 1929–30 season, when it was promoted to the first division on the strength of its surprising competitiveness over the years. The strength of the school team was due largely to the consistent support it received from such headmasters as Revd T. Lyall Speed, who had himself been a first-class cricketer, and G.B.R. Burton, who sincerely believed that cricket was almost as important as the classics in the development of human character. Burton was not at all athletic, but he firmly believed that cricket was an excellent medium through which morals and discipline could be taught. It was he who introduced the house and prefect system to Combermere and supported the notion that his school should participate in regular cricket competition, notwithstanding its lack of proper facilities. He founded the Combermere cadet corps in 1904 and the Combermere scout troop in 1912 and went far towards shaping Combermere in the image of Deighton's Harrison which he had himself attended in his youth. Under Burton, Combermere's student roll rose steadily to 180 in 1904 when it actually outstripped those of all other secondary schools in the island. It remained the most densely populated secondary school in Barbados, admitting an increasing number of black students, for the rest of Burton's tenure.[5]

Speed and Burton were succeeded by such scholar–athletes as G.B.Y. 'Gussie' Cox (1926–34), who had been one of the finest allrounders in the Caribbean at the turn of the century; Revd A.E. Armstrong (1934–46), who had represented Pickwick and St Ann's in his youth; and Stanton O'C. Gittens (1961–70), who was good enough in his younger days to play both cricket and soccer for Barbados. Major Cecil Noott, a Welsh soldier–educator who administered the school from 1946 to 1961, was not renowned for his athletic ability but he nevertheless held games and sport in equally high esteem.[6]

All of these headmasters encouraged the staff members to play with the boys and occasionally there were as many teachers as students in the Combermere XI. Such masters as Frank Collymore and Vincent 'Bull' Williams, for example, were excellent athletes during the 1920s and 1930s. Combermere also profited, after 1926, from the services of 'Graffie' Pilgrim, an Old Lodge Boy, who had represented Spartan and Barbados as a right-arm medium-fast bowler. When Combermere was promoted to the first division in 1929, Pilgrim was the only

Revd A.E. Armstrong (1881–1963) promoted cricket and athletics at Combermere

member of the team with any previous experience in playing at that level. He provided much needed guidance for many years, leading the team to a third place finish in 1937–38, when, at the age of 44, he took 13 wickets at a cost of 16 runs each.[7] He later played in the second division for Combermere until the mid 1940s when he was more than 50 years old. 'Graffie' regarded the young Derek Sealy and Frankie Worrell as his special protégés and did most to promote their cricketing careers while they were at Combermere. His role in Barbadian cricket is almost incalculable. It was under his watchful eye that such schoolboy stars as John Lucas, 'Mannie' Martindale, Derek Sealy, 'Foffie' Williams and Frank Worrell were destined to shine even more brilliantly than he himself had done.[8]

After joining the Combermere staff in 1935, Stanton Gittens played cricket for his new school for several years before returning to teach at his alma mater, Harrison College, which he had represented in both cricket and soccer in his youth. He had the distinction of playing on as many as six championship teams in the Barbadian first division cricket competition. He was a member of the two cup winning Harrison College teams in 1928 and 1931 and the victorious Combermere XI of 1941. He also played a very important role in three of the five championships won by Empire between 1933 and 1942. Stanton was a very steady right-handed opening batsman and an accomplished wicketkeeper who scored 459 runs (av: 21.85) and effected 20 dismissals in his 11 matches for Barbados. He continued to take a very keen interest in the game when he served as Combermere's first black headmaster during the 1960s. His influence on cricket at Combermere and Harrison College was immense.[9]

Stanton O'C. Gittens (1911–94) played on six championship teams

Stanton's elder brother, Lionel Gittens, and D. Ralph Perkins also played frequently for Combermere for several years after joining the staff in the 1930s. 'Gussie' Cox himself had tried to set the example when, in his first season as headmaster, at the age of 56, he scored 164 runs for the school at an average of 14.90 per innings.[10] In later years, such masters as Harold Brewster, Gladstone Holder, Ronnie

Hughes, Arthur Sealy, Harry Sealy, George Solomon, Frederick Smith, Ivan Smith and Billy Wickham were also pressed into service. It is noteworthy that the majority of these teachers had themselves been taught their first cricket lessons as students of Combermere. Of perhaps even greater significance is the fact that the ability to play cricket was then regarded by headmasters in Barbados as a useful qualification when new (or even acting) appointments were being considered.

George Learmond: The First Combermere Cricket Star

These were the circumstances that allowed Combermere, despite its numerous obstacles, to wield so much influence over Barbadian cricket from the 1890s onward. Its first great cricketer, in fact, was George Learmond, a native of Demerara, who was lured to the school by its reputation for teaching commercial and practical subjects at a time when its great rivals, Harrison and the Lodge, were still focusing too narrowly on Greek and Latin. Following his departure from Combermere, Learmond became captain of the newly founded Spartan CC and gave it very valuable leadership during its infancy. Spartan was founded in 1893 (when Learmond was 18 years old) essentially for non-white players, who had been excluded from Pickwick and Wanderers on purely racial grounds. Ironically, the club chose Learmond as its first captain despite the fact that he was white, foreign and inexperienced.[11] This proved to be a singularly fortunate choice since all reports indicate that Learmond's leadership was a source of inspiration and had much to do with the club's early successes in the Challenge Cup competition. His value to the team was publicly recognized by Sir Conrad Reeves, president of Spartan, who presented him with a silver cup just before he returned to Demerara in 1896.[12] Learmond went on to represent Barbados, British Guiana, Trinidad and the West Indies. He was a sound right-handed batsman, a very good field and a competent wicketkeeper. In his three matches for Barbados in the mid 1890s, he scored 164 runs at an average of 27.33.[13] On the surface, this appears a very moderate performance, but it included two superb exhibitions. The first came on a turning wicket in Georgetown when his first innings top score of 59 failed to save Barbados from defeat. The second was his 86 against the very first English touring team to the Caribbean. Opening with 'Gussie' Cox, Learmond established what was then a Barbadian record first wicket partnership of 151, which laid the cornerstone for an enormous innings of 517 which was the highest ever amassed by a Barbadian team up to that time.[14] Although he was not a regular wicketkeeper, contemporaries held a very high opinion of his skills with the gloves. Writing for the *Advocate* early in 1896, 'Long Leg' described him as the best wicketkeeper in the colony.[15]

Learmond's influence on Caribbean cricket is difficult to exaggerate. Apart from making two tours to England in the first decade of the twentieth century, he also gave able leadership to three separate territories. Learmond's legacy also included a son who represented British Guiana, and a grandson, Stephen Camacho, an opening batsman who played 11 Tests for the West Indies during 1967–71 and later became an important administrator on the WICBC.[16]

Learmond's contemporaries at Combermere included Henry Austin who played a key role in the early successes achieved in the Barbados Challenge Cup competition by the Pickwick Cricket Club. Austin, a capable right-handed batsman, represented Barbados on six occasions between 1897 and 1904.[17] Apart from his contributions to Pickwick and Barbadian cricket during his prime, he is famous for being the grandfather of Robin Bynoe, an even better batsman, who represented Barbados and the West Indies during the 1970s.

PRE-WAR CRICKETERS AT COMBERMERE

When Combermere joined the second division competition, its brightest star was John MacColl Kidney, a right-handed batsman of considerable promise. He eventually gained selection to the Barbados XI in 1908 and represented the island on ten occasions over the next 20 years. For more than a quarter of a century, Jack Kidney served as a powerful bulwark of the Pickwick club. He is best remembered as the manager of West Indian touring teams to Australia and England during the 1930s and was at the helm when they enjoyed their first Test triumphs in England in 1950. Jack also fathered Harold Kidney, a sound club player for Pickwick, who became one of the best cricket commentators in the Caribbean during the 1950s.[18]

Just before the outbreak of World War I, Combermere produced some able cricketers who, in due course, made noteworthy contributions to club cricket in Barbados and three of whom, B.I. Gilkes, J.S. Hoad and L.R. Hutchinson, were chosen to represent the island in intercolonial contests. A fine allrounder, Benjamin Gilkes made Empire a force to be reckoned with for many years. He played for Barbados on four occasions between 1919 and 1930. His first-class statistics, 2 runs from 4 innings and 6 wickets for 294 runs, fail miserably to do justice to one of the most successful allrounders in Barbadian club cricket throughout the 1920s. He enjoyed the important distinction of being the first Empire batsman to score a century in first division play and the first member of that club to represent Barbados.[19]

After leaving Combermere, John Hoad and Leo Hutchinson joined the Pickwick ranks and played excellent cricket for that club for many years. Hoad was a steady legbreak bowler and Hutchinson was a resourceful left-handed allrounder. Hutchinson fought briefly in World War I and then returned to teach for a short while at his alma mater. He headed the school's batting and bowling averages in 1919–20, scoring 316 runs and taking 26 wickets from the nine matches in which he participated.[20] He then proceeded to make Pickwick a powerful club in the Challenge Cup competition, which it won on no fewer than four occasions between 1923 and 1930. Despite a very poor first-class record, 30 runs from 4 innings and 1 wicket for 184 runs in two games, Hutchinson was a prolific rungetter in club cricket and a most formidable medium-fast left-arm bowler in the bargain.[21]

A potentially greater allrounder than any of these three was Thomas A. Moe, who ultimately failed to fulfil his early promise and was never invited to represent his country. After a short stay at Empire, where he bowled and batted with much success during 1917–19,[22] he threw in his lot with Spartan during the 1920s. The fact that he was partially handicapped in the field, because of a shrivelled right hand, perhaps explains why he was so often overlooked by the selectors. Moe was an enterprising batsman and a clever bowler who had performed extremely well for Combermere during 1913–16. Elevated to the captaincy of his school team in 1914, after H.F. Pilgrim's departure, Moe led Combermere to a third-place finish in the second division competition in 1915 and to a second-place result in the following year. He also had the distinction of scoring the first century for Combermere. This came against Wanderers XI during the 1914–15 season when he and Frank Collymore starred in a fine partnership of 127. Moe finished that campaign with an aggregate of 332 runs and an average of over 30, which were excellent records in those days of low scores and inadequately prepared wickets. In the following season he amassed 291 runs and averaged 26.25 while also capturing 20 wickets at 9 runs apiece. Moe's place in the history of Combermere cricket is a prominent one indeed.[23]

Much less secure, ironically, is the place of Edward Lisle Goldsworthy Hoad, who attended Combermere briefly during the first decade of the twentieth century before transferring to Harrison College. As a result, he is often regarded as an Old Harrisonian. E.L.G. (Snr) was the most successful of the five Hoads who represented Barbados and contributed so significantly to Pickwick's prosperity. One of the most difficult batsmen in the Caribbean to dislodge, this lanky, right-handed player represented Barbados in 20 matches between 1921 and 1938, recording 1,425 runs (av: 57.00), 46 wickets (av: 30.97) and 16 catches. He was, that is to say, one of the leading allrounders in the West Indies during the inter-war years. In 63 first-class matches altogether, he scored more than 3,500 runs and ended with an average of almost 39 per innings. He toured England with the West Indian teams of 1928 and 1933, but performed without much success in his four Test matches. Test cricket, in fact, came to the West Indies when Teddy Hoad was beyond his peak. But he had the satisfaction of leading the tourists with a batting average of 36.42 from his 765 first-class runs in 1928 and of exceeding 1,000 runs in first-class cricket in 1933. Against Sussex at Hove in that second summer, he made 149 not out and shared with Herman Griffith a partnership of 138 which remained a West Indian record for the tenth wicket for more than 50 years. One of the finest of all batsmen with Combermere roots, Hoad eventually made a further contribution to Barbadian cricket by producing a son, E.L.G. Jr, an Old Harrisonian, who was one of the wiliest right-arm spin bowlers in the Caribbean during the 1940s. E.L.G. Hoad Snr lived on to the ripe age of 90 and was the oldest surviving West Indian Test cricketer at that time. He had the distinction, too, of being the West Indies' first captain in a Test match in the West Indies (1929–30).[24]

Herman Griffith (1893–1980), Empire's heart and soul for more than 50 years

The Advent of Herman Griffith

By far the most famous of Combermere's early cricket heroes was Herman Clarence Griffith, a fiery right-arm fast bowler, who was a most remarkable athlete in his youth. He excelled not only on the cricket field but in football and athletics. When he left school, he was debarred from Spartan on account of his class. This prompted the more liberal members of Spartan to secede and to form their own separate club. Griffith thus became the foundation stone, as it were, of the Empire CC which gained admission to the Challenge Cup Competition in 1916. It at once became a symbol for lower middle income blacks in Barbados and was the haven for many cricketers who could not gain admission to Spartan (a middle class black and mulatto club) or any of the white clubs in the island. It was mainly Old Combermerians, such as Griffith, Gilkes and Moe, who did most to make Empire so very competitive from the very beginning.[25]

Griffith, quite simply, is the most important name in the history of the Empire club which he led for a very long time. Not only did he serve as its captain on both the cricket and soccer fields, but he became very much its leading administrator in the pavilion. He took it to the top of Barbadian cricket and soccer during the 1930s. Herman himself went on to represent Barbados and the West Indies with much distinction, even though the West Indies did not achieve Test match status until he was almost 40 years old. At the age of 48, in 1941, Griffith became the first black captain of a Barbados cricket team. Even at that advanced age, he was able to take 3 wickets for 38 runs in short spells of tidy medium-fast bowling. Altogether, in a first-class career that lasted 20 years, he represented Barbados on 18 occasions, taking 87 wickets for just under 21 runs apiece. No rabbit with the bat, Herman also garnered more than 1,200 runs in first-class cricket, including scores of 84 and 60. Griffith had a great deal to do with the success of such young Empire fast bowlers as E.A. 'Mannie' Martindale, C.D. 'Pampie' Spooner and E.A.V. 'Foffie' Williams who terrorized Barbadian batsmen during the 1930s and went on to achieve first-class status. They all publicly acknowledged him as their mentor and chief source of inspiration. Herman also produced four excellent cricketing sons, three of whom played first-class cricket. Although the fourth (Kenneth) never did so, he showed considerable promise while at Harrison College in the late 1940s and early 1950s before his emigration from the island. Herman Griffith's contribution to the game, in a word, was enormous.[26]

'Colly' and the 'Bull'

If Griffith was the heart and soul of Empire from 1916 until his death in 1980, the real driving force behind cricket at Combermere from 1907 to about 1940 was Frank Appleton Collymore. 'Colly' entered Combermere at the age of ten in 1903 and remained connected with the school in one capacity or another until 1973. At 16 in 1909, he joined the teaching staff, from which he did not retire until he had reached the age of 70 in 1963. He then served as a member of the school's governing body for the next

10 years.[27] 'Colly' was an aggressive batsman and a fiery medium-fast right-arm bowler, who often opened both the bowling and the batting for his school. He dominated Combermere's cricket averages for an incredibly long time. As early as 1908, before joining the teaching staff, he led his school to victory over the Lodge Second XI by taking 7 wickets for 8 runs in a most remarkable spell. His opponents totalled only 22 on that day.[28] In the 1915–16 season, in which he registered a scintillating century against Pickwick II, he scored 311 runs and took 22 wickets. Ten years later, he captured 38 wickets at 9.81 runs each. In 1928–29 when Combermere finished second in the second division competition and was narrowly edged out of first by Windward, 'Colly' contributed 361 runs (av: 30.08) and 20 wickets (av: 10.55). It is clear that had Collymore elected to play for Pickwick, which was an option open to him, he might well have given himself a chance to participate in first division cricket and to earn selection on the Barbadian team (like his old team-mate, Leo Hutchinson). Instead, he dedicated his entire cricket career to the development of that sport at Combermere.[29]

It was largely on the strength of Collymore's consistent play, year after year, when the school had to cope naturally with the problem of reconstruction as its oldest players left on an annual basis, that Combermere was promoted to the first division in 1929. The school never won the second division title but it was often near the top of the standings and was always regarded as one of the most competitive clubs in the junior ranks. Collymore continued to shine in the senior division. As late as 1939, at the age of 46, he was still bowling well enough to take 5 for 47 in a Harrison College innings that realized 252 runs.[30]

Collymore's most devoted partner throughout this long period was Vincent B. Williams, who returned at once to teach at his alma mater after graduating from Combermere with a Cambridge School Certificate in 1919. From 1916 to 1942, 'Bull' was a source of inspiration to the boys. A small and frail-looking man, he nevertheless played soccer and cricket with an almost reckless abandon. He was a fastish right-arm bowler of fair pace and his batting was described by the editor of the December 1964 issue of the *Combermere School Magazine* as "of an unorthodox and hilarious quality".[31] He was an excellent fieldsman, especially in the slips, where he took many "acrobatic" catches. Williams was invariably second to Collymore in both the bowling and batting averages for the school during the 1920s. In 1922–23, for instance, he scored 283 runs and took 28 wickets.[32] Four years later, he scored 258 and dismissed 25 victims.[33] After playing briefly in the senior ranks, Williams returned to the second division in the late 1930s and dominated the school's bowling and batting averages there in the 1938–39 season when he was almost 40 years old.[34] Both Collymore and Williams made enormously significant contributions to Combermere cricket and left an indelible mark on several generations of schoolboy players.

COMBERMERE CRICKETERS AFTER WORLD WAR I

'Puss' Parris, who also attended Harrison College after leaving Combermere, was a wily right-arm spin bowler who captured countless wickets for Spartan during three decades of almost oriental magic.[36] Over a first-class career that lasted from 1925 to 1947, he claimed 26 wickets for Barbados at a cost of almost 46 runs apiece. His first-class record does not appear spectacular, but 'Puss' Parris was by far the best spin bowler in Barbados for an unconscionably long time and, at his peak, was also one of the best in the West Indies. He was also a fair right-handed bat, finishing up with an aggregate of 390 first-class runs at an average of more than 21 per innings.[37]

Clarence Skinner was a right-handed batsman of some considerable promise who became a fine player for Pickwick and was somewhat unlucky to have been selected only once for Barbados. In his two first-class innings, against Trinidad in January 1936, he scored 26 and 30.[38] Like so many Barbadian first-class cricketers, Skinner went off to work in Trinidad. It was there, in the oil-fields, that he discovered the young Sonny Ramadhin and

The Combermere School XI, 1927–28. *Standing*: D. Smith, N. Stuart, C. Frost, B Emtage, R. Sealy, H. Harris, E. O'Neall (groundsman); *seated*: Mr F.A. Collymore, G.McD. Carew, Mr G.B.Y. Cox (headmaster), J.E.D. Sealy (capt.), Mr V.B. Williams

persuaded the cricket administrators to invite him to the trials in 1949–50. As everyone knows, Ramadhin proceeded to mesmerize dozens of first-class batsmen throughout the 1950s. Skinner's contribution to Trinidad and West Indies cricket is thus much more significant than his own first-class statistics would suggest.[39]

During the 1920s, just before Combermere gained admission to the first division, it produced such fine cricketers as George Carew, Leon Foster, Russell Griffiths, Arnott Harris, Frank C. Lobo, E.A. Martindale, the Rogers brothers (C.C. and H.M.), and C.D. Spooner. All of these players ultimately represented Barbados and two of them, Carew and Martindale, were destined to gain selection to West Indian Test teams. Martindale and Spooner, both right-arm fast bowlers of immense promise, gravitated towards Empire and contributed enormously to the five championships won by that club between 1932 and 1942 in the BCA first division competition.[40] Leon Foster and Cecil and Herbert Rogers played for some years for St Ann's during the 1930s before that club breathed its last.[41] It was early in that same decade that Lobo, a very good allrounder, gave valuable service to Pickwick and then Wanderers.[42] He later migrated to Trinidad and was lost to Barbadian cricket thereafter.

'Mannie' and Carew

George Carew was an aggressive right-handed opening batsman who specialized in back-foot play. His best strokes were therefore the square cut and the hook. He helped to make Spartan one of the strongest teams in the BCA during the 1930s and 1940s. Carew and Parris were major cogs in the Spartan machine which won three first division titles between 1932 and 1939.[43] For Barbados, Carew played 27 matches, scoring 1,288 runs at an average of 33.89 per innings. In a first-class career encompassing 39 matches over a period of 14 years (1935–49), he registered 2,131 runs (av: 34.27), 13 wickets (av: 46.15) and 17 catches. For the West Indies, he was selected in only four Tests. In one of these he struck a memorable century against England at Port-of-Spain in 1948, sharing an opening partnership of 173 with Andy Ganteaume. This remained the record for the West Indies against England until February 1974 (when Roy Fredericks and Lawrence Rowe led off with 206 at Kingston).[44]

'Mannie' Martindale was arguably the fastest bowler produced by Barbados before the advent of Wesley Hall. Standing only 5 ft 8 in., he was not as robust as the modern West Indian fast bowlers, but he yet propelled the ball with amazing velocity. He was a formidable force at every level of the game. He helped Griffith make Empire almost invincible in Barbados, Barbados respectable in the Caribbean, and the West Indies very competitive on the international stage. He went on to play professionally in the north of England from 1937 until 1962. For the island, 'Mannie' played only nine matches, but he took 30 wickets, scored 355 runs and held eight catches. In ten Tests for the West Indies, he captured 37 wickets at a cost of 21.72 runs each. Martindale died in 1972 but his name remains a legend in Barbadian cricket.[45]

'Mannie' Martindale (1909–72), the fastest bowler of his generation. He is seen here being presented to King George VI during the Lord's Test of 1939

Charles Daniel 'Pampie' Spooner played only four times for Barbados, but that was mainly because he emigrated to Trinidad during the 1930s and did not return to his native island until several years later. He played once for Trinidad and also represented St Vincent where he worked briefly. But his start as a first-class cricketer was quite an impressive one, as he and Martindale had most to do with a resounding victory over British Guiana in 1934. This was the first time that Barbados had beaten British Guiana in seven years. Spooner was the fourth member of that famous Empire quartet of fast bowlers during the 1930s, when Herman Griffith pioneered the concept of a four-pronged pace attack that has recently become so significant a feature of West Indian cricket. After returning to Barbados in 1944, 'Pampie' rejoined Empire for which he bowled consistently well, despite his gradual loss of pace. He moved later on to Leeward and in 1973, at the age of 64, was still taking part in competitive cricket in the second division.[46]

The Legacy of Derek Sealy

When Combermere gained promotion to the first division, it immediately created a favourable impression thanks to the exploits of a schoolboy prodigy by the name of James Edward Derek Sealy. He was one of the greatest athletes in the history of Combermere School. He excelled at cricket, soccer and track and field and was a most stylish performer in everything he did. Derek was an elegant batsman with a fine array of scoring strokes, a brilliant fieldsman, a competent wicketkeeper and a right-arm medium-fast bowler of almost unplayable quality on a helpful pitch. He was promising enough to earn a berth on the West Indies Test team before he was 18 years old and his mark of 17 years, 112 days still stands as a West Indian record. In fact, he was the first schoolboy to play Test cricket for the West Indies and the first to score a century against an MCC touring team. For Barbados, Derek played 22 matches, scoring 1,135 runs (av: 27.68) and taking 33 wickets (av: 23.36). He also played first-class cricket for Trinidad after migrating there in the early 1940s. As the leading Trinidadian allrounder, he returned to the Kensington Oval in 1949 to play three superb innings of 87, 112 and 53 in two matches against Barbados. He represented the West Indies in 11 Tests between 1928 and 1939, scoring 478 runs, taking 3 wickets and effecting 7 dismissals.[47]

Like Frank Collymore and Vincent Williams, Sealy joined the Combermere staff immediately after leaving school and helped to shape the careers of such promising cricketers as Charles Alleyne, Harold Brewster, Cuthbert Crick, Alan Ishmael, the Lucas brothers, Frank Thomas and Frankie Worrell. Occasionally, too, he turned out for Spartan. But Derek is best remembered perhaps as the fast bowler who, in January 1942, on a devilish Kensington pitch, took 8 wickets for 8 runs as Barbados skittled out Trinidad for 16 – the long-standing record for the lowest score in Caribbean first-class cricket. It is still fervently held throughout Barbados that Sealy was "the best bad-wicket bowler in the world" and that had he been given a chance to bowl against England in that crazy Test at Bridgetown in January 1935, when 29 wickets fell for a total of 309 runs, the West Indies would never have lost. As it was, the skipper, G.C. Grant, placed his confidence in L.G. Hylton, whose 8 overs cost 48 expensive runs while Martindale was capturing 5 for 22 at the other end.[48] Needing only 73 runs to win, England scraped home by 4 wickets in one desperate scramble. Older Barbadians now bluntly state that no team in the world would have scored 50 runs against 'Mannie' and Derek on that day.

For the sociologists seeking evidence of the primacy of cricket in the Barbadian ethos of the inter-war years, the story of J.E.D. Sealy is most illustrative. His academic qualifications (a Junior LCC certificate) would not, in normal circumstances, have been considered sufficient to merit appointment to the teaching staff of one of the island's major secondary schools. This was clearly pointed out to the headmaster (on several occasions) by the school's governing body. Yet Armstrong, the headmaster, persisted. He felt that Sealy, one of Combermere's most renowned alumni and an idol of all Barbadian teenagers, was bound to be more effective in the junior class rooms than a superior scholar lacking Sealy's athletic gifts. This is one classic example of the system of rewards and punishments which kept cricket in the forefront of Barbadian boyhood dreams in those days. Armstrong was to behave in exactly the same manner when he replaced Sealy with Harold Brewster in the early 1940s. Brewster, a brilliant athlete, would not otherwise have been considered an appropriate candidate for a vacancy on the staff of a prestigious secondary school. At a much later period, too, such Old Combermerians as Rawle Brancker and Wes Hall could be regarded as worthy of promotion to the national senate largely on the strength of their cricketing records.

While playing for Combermere, Sealy took the school to the top of the BCA competition in 1940–41. He was joined by another master, Stanton Gittens, who had already contributed to championships won by Harrison College and Empire.[46] Among the boys who made the greatest impression in the early days of first division cricket for Combermere were Kenneth Hurley, O.M. Robinson, H.A. Stuart and E.A.V. 'Foffie' Williams. 'Bunny' Hurley was a most promising wicketkeeper who was selected to tour Antigua with an unofficial Barbados team, led by E.L.G. Hoad, in 1935. He performed extremely well behind the stumps but, unfortunately, was never invited to represent Barbados in a first-class match. He too played for Empire after leaving school.[50] An exceptionally gifted left-arm spin bowler, Harold Stuart faded rather disappointingly from the game after his departure from Combermere. He played briefly for Spartan before migrating to the United Kingdom.

Sealy's Soldiers

By the time of Armstrong's tenure, Combermere was fast becoming the Barbadian institution most famous for catering to the needs of lower-middle class blacks. The students were intensely competitive and seemed somehow inspired by that black renaissance that would eventually produce a BLP and a BWU. They competed with incredible success on the cricket and soccer fields and miraculously won four of five interschool championships between 1936 and 1940 despite the absence of adequate classroom space and playing fields.[51] The school began to produce an imposing array of black cricketers, led by such stars as Merton Robinson and E.A.V. 'Foffie' Williams.

O.M. Robinson was a sound and patient right-handed opening batsman and a very good wicketkeeper. Like so many Old Combermerians, he went on to become a tower of strength for Empire in both cricket and soccer. He played five matches for Barbados in the 1940s, once hitting a superb 148 against British Guiana. He performed well behind the stumps, catching 2 batsmen and stumping 4 others.[52] His batting average of 31.66 was also reasonable enough. Robinson, however, was most unfortunate to have emerged at a time when he had to compete with Clyde Walcott and Gerald Wood for a wicketkeeping place in the Barbados XI. Other great opening batsmen, such as George Carew, Roy Marshall and Charlie Taylor, were also available for selection. Even so, Robinson is still considered one of the best wicketkeepers and one of the best opening batsmen ever produced by Combermere.

'Foffie' Williams was an aggressive allrounder who bowled fast, fielded well and batted violently. He had not played cricket for several years, but remained a most popular Barbadian idol until his death in 1997. A flamboyant character, he was a favourite with the crowds, especially at Bank Hall where Empire played its home games. During the 1930s, he combined with Griffith, Martindale and Spooner to form the most awesome quartet of fast bowlers in the history of the BCA. For Barbados, 'Foffie' played 27 matches between 1934 and 1949, scoring 989 runs (including one century) and taking 89 wickets. It was he who helped Derek Sealy dismiss Trinidad for 16 in 1942. He also played in four Tests for the West Indies. In the most memorable of these, against England at Bridgetown in 1948, he registered a swashbuckling 72 in 63 minutes. His first four balls, received from Jim Laker, were dispatched for 6, 6, 4 and 4. He thus probably became the first batsman ever to score 20 runs from the first four deliveries of a Test match innings. 'Foffie' had an incredibly large following among the youth, hundreds of whom tried to imitate his cricketing style and method. The one who came closest perhaps was Keith David Boyce, of Barbados, Essex and the West Indies, with his infectious intensity and enthusiasm.[53]

By the mid 1930s, Combermere could well feel satisfied with the role it was playing in the development of Barbadian cricket. The editor of the *Combermerian* for 1934–35 was delighted to report that of the 14 cricketers chosen to represent the island against the MCC that year, no fewer than 11 were Old Combermerians: George Carew, C.S. Foster, Herman Griffith, Arnott Harris, E.L.G. Hoad, 'Mannie' Martindale, 'Puss' Parris, Derek Sealy, 'Pampie' Spooner, Leslie Walcott and 'Foffie' Williams. It is true that three of them (Hoad, Parris and Walcott) had played more cricket for Harrison College than for Combermere, but they had all learnt their cricket on Constitution Hill. Moreover, the three Barbadians chosen to represent the West Indies (Carew, Martindale and Sealy) were all Old Combermerians.[54]

A CHAMPIONSHIP AT LAST

After finishing third in the BCA competition in 1938, Combermere rose all the way to the top of the proverbial 'greasy pole' during the 1940–41 season. The school lost its first match narrowly to Harrison College, after leading on first innings, but escaped unscathed for the rest of the season. It defeated Pickwick by an innings and 47 runs at Kensington Oval, where Alan Ishmael and Derek Sealy registered centuries. At the Bay, Combermere won by 9 wickets after dismissing Wanderers for 75 and 179, with Crick taking 8 for 65 and Stanton Gittens scoring 43 and 103 not out. Spartan managed to avert defeat, but Empire did not. This was a truly remarkable run of consistent cricket and Combermere deserved the title even though it was probably not as powerful as the Harrison College XI

The Combermere School XI, BCA first division champions, 1940–41. *Standing:* C.G. Alleyne, A.F. Ishmael, F.G. Thomas, J.H., Lucas, C.O'B. Crick; *seated:* Mr J.E.D. Sealy, Mr S.O'C. Gittens, H.G. Brewster (capt.), Mr L.L. Gittens; *front:* F.M. Worrell, G.H. Sealy

which then included such talented individuals as H. St C. Cumberbatch, Harold Griffith, Val McComie, Clyde Walcott and Keith Walcott. Almost incredibly for a school team in those days, the XI remained unchanged throughout the season.[55]

When Combermere enjoyed its greatest BCA triumph at the beginning of the 1940s, its team included some outstanding cricketers who left an indelible mark on the game. The captain was Harold Gittens Brewster, a renowned athlete, who later joined the teaching staff, studied physical education at Loughborough and returned to coach another generation of cricketers.[56] He belonged to a family of gifted athletes, three of whom were famous track stars at Combermere. His younger siblings, Hal and Lisle, were among the fastest schoolboy sprinters of their generation. Brewster was a stylish right-handed batsman and a penetrative right-arm medium pacer, who made very clever use of the seam. He took 24 wickets (av: 10.08) in 1940–41 to finish second to Crick in the averages.[57] In the previous season, he had made a mark for himself as a batsman by scoring an attractive century against Police.[58] He is, of course, better remembered in Barbados for his sprinting and long jump records at the interschool sports and as the brother-in-law of the late Sir Frank Worrell.

Charles Alleyne was a fine allrounder, who was invited several times to the trials but was most unlucky never to have gained selection for Barbados. He is still considered perhaps the finest Barbadian cricketer never to have acquired first-class status. He was an aggressive right-handed batsman, a useful spin bowler and an excellent fieldsman. He ended up making a great contribution to Empire as a player and to the BCA as an administrator.[59] His leadership skills were recognized in a curious kind of way when the BCA invited him to captain the 'Rest' vs 'Barbados' in the final trial match at the Bay before the tour of British Guiana in 1951. Many pundits felt that the 'Rest' were superior to 'Barbados' and that most of them, including Alleyne himself, ought to have been selected. In fact, this infamous trial match ended prematurely and in much confusion when Frank King, by far the most dangerous fast bowler throughout the Caribbean, was threatening to decapitate all of the island's batsmen while angrily representing the 'Rest'.

Harry Sealy was an elegant batsman with enormous potential. He was also a steady right-arm slow bowler and a brilliant fieldsman. He abandoned the game early because of recurrent migraine headaches, but was a great inspiration to countless youngsters while he served as a member of the Combermere teaching staff from 1943 to 1981. During the 1950s, he occasionally took part in some of the school's second division matches which he found more relaxing. He was another of Armstrong's assistants whose appointment owed almost as much to his athletic accomplishments as to his academic qualifications. It must be quickly added, however, that Sealy proved himself an excellent teacher and an able administrator after having been asked by Major Noott to assume the duties of master in charge of the Junior School.[60]

The wicketkeeper in the championship team was Alan F. Ishmael who carried the gloves for Combermere with much success for about three seasons. He was also a promising opening batsman, who struck a fine century against Empire in 1939.[61] In the championship year he hit another hundred, this time against Pickwick, while amassing 212 runs and averaging 23.55 per innings.[62] He was one of the finest wicketkeepers produced by Combermere and one of the best never to have gained selection for Barbados.

But the truly great stars of that victorious Combermere team, apart from the masters (Derek Sealy and Stanton Gittens), were C. O'B. Crick, John H. Lucas, Frank G. Thomas and Frank Maglinne Worrell, all of whom were destined to achieve first-class status. Cuthbert Crick was a very good right-arm fast bowler with exceptional stamina. He headed the BCA bowling averages in 1940–41, with 34 wickets at a cost 9.29 runs each, and earned a berth on the Barbados team which toured Trinidad under Herman Griffith in 1941.[63] He was the most impressive bowler on that tour, taking 10 wickets for 227 runs in a losing cause.[64] One of the most promising fast bowlers produced by Combermere, Crick very soon emigrated and was lost to Barbadian cricket for ever. He eventually died in St Lucia in 1991.[65]

'Fluffy' Thomas was a right-handed batsman and a right-arm fast bowler, who later played football and cricket for Empire. He played only once for Barbados, against Trinidad in 1945, and might have done so more often had he not migrated to St Vincent. There he did a great deal for several years to promote both cricket and soccer. He was appointed vice captain of the first ever Windward Islands' Cricket XI which toured British Guiana in 1948.[66] Frank Thomas was eventually honoured in 1994 when a stand at the Arnos Vale Ground in St Vincent was named after him.

The young allrounder, 'Johnnie' Lucas, seemed to have almost unlimited potential. He was a graceful stroke player, a good field especially close to the wicket, and a steady right-arm offbreak bowler. He played only 12 matches for Barbados between 1945 and 1950, but exceeded 1,000 runs and averaged almost 65 per innings. Of all the great batsmen performing for Barbados since 1865, only Sobers (75.96) and Worrell (73.66) have ended with a better average than Lucas, who was clearly one of the finest batsmen in the West Indies during the 1940s. 'Johnnie' is still fondly remembered as one of the most successful and stylish of all Barbadian strokeplayers and as one of the pillars of YMPC. When YMPC was demoted from the first division, Lucas proceeded to play brilliant cricket for Pickwick. For Barbados against Trinidad in 1949, he exhibited some of the most elegant strokes ever seen at the Kensington Oval when he scored 216 not out, 92 and 158 in consecutive innings. But he was so disappointed at having been excluded from West Indian tours to India in 1948–49 and to England in 1950 that he migrated to British Columbia. He made a tour to England with a Canadian team in 1954 but by then had lost his form.[67]

Sir Frank Worrell (1924–67), the greatest Combermerian of them all

Frank Worrell and his Colleagues

Sir Frank Worrell is, of course, the greatest name in the history of Combermere cricket. He was so promising as a youngster that he was promoted to the first XI when he was only 13 years old. At football, he was equally gifted and would most certainly have made a name for himself in that sport had he been born elsewhere. As a cricketer, young 'Tae' (as he was for a long time called) was then an excellent left-arm spin bowler and he gradually became one of the best spinners in the island. It was 'Graffie' Pilgrim who first spotted Worrell's talent as a batsman and lived to see his protégé develop into one of the greatest batsmen in the world. Worrell advanced steadily up the batting order, finally opening for the West Indies in England in 1957 when he carried his bat right through an innings on one memorable occasion at Trent Bridge. Against Brian Statham, Fred Trueman, Trevor Bailey and Jim Laker, Worrell scored 191 not out in a West Indies total of 372, after having fielded throughout a monumental England innings of 619 for 6 declared. As he opened again in the second innings, when he batted another hour for 16 runs, he established an interesting record for enduring 20½ hours of continuous play.[68]

Worrell's progress as a batsman in the early 1940s was most dramatic. He was not yet 20 years old when he struck a glorious 308 not out against Trinidad at Bridgetown and, with John Goddard, established a world record of 502 for the fourth wicket in 1944. His triple century is still regarded as one of the most delightful innings ever played at Bridgetown. With Clyde Walcott he shattered the world record two years later, establishing a new standard of 574. His share was 255 not out. His 308 had been a new West Indian record. Walcott broke that by scoring 314 not out. Worrell proceeded to play brilliantly at the international level, amassing 3,860 runs (av: 49.48), capturing 69 wickets (av: 38.73) and holding 43 catches in 51 Tests for the West Indies. For Barbados his statistics were even more impressive. In 15 matches during 1941–47, before he migrated to Jamaica, he scored 1,547 runs at an average of almost 74 per innings, held 15 catches and claimed 43 wickets at just under 27 runs each.[69]

Worrell died at 42 in 1967 but his name is still revered all across the Caribbean. He is remembered as the first black cricketer to lead a West Indies team on tour and the first person (of any colour) to campaign vigorously for an end to the parochialisms that had previously undermined West Indies cricket. He argued that the best team should always be selected, irrespective of quotas and nationality and insisted that the smaller islands, like Antigua and Dominica, be given more serious consideration in the selection of Caribbean teams. Whereas previous West Indies teams had been collections of individual stars, Worrell's teams in the 1960s were well led and closely knit. He took the West Indies to the top of the cricketing world and was knighted for his services to the game. Sir Frank Worrell is still regarded as one of the greatest of all Combermerians. Such was the universal respect in which he was held that he was awarded an honorary doctorate of law by Punjab University in India, where the government later proclaimed a Frank Worrell Day. On another continent, he was elected to 'Black America's Hall of Fame' in the USA. The Australians sought to cherish his memory by giving his name to a trophy for which Australia and the West Indies have been contending ever since 1961. There are Frank Worrell mementos in the cricket museum at Lord's and a Frank Worrell Memorial Gardens in Barbados. The Sir Frank Worrell Pavilion was built on the Combermere grounds at Waterford as part of that school's celebration of its 300th anniversary in 1995; and in Trinidad, the playing fields of the St Augustine campus of the UWI have been renamed the Frank Worrell Grounds. At Bank Hall, the Frank Worrell Gate was erected in his memory; and in Radcliffe, the street on which he lived while playing professional cricket in the Central Lancashire League was renamed 'Worrell Close'.[70]

In Worrell's last days at Combermere, he was joined by such budding cricket stars as Hughley Barker, E. Winston Grant, Noel S. 'Brickie' Lucas, K.B. 'Tootie' Warren and the four Atkinsons. Grant is best remembered as an outstanding soccer player who was probably the best defender in the Caribbean during the early 1950s. In that sport, he captained the Barbados and Empire teams for many years, leading Empire to the first division championship no fewer than five times between 1953 and 1959.[71] Like Grant, a useful right-handed batsman who ultimately delivered less than he had earlier promised, Barker joined Empire after leaving school. Hughley was a rather large and ungainly boy who did not appear at all athletic, but he could bowl fast. He had more speed than accuracy and often produced menacing beamers which mesmerized both the batsman and the wicketkeeper. He played four matches for Barbados in the early 1950s, taking 12 wickets for 368 runs.[72] These are not very impressive results but, at his peak, Barker was one of the most feared fast bowlers in the island.

N.S. Lucas, John's younger brother, was an aggressive right-handed batsman, a brilliant fieldsman and an excellent soccer player. He joined YMPC following his departure from Combermere but later became one of the greatest sportsmen in the history of Carlton. 'Brickie' did not altogether do justice to his enormous talent. He gained selection only to three Barbadian teams and produced only moderate results. His highest score was 91, against British Guiana at Bridgetown in 1955, while his batting average was 27.60.[73] In their youth it certainly appeared that the Lucas brothers would have gone much further in the game. They were two of the classiest batsmen in Barbados during the 1940s. Yet, by 1955, they had both retired from the first-class ranks without having left the significant mark that their supporters had so confidently expected. 'Brickie' is best remembered now as one of the most accomplished soccer players in Barbados during the 1940s and 1950s.

One of 'Brickie's' most important teammates at Carlton was Kenny Warren, a useful allrounder, who played consistently good cricket in the BCA first division competition. 'Tootie' was a very steady right-arm medium-pace bowler, a safe field and a competent bat. Despite the many years of yeoman service which he rendered Carlton, however, he was selected only once to represent Barbados.[74] Warren simply emerged at the wrong time. The Barbadian selectors had too many excellent allrounders from whom to choose during the 1940s and 1950s.

The Four Atkinsons

Denis Atkinson earned a memorable draw by the sweat of his brow.

The Atkinson brotherhood made Combermere a very powerful force in interschool athletics during the late 1930s and early 1940s. All four of them played cricket and soccer as well. They continued an Atkinson tradition by attending Combermere even though their parents might well have afforded to send them to Harrison College. Their great-grandfather, W. St Eval Atkinson, had been a student at the Boys' Central School (which was renamed Combermere in 1879) in the middle of the nineteenth century.[75] This long-lasting attachment of a white family to Combermere was most unusual; it was all the more so when one considers that most white children had ceased to enrol at this school which, under Armstrong, was steadily becoming predominantly black. William Atkinson, the eldest among his siblings, established a long-standing schoolboy high-jump record and ended up serving the BCA for over 20 years as its treasurer.[76] Richard, better known throughout the Bay Land as 'Timoshenko', did not reach the same heights as his brothers but, like them, became a staunch supporter of Wanderers. Eric was a superb all-rounder. He bowled his right-arm out-swingers at a lively medium pace and, throughout the 1950s, was one of the most skilful users of the new ball in Barbados. He was a fine fielder and an aggressive batsman. It was largely due to his skills that Wanderers won seven BCA first division cups between 1948 and 1961. He played 12 matches for Barbados and 8 Tests for the West Indies during 1949–59. Eric was a participant in the famous Test at Sabina Park in 1958 when Gary Sobers hit his historic 365 not out. In the excitement surrounding Gary's world record, it is not often remembered that Eric was one of the stars of the West Indian victory. His fine match analysis, on a batsman's paradise, was 8 wickets for 78 runs. Eric Atkinson's first-class record is more satisfactory than many cricket fans realize. In 29 matches, he scored 696 runs (av: 21.75), captured 61 wickets (av: 26.72) and held 14 catches. For the West Indies, he took 25 wickets (av: 23.26) and scored 126 runs (av: 15.75) during his Test career.[77]

The best cricketer among the numerous Atkinsons was Denis St Eval, for a long time one of the top allrounders in the Caribbean. In 19 matches for Barbados he scored more than 1,100 runs and captured 45 wickets. He was an aggressive batsman, a steady right-arm medium pace bowler with a penetrative offcutter and a brilliant fieldsman in any position. He rose to the captaincy of the West Indies Test team in 1955 when, in a remarkable innings against Australia at Bridgetown, he scored 219 runs to save his side from total disaster. He and Clairmonte Depeiza came together at 147 for 6 in reply to a mammoth first innings total of 668. They batted through an entire day in a world record seventh wicket partnership of 347 runs that still stands after more than 40 years. Denis also took 7 wickets for 164 runs in that very high-scoring game. In his 22 Tests, he collected 922 runs (av: 31.79) and claimed 47 wickets (av: 35.04). These were very respectable statistics indeed. It often comes as a great surprise to ordinary cricket historians to discover that Atkinson's Test record was so much better than Learie Constantine's, despite the latter's awesome reputation. Sadly, however, this superb athlete, is often remembered simply as one of the last of the "white captains" who should never have been invited to lead an international squad that included the vastly superior and more experienced "W Formation".[78]

SOME PROMISING STARS OF THE FORTIES

Combermere produced two very promising spin bowlers during the 1940s. One was Adzil Holder, a left-hander, who spun offbreaks at a pace that was almost medium. He eventually made a huge contribution to Empire cricket and played 11 times for Barbados between 1951 and 1959. Steady rather than penetrative, Holder took 26 first-class wickets at a cost of 34.92 runs each and once captured 7 for 38 in a single innings. He was also good enough as a batsman to register a half-century and to average more than 20 runs per innings in first-class cricket.[79] It is interesting now to reflect that he could hold his own for such a long time on the Barbados team, despite obviously fierce competition from such very good spin bowlers as Keith Bowen, Horace King, Eddie Perkins, Gary Sobers, Gray Wilkie and 'Boogles' Williams. In fact, he was invited to the West Indian trial matches at Port-of-Spain early in 1957 and must have come agonizingly close to selection for the tour of England that year as he was certainly one of the most successful of all the bowlers on display.

Kenneth A. 'Honey' Branker enjoyed much early success as a cunning right-arm spinner before he improved into a very capable right-handed batsman. He seemed destined to become a formidable allrounder but played only twice for Barbados without success with either bat or ball. He migrated to Canada shortly after leaving Combermere and occasionally represented Canada against MCC and USA teams. At Toronto in 1963, he led Canada to a resounding victory over the USA by capturing 11 wickets for 87 runs from 55.4 overs after having scored 41 not out in his team's only innings.[80]

Four other Combermerian cricketers stood out like beacons during the late 1940s when the school team itself was achieving very poor results: V.S. Babb, Neville Grant, Rudolph 'Huffie' Knight and Orman H. Wilkinson. Vendall Babb was a fine strokeplayer and a good fieldsman, who captained the school's First XI in his final year at Combermere.[81] His career, however, did not evolve in the expected manner. Neither did Wilkinson's. 'Wilkie' was an attractive right-handed batsman with very good technique and excellent temperament. He was also a brilliant fieldsman. He played some good cricket for Empire following his departure from Combermere but could not gain selection for Barbados. A big and powerful lad, 'Huffie' was an aggressive fast bowler capable of generating exceptional pace. But he was lost to Barbadian cricket after emigrating to the USA.

The most promising and stylish of this group was G.N.B. Grant, the best schoolboy batsman in Barbados between 1949 and 1952. Neville was a diminutive player but his timing was so good that he could despatch balls to the boundary with astonishing speed and power. He commanded a wide variety of elegant strokes and was one of the most popular batsmen in the island during the early 1950s. He was capable of playing on all types of pitches and gave several exhibitions of excellent batting technique on sticky wickets during his stay at Combermere. He was only 14 years old, for instance, when he defied John Goddard, Hampton King, Theodore Birkett, John Lucas and Harold Jordan for more than two hours on a devilish strip while scoring 29 not out in an innings of 72. He joined Spartan after leaving school and scored heavily in first division cricket for a few years. He was one of the very best batsmen never to have won a Barbados cap although he was occasionally invited to the trials and was once given the task of twelfth man. He eventually migrated to Canada and became one of the leading stars of Canadian cricket, representing that country in its annual match against the USA in 1963. On this occasion he found himself playing in the same team as 'Honey' Branker with whom he had so often played at Combermere. His contribution to the Canadian victory was an attractive 30 in a second wicket partnership of 80 runs with R. Nascimento who established a record for the Canada–USA series by scoring 176.[82] In addition to his batsmanship, Grant was an excellent fieldsman and a useful right-arm offbreak bowler who occasionally achieved good results on helpful wickets.

Hughes at the Helm

During the 1950s, when Ronnie Hughes served as cricket master, Combermere was most competitive in the BCA first division largely because its headmaster, Major Cecil Noott, had taken the unusual step of hiring a first-class right-arm fast bowler, Frank King, to serve as head groundsman and cricket coach. King was then the fastest bowler in the Caribbean and remained the outstanding fast bowler in BCA competition until he left his native island for good in the late 1950s. For Barbados, King played 12 matches between 1947 and 1957, capturing 49 wickets at an average cost of 21.42 runs each. He went on to play 14 Tests for the West Indies, capturing 29 wickets at just under 40 runs apiece. But he emerged at a time when there was no other genuine fast bowler to join him in the attack and when the standard of West Indian out-cricket was low. Several of King's catches behind the wicket and in the slips were dropped and his Test record consequently does not reflect the quality of his fiery bowling. He ended his career as a professional in Scotland where he died in 1990 at the age of 64.[83]

Hughes and King proved to be an effective combination and the school soon produced a number of capable players, including Rawle Brancker, Victor Callender, Ossie Gill, Wesley Hall, Errie Inniss, Peter Lashley, Anton Norris, Rodney Norville, Francis Scott, Donald Weekes and Lionel Williams. Norris and Williams were two right-arm fast bowlers who between them played three first-class matches for Barbados and ended up contributing substantially to Empire's cause.[84] One of the best

Rawle Brancker who toured England with the West Indies in 1966

wicketkeepers produced by Combermere, Gill's opportunities were later limited by his early emigration from Barbados. Weekes, who might have gained first-class status as an attacking right-handed batsman, also emigrated early. He played regularly for the USA in the early 1970s, twice serving as captain in the annual fixture against Canada.[85] Inniss and Scott were two of the most handsome strokeplayers in Barbados in their youth but failed to fulfil their early promise. Errie, who captained the school eleven during the 1954–55 season, was a sound right-handed opening batsman and a reliable fielder. 'Nittie' Scott was not only an attractive middle-order batsman but a clever spinner of right-arm offbreaks. Callender, a fine left-handed allrounder, and Norville, an accomplished wicketkeeper, gravitated towards Empire. Norville, who shortly left for the United Kingdom, was also a brilliant footballer.

Two other interesting cricketers who played for the Combermere First XI while Hughes was at the helm were Wilfred Denison Wood and Erskine A. Simmons. Neither of them left any particular mark on the cricket field but shone prominently in entirely different arenas. 'Froggie' Wood, the captain for the 1953–54 season, became famous as an Anglican priest and earned the enviable distinction of being the first black Barbadian to be promoted to a bishopric.[86] Erskine Simmons, who later became a medical doctor and an important member of the national senate as well as co-chair of the European Economic Community, was, like Wood, a patient opening batsman totally devoid of scoring strokes. He was mainly interested in surviving long enough to exhaust the opening bowlers and accumulated what few runs he did record in little nudges here and deflections there. It was perhaps just as well that Dr Simmons and Bishop Wood did not pursue cricketing careers after all.

THREE STALWARTS OF THE 1950s

The three Combermere stalwarts of the 1950s who left a noticeable imprint on the game were Brancker, Hall and Lashley who actually toured England together with the West Indies team of 1966. Rawle Brancker was a graceful left-handed batsman who drove exquisitely off the front foot. He was a safe fieldsman in almost any position, and he was also a competent purveyor of left-arm spin with a very high action. He played 31 matches for Barbados during 1955–70, scoring 1,337 runs (av: 31.09 with five centuries) and taking 73 wickets (av: 27.87). His first-class career encompassed 47 matches in which he scored 1,666 runs, including five centuries, and captured 106 wickets. It produced the most unusual statistical quirk in that

Wes Hall, the fastest bowler in the world during the 1960s

he averaged exactly 27.31 both with the bat and the ball. Brancker joined Empire in 1956 and helped to make that club a powerhouse in the BCA. He led it to first division championships in 1962, 1963 and 1965. After retiring from the game, he also served briefly on the BCA board of management.[87]

Wes Hall was a promising wicketkeeper/batsman at Combermere. He took up fast bowling only when he joined the staff at Cable & Wireless (now BET) in 1955. He improved so rapidly that within a year he was selected to represent Barbados as an opening bowler and by 1957 was a member of the West Indies team to England. By 1960, 'Big Wes' had become generally acknowledged as the world's fastest and most feared bowler. He only represented Barbados on 13 occasions, but his best work was done at the highest level. He played 48 Tests for the West Indies, capturing 192 wickets at 26.38 runs apiece. With Charles Griffith in the 1960s, he combined to form one of the greatest opening attacks in the history of West Indies cricket. Altogether, in 170 first-class matches, 'Big Wes' scored 2,674 runs (av: 15.11), took 546 wickets (av: 26.14) and held 58 catches.[88]

Hall was a fine ambassador for Barbados. He was a crowd favourite wherever he played. He achieved success in Lancashire (where he captured more than 100 wickets in each of three consecutive seasons for Accrington) as well as in Australia, where for two years he played for Queensland in the Sheffield Shield competition. In 1961–62, he established a state record by capturing 43 wickets and taking an otherwise undistinguished Queensland squad to second place in the Australian championship. After his retirement from first-class cricket, Hall coached in Trinidad and Tobago. He also managed a few West Indian touring teams. He ended up as a successful politician and was for many years a member of the Democratic Labour Party (DLP) cabinet in Barbados. He returned to cricket in 1995 to manage the West Indian team in England and was also at the helm during the controversial expedition to the World Cup in

1996. Later in this same year, he was elected to serve the reconstructed West Indies Cricket Board (WICB) as a selector.[89]

Although Lashley did not have Hall's success at the Test match level, he left an even greater impression on cricket in Barbados. Starting his career as a right-arm spinner, he gradually developed into a very sound and prolific left-handed batsman. He was most unlucky to have gained only four West Indian Test caps, considering his fabulous achievements in the Caribbean Shell Shield competition. For the island, he established a number of significant records that have only recently been broken. His marks included most games played for Barbados (58) and most runs scored (3,994). He also succeeded in equalling the record of eight centuries for Barbados that Challenor and Weekes had established. His average of 48.70 per innings in these matches is also very good. In 85 first-class matches altogether, he registered 4,932 runs (av: 41.44), 27 wickets (av: 35.48) and 66 catches. His finest innings perhaps was the solid 204 he struck at Guyana's expense in March 1967. He had the good fortune, like Hall, to participate in that memorable tied Test at Brisbane in December 1960. Lashley also played consistently well for Spartan for many years and eventually became one of the most important of the BCA administrators. It was he who instigated, masterminded and administered the Instant Money Game (IMG), a popular national lottery, which has allowed the BCA to become easily the most successful sporting institution in the Caribbean. He has been a BCA vice president since 1988 and a member of its board of management since 1973.[90]

'Peter' Lashley has masterminded the Instant Money Game in Barbados since 1978

SLIM PICKINGS AFTER 1955

After the 1950s, Combermere (like Harrison College and the Lodge) became significantly less conspicuous as a Barbadian cricket nursery. By the

1970s, indeed, the three élite schools had become so outmatched by the senior clubs, that the BCA decided to demote them from the first division. A Combined Schools' XI gradually emerged to take their place but without ever really threatening to win any trophies. Some competitions were established for the secondary schools themselves. The earliest of these was the Ronald Tree Cup, first introduced in 1959 and vied for by Combermere, Harrison and the Lodge. That competition tended in the early days to be dominated by the other two élite schools and Combermere was therefore delighted to win it for the first time in 1963, when Ishmael Roett and Earle Williams performed with some distinction.[91] When the CIBC Schools Under 19 competition was inaugurated in 1984, Combermere proceeded to win the trophy on the first two occasions and to reach the finals in the third. But generally speaking, Combermere, as a team, has not distinguished itself in any of the BCA competitions for a long time.[92]

Whereas by 1955, Combermere School could look back with great satisfaction on its cricketing past and point with justifiable pride to about 35 to 40 of its alumni who had been selected to represent Barbados, it has not been able to sustain such a rich tradition over the past 40 years. This is an even more puzzling phenomenon when one considers that Combermere finally received adequate playing fields when it moved from Constitution Hill to Weymouth in 1944 and when it relocated to Waterford in 1958.[93] The irony is that Combermere produced better cricketers when it catered to a smaller pool of children and lacked adequate amenities. Since the mid 1950s, in fact, Combermere has produced only about a dozen cricketers of unusual quality. These include Winslow Ashby, John Burke, Pedro Corbin, Anderson Cummins, Ricky Ellcock, John Holder, Roland Holder, Henderson Simmons, Gladstone Small, Henderson Springer and Lawrence Worrell.

Ashby was an outstanding schoolboy opening batsman who led Combermere to one of its best first division results in the 1970–71 season when he himself headed the BCA batting averages with 53.66. His aggregate was 483 and included an innings of 150 not out. He gained selection to the West Indies Youth team which toured England under Wes Hall's management in 1970. His manifest leadership qualities prompted the BCA to appoint him captain of the Barbados Youth team which took part in the Benson & Hedges competition in 1971.[94] He made a substantial contribution to Empire's cause during the 1970s but his first-class record still makes disappointing reading. In his 11 matches for Barbados during 1971–75, he managed only 268 runs and wound up with an average of 14.88 per innings.[95] These are very meagre returns indeed for a batsman of his reputation and potential.

Although not particularly robust, Burke was a tireless, right-arm medium-fast bowler who gave yeoman service to Carlton during the 1970s. He was also a capable batsman and a good fielder. But he never climbed to first-class status although playing consistently well in BCA competition. Similarly, Corbin was a very good right-handed opening batsman who could never challenge Desmond Haynes or Gordon Greenidge for a regular place in the Barbados team during the 1980s. He played for Carlton with considerable success as Haynes' opening partner for some years and was occasionally invited to the trials. Eventually he gave up and migrated to Antigua where he is currently serving on the cricket board of control.

John Holder and Larry Worrell never represented Barbados but they played briefly for Hampshire in the 1970s. A cousin of the great Sir Frank, L.R. Worrell was a right-arm off-break bowler and an attacking lower order right-handed batsman. In 32 matches for Hampshire, he scored 289 runs and took 65 wickets before throwing in his lot with Dorset in the Minor Counties.[96] Holder was a right-arm fast-medium bowler, who took 139 first-class wickets (av: 24.56) in his five seasons for Hampshire. He later made a name for himself as a proficient Test umpire. He joined the umpires' list in 1983 and eventually became the first black umpire to be appointed on the English Test match panel and was among the first of the neutral umpires to be named by the ICC. His first 10 Tests as umpire included 4 in Pakistan in 1989–90.[97]

The promising right-arm fast bowler, Ricky Ellcock, who earned only three caps for Barbados, in which he took 6 wickets for 185 runs, played the bulk of his first-class cricket for Middlesex and Worcestershire, capturing 109 wickets all told at 29 runs apiece.[98] He was also selected to an England touring team in the 1980s but was prevented by injury from undertaking the tour. Much more fortunate was Gladstone Small, a clever medium-fast right-arm bowler, a hard-hitting lower-order batsman and a brilliant fieldsman, who became the first Old Combermerian to play Test cricket for England. Up to September 1995, he had represented Warwickshire in 17 seasons of county cricket, scoring more than 4,000 runs and capturing over 800 wickets in his first-class career. In 17 Tests he scored 263 runs (av: 15.47) and claimed 55 wickets (av: 34.01). He has been most effective as a player in One-Day Internationals (ODIs) because of the steadiness of his bowling and the quality of his fielding. He has represented England in 53 such matches already.[99]

The cricket career of Henderson Simmons was rather unusual. After a promising start as a right-arm medium pace bowler in the late 1950s, he enjoyed an outstanding career as a professional in the Scottish League. He returned to Barbados to represent Empire in the 1970–71 season. His 59 wickets at a cost of 8.82 runs each not only brought Empire the BCA championship but earned Simmons a berth on the Barbados Shell Shield team for the last match of the season. He proceeded to bowl Barbados to a convincing victory over Jamaica, taking 5 wickets for 87 runs. But he was never invited to represent Barbados again. In fact, his performance for Empire in the 1971–72 season was quite disappointing and his career soon fizzled out rather inexplicably.[100]

More durable was Henderson Springer, a right-arm off-break bowler, who played 18 times for Barbados between 1988 and 1992, taking 36 wickets at 31.56 runs apiece. He was a good fielder and a useful batsman who looked like becoming an effective allrounder. During the 1980s he performed extremely well for Spartan, but he did not make his first-class début until he was 24 and his first-class career had ended by the time he was 30. He at least had the satisfaction, however, of contributing to Barbados' first Red Stripe Cup triumph in 1991 and to Spartan's BCA championship in 1990.[101]

Anderson Cummins and Roland Holder

Among the most recent Combermerians, by far the most promising and easily the best are Anderson Cummins and Roland Holder who have not only represented Barbados but have been selected to West Indian touring teams. Holder is an exciting right-handed batsman with fine technique and equable temperament. He is also a dependable fieldsman. A precocious player, he made his first-class début in 1986 when he was only 18 years old. He has represented Barbados in more than 40 matches thus far and maintained a first-class batting average of approximately 40 runs per innings. He has only very recently (1997) been invited to play Test cricket but many pundits claim that he ought long ago to have been. He justified his selection (as his supporters knew he would) by scoring a priceless 91 at Port-of-Spain in his second Test against India. Before the start of the New Zealand tour to the West Indies in 1996, he had already scored almost 3,000 first-class runs, including 10 centuries. Holder has established himself as a reliable performer in ODIs. In one such game in 1993 he struck a very good 50 against Zimbabwe at Hyderabad; but he was consistently overlooked by the West Indies Test selectors, even though he was a bulwark of Empire and Barbados for more than a decade and had often served as captain of both his club and his country.[102]

Cummins is a very good right-arm fast bowler whom some Barbadians thought worthy of selection in the historic Test against South Africa in 1992. When he was omitted from the West Indies team on that occasion, they organized a massive and highly successful boycott. This may well be his greatest claim to cricket fame. Cummins is not a devastatingly fast bowler, but he is clever, accurate and effective with both the old ball and the new. He is also a safe fielder and a competent batsman, who regularly opens the innings for YMPC in BCA competition. The selectors have therefore given him the chance to play in more than 60 ODIs, although they have so far invited him to play in only 5 Tests. He has performed consistently well (though not brilliantly) at the international level and therefore continues to hover on the brink of Test selection. But he is already (1997) 31 years old and is not likely, as a fast bowler, to have many years left. His finest efforts for the West Indies thus far have been 4 wickets for 54 runs in the one innings which the weather permitted against Pakistan in the Test match at St John's in 1993 and, as a batsman, a fine 107 against Otago at Dunedin in January 1995. Playing English county cricket with Durham for two years allowed him to lift his first-class record to 1,593 runs (av: 20.68) and 188 wickets (av: 30.87) by the end of the 1995 season.[103]

COMBERMERE'S CONTRIBUTION

For a school that has traditionally catered mainly to lower-middle income blacks, Combermere's performance both in the classroom and on the playing field is very impressive. Its contribution to the development of cricket in Barbados is almost staggering when one considers the quality of its players who have gone on to represent the West Indies and the quantity of its alumni who have helped to administer the sport. Charles Alleyne, Jack Kidney and Peter Lashley between them served more than 20 years as BCA vice presidents. Apart from them, such Old Combermerians as William Atkinson, Rawle Brancker, Chrissie Brathwaite, George Carew, Herman Griffith, Wesley Hall, 'Foffie' Williams and Vernon Williams have given invaluable service on the BCA's board of management. In addition, Denis Atkinson, Wes Hall, Stanton Parris and 'Foffie' Williams have been awarded honorary life memberships by the BCA.[104]

The school has also contributed to the growth of the sport in other ways. It produced, for instance, two of the finest umpires yet spawned by the Caribbean: David Archer and John Holder. While the latter made his mark in England, Archer was the leading umpire in the West Indies throughout the 1980s and up to the time of his sudden death on 24 October 1992 at the age of 61. He officiated in 76 first-class matches and 23 ODIs. Altogether, between 1981 and 1992, he stood in 28 Tests, the last of which was the historic confrontation between South Africa and the West Indies at the Kensington Oval. Such was the respect in which he was universally held that he was invited to officiate in the Australasian Cup in Sharjah in 1986 and the World Cup in India and Pakistan in 1987. As a cricketer at Combermere during the 1940s, he showed some promise as a right-arm leg-spinner before joining YMPC. Migrating later on to Grenada, he represented that island during 1965–68 and was able to gain selection for the Windward Islands in one match against Trinidad and Tobago in 1967.[105]

Combermere also provided cricket with a number of sports editors and reporters, the chief of whom perhaps were O.S. Coppin, Clyde A. Walcott and Sam Wilkinson. Coppin, universally known as 'Santa Claus', served the *Barbados Advocate* as a cricket writer and sports editor for several years and also reported the local scores on Saturday nights over the Barbados Rediffusion during the 1950s. Unlike Walcott and Wilkinson, he had been an active player in his youth and turned out often for the Volunteers and the Empire Second XI during the 1940s when he also played regularly in the Combermere Past vs Present fixture.[106]

In evaluating Combermere's contribution to the development of cricket in Barbados, one of the difficulties is the fact that so many boys began their school careers at Combermere before attending first-grade secondary schools in the hope of winning island scholarships. This huge list includes Lyall Speed, Leslie Walcott, E.L.G. Hoad, Snr, L.S. Birkett, C.R. 'Snuffie' Browne, Stanton Gittens, 'Puss' Parris, Clyde and Keith Walcott, Horace King, Cammie Smith and David Holford. All of them were good enough to represent Barbados and some of them eventually played Test cricket. While Lyall Speed is often considered a Lodge School product, the others are always classified as Old Harrisonians. They spent more time at that school than at Combermere, it is true, but they also took something from Combermere with them.

Combermere has made an incalculable contribution to Empire's cause. The link between Combermere and Empire has never really been broken although the circumstances in which Empire was born in 1914 have significantly altered. Affinities of class and race bound these two institutions very closely together from the beginning. The vast bulk of Empire's administrators, captains and players over the years, from Herman Griffith to Roland Holder, have been Old Combermerians. In fact, until about 1970, Empire could just as easily been referred to as the Combermere School Old Boys. To Spartan, too, Combermere gave, among a host of others, George Carew, Neville Grant, Wesley Hall, Peter Lashley, George Learmond, Thomas Moe, Jim Parris and Derek Sealy. White cricketers from middle income backgrounds who had attended Combermere in their youth, for a long time had no haven but Pickwick. So the school provided that club with such distinguished members as Henry F. Austin, Edward and John Hoad, Leo Hutchinson, Jack Kidney, and Clarence Skinner. John Burke, Pedro Corbin, Noel Lucas and Kenny Warren were Old Combermerians who helped to make Carlton a great sports club. In the early days, because of its very nature, YMPC was composed to a large extent of Old Combermerians, led by the Burkes, Fosters and Lucases. The prestigious Wanderers club for a long time represented the wealthiest white families in Barbados. There was a social gulf between that institution and Combermere School. Yet Combermere provided it nevertheless with F.C. Lobo and the four Atkinson brothers.

In short, Combermere made a noteworthy contribution to all the major cricket clubs in the BCA. It also was directly responsible for the establishment of the BCL in 1937. It was due to the untiring efforts of such Old Combermerians as Chrissie Brathwaite, J. Mitchie Hewitt and J.T.C. Ramsay that the BCL emerged and ultimately flourished. The BCL was deliberately intended to cater to those rural and working class cricketers who had not the social clout or connections to gain admission to any of the BCA clubs. Within just over 30 years, more than 100 clubs had become affiliated with the BCL which produced such eminent players as Clairmonte Depeiza, Charles Griffith, Conrad Hunte, Frank King, Seymour Nurse, Gary Sobers and Everton Weekes.[107]

Combermere's Best

Combermere's influence can perhaps best be gauged by considering the number of its alumni who eventually played well for the West Indies at the highest level and by trying to select its proverbial dream team. Old Combermerians who starred in Test cricket were Denis and Eric Atkinson, George Carew, Anderson Cummins, Herman Griffith, Wes Hall, Edward Hoad, Roland Holder, Peter Lashley, 'Mannie' Martindale, Derek Sealy, E.A.V. 'Foffie' Williams and Frank Worrell. Rawle Brancker and George Learmond did not gain selection to Test teams but they were good enough to accompany West Indian touring teams abroad. For a school of this nature and size to be able to boast a dozen international stars is quite exceptional.

The batting order of an All-Time Combermere cricket XI might well be: George Carew, Edward Hoad, Peter Lashley, John Lucas, Frank Worrell (captain), Derek Sealy (wicketkeeper), Denis Atkinson, Rawle Brancker, Herman Griffith, Wesley Hall and 'Mannie' Martindale. This team is so powerful that no place can be found in it for such international stars as Eric Atkinson, Roland Holder, George Learmond and 'Foffie' Williams. Its strengths are immediately apparent. Combermere is famous for producing great fast bowlers, stylish batsmen and excellent allrounders. That it has spawned fast bowlers in greater bulk than the two first-grade schools may arguably be of some sociological significance. This may confirm the age-old suspicion that members of the lower strata of society tend to be more assertive and aggressive on the field of play where they can relieve their frustrations and sense of alienation in legitimate and constructive ways. If Barbadian fast bowlers have generally sprung from modest roots, this is certainly in keeping with the sociology of Australian and English cricket. In fact, for many years, English amateurs spurned fast bowling and wicket-keeping as drudgery beneath the dignity of gentlemen. The lower class professionals were therefore expected to perform these menial tasks.[108]

Such sociology, however, cannot explain the Combermere tradition of stylish batsmanship which has historically been the hallmark of patricians. Nor will it account for Combermere's failure to provide Barbados with more than a handful of first-rate wicketkeepers. Combermere has churned out a sizeable cluster of elegant strokemakers over the years, including such luminaries as Lucas, Sealy and Worrell, three of the greatest stylists in Barbadian cricket history. The array of outstanding allrounders produced by this school is also extraordinary. Combermere has provided Barbados, however, with precious few wicketkeepers or spin bowlers of quality. Apart from Robinson, its best keepers perhaps were Ossie Gill, Alan Ishmael, Kenneth Hurley and Rodney Norville, none of whom made it to the first-class ranks. Learmond and Sealy kept wicket competently but they did so only occasionally – even though Sealy's supporters still claim that he was one of the finest wicket-keepers of his generation. Hall, who showed much promise behind the stumps as a schoolboy, changed disciplines in his late teens. The best spinners ever to play for Combermere might well have been Rawle Brancker, Adzil Holder and 'Puss' Parris. But while they represented Barbados effectively they failed to gain selection to West Indies Test teams.

On the credit side, few schools anywhere in the world can claim to have produced fast bowlers to equal the quantity and quality of Barker, Crick,

Cummins, Ellcock, Griffith, Hall, Martindale, Norris, Small, Spooner, E.A.V. Williams and Lionel Williams. Nor can many schools have produced allrounders to match the Atkinson brothers, Brancker, Hoad, Lucas, Sealy and Worrell. It is by taking all these things into consideration that one can appreciate the measure of Combermere's influence and contribution over the years. The All-Time Combermere XI is perhaps the strongest that any school can muster.

Up to July 1997, in purely statistical terms, 13 Old Combermerians represented the West Indies in 191 Tests. They went to the crease on 298 occasions (with 44 not outs), scored 7,281 runs (including 11 centuries), and averaged 28.67 per innings. They captured 435 wickets at 29.19 runs apiece. They also achieved 99 dismissals, including 1 stumping. These are incredible statistics for a secondary school that was classified as 'second grade' until 1961 and which catered to fewer than 400 students until the 1940s.

NOTES

1 Keith A.P. Sandiford and Earle H. Newton, *Combermere School and the Barbadian Society* (Kingston, 1995), passim. See also Keith A.P. Sandiford, " 'Sons in the Sun': The Cricket Story of the Combermere School of Barbados", *Cricket Lore* 2, no. 5 (1995): 41–5.

2 Sandiford and Newton, *Combermere School and the Barbadian Society*, 140.

3 Thorn failed to notice, however, that Norman Marshall (Roy's brother) had been educated at Foundation and Roy himself spent a short time there before moving on to the Lodge for the sake of his cricket.

4 Sandiford and Newton, *Combermere School and the Barbadian Society*, 63.

5 Ibid., 23–47. See also Keith A.P. Sandiford and Brian Stoddart, "The Elite Schools and Cricket in Barbados: A Study in Colonial Continuity", *International Journal of the History of Sport* 4 (December 1987): 337–38; *Combermere School Magazine*, 1913–26; *Barbados Blue Books*, 1896–1926.

6 Sandiford and Newton, *Combermere School and the Barbadian Society*, 15, 41, 48, 55, 85–6, 104.

7 *Combermerian* (1937–38), 33–6.

8 *Combermerian* (1926–49); BCA, *100 Years of Organised Cricket in Barbados, 1892–1992* (Bridgetown, 1992), 108–9.

9 BCA, *100 Years*, 75–6.

10 *Combermerian* (1926–27), 61.

11 Keith A.P. Sandiford, "The Spartan Cricket Club 1893–1993", *Journal of the Cricket Society* 16, no. 3 (Autumn 1993): 44.

12 *Barbados Advocate*, 4 September 1896, 5.

13 Philip Thorn, *Barbados Cricketers, 1865–1990* (West Bridgford, 1991), 27.

14 Bruce Hamilton, *Cricket in Barbados* (Bridgetown, 1947), 49, 52.
15 *Barbados Advocate*, 19 February 1896, 6.
16 BCA, *100 Years*, 98.
17 Thorn, *Barbados Cricketers*, 7, 21.
18 BCA, *100 Years*, 93–4.
19 Empire Cricket Club, *The Empire Club, 1914–1989* (Bridgetown, 1989), 16–23; Hamilton, *Cricket in Barbados*, 98, 106, 109, 110, 114; Thorn, *Barbados Cricketers*, 24.
20 *Combermere School Magazine* (Second Term 1919–20), 12
21 Hamilton, *Cricket in Barbados*, 106, 111, 112, 114; Thorn, *Barbados Cricketers*, 26.
22 Hamilton, *Cricket in Barbados*, 98–100.
23 *Combermere School Magazine* (Second Term 1914–15), 18–22; *Combermere School Magazine*, Second Term 1915–16, 18–21.
24 Philip Bailey, Philip Thorn and Peter Wynne-Thomas, *Who's Who of Cricketers* (London, 1984), 489; Thorn, *Barbados Cricketers*, 13, 15; *Wisden* 1987, 1236–37.
25 Empire, *The Empire Club*, 16–26.
26 BCA, *100 Years*, 83.
27 Sandiford and Newton, *Combermere School and the Barbadian Society*, 35.
28 *Barbados Advocate*, 27 October 1908, 8.
29 *Combermere School Magazine* (1913–25); *Combermerian* (1926–47).
30 *Combermerian* (1938–39), 45.
31 *Combermere School Magazine* (December 1964), 43.
32 *Combermere School Magazine* (Second Term 1922–23), 18.
33 *Combermerian* (1926–27), 61.
34 *Combermerian* (1938–39), 50.
35 BCA, *100 Years*, 58.
36 *Combermerian* (1934–35), 32.
37 Thorn, *Barbados Cricketers*, 28.
38 Ibid., 29.
39 Jeffrey Stollmeyer, *Everything under the Sun* (London, 1983), 107–8.
40 Empire, *The Empire Club*, 24–6.
41 Hamilton, *Cricket in Barbados*, 118, 131, 138.
42 Ibid., 134.
43 Sandiford, "The Spartan Cricket Club", 44–5.
44 BCA, *100 Years*, 63–4; Thorn, *Barbados Cricketers*, 22; *Wisden* 1975, 919–21.
45 BCA, *100 Years*, 104.
46 *West Indies Cricket Annual 1989*, 88.
47 BCA, *100 Years*, 110.
48 Bill Frindall, *The Wisden Book of Test Cricket 1877–1984* (London, 1985), 250.
49 Sandiford and Newton, *Combermere School and the Barbadian Society*, 62–4.
50 *Combermerian* (1935–36), 57.

51 Sandiford and Newton, *Combermere School and the Barbadian Society*, 62.
52 Hamilton, *Cricket in Barbados*, 148, 160, 166; Thorn, *Barbados Cricketers*, 28.
53 BCA, *100 Years*, 128.
54 *Combermerian* (1934–35), 32.
55 *Combermerian* (1940–41), 24–39.
56 Sandiford and Newton, *Combermere School and the Barbadian Society*, 62, 86, 118.
57 *Combermerian* (1940–41), 35.
58 *Combermerian* (1939–40), 45.
59 Empire, *The Empire Club*: Alleyne appears in every photograph of the club's cricket and soccer teams for the period 1941–56; BCA, *Report and Statement of Accounts 1st April 1994 to 31st March 1995*, 75–6.
60 Sandiford and Newton, *Combermere School and the Barbadian Society*, 65, 108, 127–28.
61 *Combermerian* (1939–40), 45.
62 *Combermerian* (1940–41), 30, 35.
63 Ibid., 35.
64 Thorn, *Barbados Cricketers*, 23.
65 BCA, *Report and Statement of Accounts 1st April 1991 to 31st March 1992*, 63.
66 *Combermerian* (1948), 127; Thorn, *Barbados Cricketers*, 18, 30.
67 BCA, *100 Years*, 99.
68 Ibid., 122–23.
69 Ibid.; Sandiford, *Frank Mortimer Maglinne Worrell: His Record Innings-by-Innings* (West Bridgford, 1997).
70 Ernest Eytle, *Frank Worrell* (London, 1963); Torrey Pilgrim, *The Sir Frank Worrell Pictorial* (New York, 1992); Ivo Tennant, *Frank Worrell: A Biography* (Cambridge, 1987); Frank Worrell, *Cricket Punch* (London, 1959); Sandiford, *Frank Mortimer Maglinne Worrell*.
71 Empire, *The Empire Club*, 45.
72 Thorn, *Barbados Cricketers*, 21.
73 Ibid., 27.
74 Ibid., 30.
75 Sandiford and Newton, *Combermere School and the Barbadian Society*, 8.
76 BCA, *Reports and Statement of Accounts 1st April 1994 to 31st March 1995*, 75.
77 Ibid., 34; BCA, *100 Years*, 55.
78 BCA, *100 Years*, 54. By way of apt comparison, it should be noted that Learie Constantine, in 18 Tests for the West Indies, registered 635 runs (av: 19.24), 58 wickets (av: 30.10) and 28 catches.
79 Thorn, *Barbados Cricketers*, 26.
80 Ibid., 22; *Wisden* 1964, 879–80.
81 *Combermerian* (1948), 38.
82 *Wisden 1964*, 879–80.
83 BCA, *100 Years*, 95; *West Indies Cricket Annual 1991*, 19.
84 Thorn, *Barbados Cricketers*, 28, 30.
85 *Wisden 1970*, 970–71; and *Wisden 1971*, 976–77.

86 Sandiford and Newton, *Combermere School and the Barbadian Society*, 86, 147.
87 BCA, *100 Years*, 60.
88 Ibid., 84.
89 *Red Stripe Caribbean Cricket Quarterly* (April/June 1996): 8–12; and (January/March 1997): 5. See also Keith A.P. Sandiford, *Wesley Winfield Hall: His Record Innings-by-Innings* (West Bridgford, forthcoming).
90 BCA, *100 Years*, 97.
91 *Combermere School Magazine* (December 1964), 23.
92 BCA, *Report and Statement of Accounts 1st April 1994 to 31st March 1995*, 41.
93 Sandiford and Newton, *Combermere School and the Barbadian Society*, 60, 95.
94 *West Indies Cricket Annual 1972*, 56–7, 62.
95 Thorn, *Barbados Cricketers*, 21.
96 Bailey, Thorn and Wynne-Thomas, *Who's Who of Cricketers*, 1129–30.
97 Ibid., 494; *Playfair Cricket Annual 1994*, 238.
98 Thorn, *Barbados Cricketers*, 24.
99 *Playfair Cricket Annual 1996*, 168, 176, 181, 182, 191.
100 *West Indies Cricket Annual 1971*, 56, 82–4; *West Indies Cricket Annual 1972*, 60.
101 *Barclays West Indies Players' Guide 1993*, 3.
102 *Barclays West Indies Players' Guide 1996*, 3.
103 Ibid.; *Playfair Cricket Annual 1996*, 164, 172.
104 BCA, *Report and Statement of Accounts 1st April 1995 to 31st March 1996*, 77–8.
105 *Caribbean Red Stripe Cricket Quarterly* (January/March 1993), 7.
106 *Combermerian* (1939–48).
107 L. Walcott, "The Barbados Cricket League: Forty Years of Service", UWI undergraduate paper, Cave Hill, 1978.
108 Keith A.P. Sandiford, *Cricket and the Victorians* (Aldershot, 1994), 130.

5

Epilogue

Quo Vadis?

To Barbadians, cricket has long been much more than just another game. It has been a craze. Some would say it has been a religion. Up to the time of independence, there was never any doubt about cricket's position in Barbadian life. In a society that was still to a large extent Victorian and somewhat puritanical in its outlook, most sports were dismissed as mere forms of 'skylarking'. Cricket was played, less because it was a sport than because it was viewed as the most effective socializing agent and by far the best means of social control. Track and field made boys better prepared for bowling, fielding and running between the wickets; and soccer was a form of exercise to keep cricketers fit during the off-season. Not surprisingly, Jim Wedderburn is still the only Barbadian ever to have won an Olympic medal, and he did so at Rome in 1960 while running as a member of a West Indian 4 x 400 metres relay team during the brief and unhappy life of the British West Indian Federation. That quartet, inevitably, included no fewer than three Jamaicans.[1] Expensive pastimes such as golf, horse-racing, tennis and yachting were the preserve of the select few. Not many youngsters played basketball seriously in those days, and field hockey was a relatively new sport which Combermere School, Pickwick and the Polo Club had introduced and popularized during the 1950s.[2]

Cricket, in other words, faced no challenge as the national sport par excellence in Barbados during the last century of British colonialism. To such historical sociologists as Hilary Beckles, C.L.R. James and Brian Stoddart, this is a most intriguing phenomenon demonstrating the awesome power of cultural imperialism.[3] The establishment had delivered a number of ambiguous messages: on the one hand, cricket was a medium through which colonists could be civilized and brought more meekly into the imperial fold. Those subjects who accepted the cricket culture were least likely to reject the other elements of Anglo-Saxonism. On the other hand, a very deliberate attempt was made by the local élite to deter the poorer blacks in Barbados from enjoying the benefits of civilization on the same sward as the white minority. Complicated questions of class and colour thus operated to maintain old-fashioned distinctions of order and degree. On the one hand, the BCCC refused to admit Fenwick into the regular competition; on the other, it encouraged the growth of this lower class black club by allowing its players occasionally to use the regular grounds and facilities of BCCC affiliates and by seeking the services of the "professionals" to hone the skills of its own gentleman-players (especially when preparing for intercolonial competition).[4]

In colonial Barbados, nobody questioned the right of the unwashed multitude to play the greatest game that civilized man had yet invented. The talents of Delmont Hinds, Oliver Layne and William Shepherd were universally admired by most white Barbadians who only wished that these cricketers had been white and therefore eligible to join their respective clubs. The blacks themselves bought enthusiastically into the Anglo-Saxon ideology and placed great store not only on cricketing prowess but on cricketing forms and formalities. On certain fundamentals, consequently, there was obvious consensus among all classes and colours. Not only was cricket the best of all kinetic activities but it taught invaluable lessons about ethics and justice. Its values transcended race and class, but this did not mean that it could remove racial, social or economic barriers. If the Barbadian whites played cricket to signify their gentility, the blacks did so to demonstrate their equality with their social superiors. The supreme irony then was the ability of a deeply divided society to unite on the cricket field for the singular purpose of proving its moral superiority over all others while, at the same time, tenaciously adhering to old-fashioned snobberies beyond the boundary. This ability had much to do with the forging of a Barbadian sense of nationalism even before the coming of independence. Cricket gave to Barbados an identity and a sense of pride and purpose which nothing else could have ever have done.[5] Just as the Barbadian public as a whole had basked in the 1920s in Challenor's glory, 40 years later its descendants all applauded the mighty deeds of Gary Sobers with equal and universal warmth.

THE ADVENT OF KINETIC RIVALS

Nowadays, however, cricket's hegemony appears (at least on the surface) to be seriously threatened. Many of the youth, no doubt influenced by American television, consider cricket too dull, too old-fashioned and too English. They are turning their attention to other forms of recreation. Far more popular now than ever before are such sports as athletics, basketball, body-building, golf, hockey, soccer, swimming and tennis. The Barbadian standard of play in each of these sports has risen by leaps and bounds since independence. Barbadians can now compete, on relatively even terms, with most other Caribbean countries in soccer and field hockey; and the vast gulf between Barbados and Jamaica in track and field has been significantly narrowed. Over the past 30 years or so, Barbados has also produced a number of world-class body-builders and weightlifters. It is arguable, therefore, that Barbadian nationalism is no longer bound up with the singular devotion to cricket, and a great deal of anxiety was spent in 1996 on Obadele Thompson, by far the greatest sprinter that the society has yet spawned. Most Barbadians were praying for him to win a medal of some kind at the Atlanta Olympics. Now they are looking forward hopefully to the year 2000 (especially since the news that their beloved 'Oba' had smashed the world indoor record for 55 metres in the winter of 1996–97). The young swimmer, Leah Martindale, too, is attracting considerable attention – especially since becoming, at Atlanta in 1996, the first black of either gender to reach a final in any Olympic aquatic competition.

While these are positive signs of progress, there are those Barbadian critics who equate the health of the Barbadian society with the quality of its cricket and lament the fact that Barbadians have not been as dominant on the cricket field in the last decade (1987–97) as they traditionally had been. During the last 11 years, Barbados has won only three territorial championships (1991, 1995 and 1997). This stands out in sharp contrast to the Barbadian performance during 1966–86. During those first 20 years of the Shell Shield competition, Barbados won the trophy outright on no fewer than 12 occasions and shared it once (1975–76) with Trinidad and Tobago.[6] Barbados was then easily the most difficult team to beat in the Caribbean and was almost invincible at home. Touring cricketers from Australia, England, India, Pakistan and New Zealand often commented that the Barbadian XI was a tougher nut to crack than the West Indies Test squad itself. When the Barbadians lost that cheeky and infamous challenge (by 262 runs) to the remainder of the planet in 1967, there was, as J.S. Barker observed, considerable surprise throughout the West Indies "that any combination of cricketers could defeat Barbados in Barbados".[7]

THE WORLD'S LEADING EXPORTER OF CRICKET TALENT

This Barbadian dominance was not only reflected in Shell Shield results but also in the composition of the West Indian teams. The sides which left the Caribbean were invariably led by a sizeable Barbadian contingent and the Test XIs were dominated by Barbadian representatives. It was common for West Indian teams to contain as many as five or six Barbadians, especially after the notorious 'quota system' was abandoned altogether after World War II. When John Goddard led his victorious squad to England in 1950, 6 of the 16 tourists, including the captain himself, were Barbadians.[8] Seven years later, seven of the 17 West Indians whom Goddard captained in England with less positive results were natives of Barbados.[9] Six of the 17 West Indians who toured Australia and New Zealand in 1951–52 were Barbadians.[10] The team of 17 West Indians, whom Frank Worrell led so memorably to Australia in 1960–61, included no fewer than 7 Barbadians.[11] The peak of such dominance had actually come in 1955 when eight Barbadians (Denis Atkinson, Clairemont Depeiza, Frank King, Norman Marshall, Gary Sobers, Clyde Walcott, Everton Weekes and Frank Worrell) were selected to play against Australia in the third Test at Georgetown, British Guiana.[12]

Not only have Barbadians traditionally dominated the West Indian elevens but they have also been prominent in professional as well as amateur cricket wherever it has been played. When the English counties opened their doors to foreign players in 1968, the Barbadian professionals immediately became some of the most eagerly sought after. In 1971, for example, there were as many as four of them (Gordon Greenidge, John Holder, Roy Marshall and Lawrence Worrell) on the Hampshire county cricket staff alone.[13] In 1989, when the Netherlands for the very first time in their cricket history defeated an England XI in a 40-over ODI at Amstelveen, just outside Amsterdam, the hero was a 41-year-old

The 1957 West Indies Cricket Team in England. *Standing*: W. Ferguson (scorer), A. Ganteaume, N. Asgarali, F.C.M. Alexander, G. Sobers, W. Hall, T. Dewdney, B.H. Pairaudeau, R. Gilchrist, O.G. Smith, R.B. Kanhai; *seated*: T.N. Peirce (manager), S. Ramadhin, D. Atkinson, F.M. Worrell, J.D.C. Goddard (capt.), C.L. Walcott, E.D. Weekes, A.L. Valentine, C. deCaires (manager)

Barbadian, Nolan Clarke, who scored a scintillating 77 of his team's 176 runs.[14] Barbadians were also naturally among those who made 'rebel' tours to South Africa while that country was still being officially boycotted by the rest of the sporting world because of its commitment to apartheid. The knowledge that their Test careers could be destroyed by touring this forbidden land did not prevent such Barbadians as Gregory Armstrong, Sylvester Clarke, Geoffrey Greenidge, Collis King, Ezra Moseley, David Murray, Albert Padmore, John Shepherd and Franklyn Stephenson from travelling thither.[15]

This means, in effect, that Barbados had become famous on the international stage more for exporting cricketers than for exporting rum or sugar. It has always produced the latter commodities in modest bulk commensurate with its diminutive stature. But it has bred more brilliant cricketers per capita and per square mile than any other community. Its natives have played the game at the highest level in all parts of the world, and indeed there were more Barbadian-born players on the Canadian national team in the 1979 World Cup competition than Canadian-born players themselves. The fast bowler, John Valentine, was the only indigenous Canadian and the only white member of the team that actually reached the finals, to everyone's astonishment, in that memorable summer. When Canada opposed England on 13 and 14 June, such Barbadian natives as R.G. Callender, C.A. Marshall, G.R. Sealy and J.C.B. Vaughan performed as representatives of Canada.[16] The team's coach, too, was none other than Everton DeCourcey Weekes who had spent a good portion of the previous summer watching the provincial teams and helping with the process of selection.[17]

CRICKET AND BARBADIAN NATIONALISM

Such a phenomenal output of talented cricketers, generation after generation, by such a small community occupying such a small area of the globe, is one of the teal curiosities of modern sociology. It is naturally also one of the key sources of Barbadian nationalistic pride. The whole Barbadian sense of nationalism has been intertwined with its cricket from as long as anyone cares to remember. As long ago as the nineteenth century, local newspapers such as the *Barbados Agricultural Reporter*, the *Barbados Bulletin*, the *Barbados Globe* and the *Barbados Herald*, unabashedly cheered for the national heroes during intercolonial cricket tournaments;[18] and the local press, led now by the *Barbados Advocate*, had much to criticize the West Indian selectors for when Barbadian champions were omitted from teams to tour England in 1900, 1906, 1923 and 1928.[19]

The traditional jingoism of the Barbadian press was never as pronounced when dealing with non-cricketing matters. It was cricket which furnished the journalists with all the fuel they needed for their patriotic fire. It was cricket, too, which was favoured above all other physical exercises by the academic, political, economic and religious institutions. Thus the island teams, sponsored as they were by the business firms, inspired as they were by schools and churches, and encouraged as they were by the legislature and the press, took to the field as so many upholders of the Barbadian national image. They fought each cricket match as though they were participating in a modern crusade. Barbadians brought a level of intensity to their cricket that was clearly absent from everything else that they did.

It was precisely this kind of intensity which produced the jingoism that other West Indians have found so very abrasive. Even Sir Frank Worrell, a favourite son, often criticized this approach. Having committed himself totally to the notion of a "West Indian nationalism", he dismissed the Barbadian challenge to the Rest of the World in 1966 (by way of celebrating its achievement of political independence) as savouring of "bigotry, vanity and insularity". Worrell thought that the "only possible reason for this match seems to be to permit the Barbadians to prove that the Barbados team is better than West Indies".[20] Sir Frank, of course, was right. The Barbadians have never been content with the treatment meted out to their cricketing crusaders by the WICBC (recently reconstituted as the WICB). They have tended to put their cricketing stars on a pedestal and marvel at the myopia of the authorities. They generally fail to understand how it is possible for selectors to overlook the obvious genius of a Carlisle Best or a Roland Holder while choosing such "palpably inferior" players as a Philip Simmons or an Augustine Logie to fill places in the West Indies Test XI. This feeling of paranoia produced an explosion, for instance, when Franz Alexander, an inexperienced Jamaican, was chosen ahead of Frank Worrell to lead the West Indies team in the late 1950s. It rose again dramatically to the surface in 1991 when the West Indian selectors announced that the Antiguan batsman, Richie Richardson, would succeed Viv Richards as the Test captain.

Many Barbadian chauvinists regarded this latter decision as an insult to their own Desmond Leo Haynes who had been a good vice captain to Richards in the past and had also shown excellent leadership qualities in captaining Barbados to a Red Stripe triumph in 1990–91. To add insult to injury, the WICBC then bypassed Haynes yet again when it asked Gus Logie of Trinidad to serve as vice captain to Richardson on the 1992–93 tour to Australia. Gus Logie's place in the Test team, after all, was not

Desmond Haynes has exceeded 7,000 runs in Test cricket

automatic or even secure. Their protests seemed justified since Logie appeared in none of the five Tests that winter.[21] When, in addition to these frustrations, the West Indian selectors chose to overlook the impressive claims of the young Barbadian fast bowler, Anderson Cummins, whom they omitted from the historic Test against South Africa at the Kensington Oval in 1992, the Barbadians could contain their anger no longer. They rose in revolt and organized by far the most massive and effective of all boycotts in the history of cricket. That Test was witnessed by a pitifully small audience on every day, despite the pulsating nature of the cricket.[22]

The great boycott of 1992 served as a spectacular testimony to the linkage between cricket and Barbadian nationalism. The society did not so much feel that Cummins and Haynes had been overlooked as cricketers. To the patriots, it was a far more serious question of the Barbadian national honour being sullied. To emphasize their total dissatisfaction with the WICBC, the members of the BCA voted David Holford off its board of management in July 1992. He received the least votes among the nine persons nominated to fill eight positions.[23] As one of the West Indian selectors, Holford became the immediate target and suffered the scapegoat's fate. This was the only way in which Barbadian nationalists could exact redress for a whole litany of grievances, both real and imaginary.

A Crisis of Social Culture

So fierce is the Barbadian commitment to cricket and to cricketing excellence that there has always been a great deal of wailing and gnashing of teeth in the island when the national team fails to win the territorial cricket championship. There is considerable alarm now, for example, that the nation finds itself in the midst of an unusual drought. It has failed to win the territorial competition no fewer than eight times since 1986 and many inhabitants interpret this as a symptom of national malaise, a sure sign that the fibre of the society is not what it should be and/or once was. The nation, which had never before lost more than three cricket championships in a row, proceeded to lose four between 1986 and 1990. This produced a stifling sense of gloom and despair which was reflected, for example, in an article which appeared in the BCA's 100th anniversary publication in 1992. Written by Dr Hilary Beckles, perhaps the most celebrated of all Barbadian social historians, it was entitled "Barbados Cricket and the Crisis of Social Culture". It is nothing short of a national calamity that Barbados has won the Caribbean cricket championship twice since 1991.

Like other leading sociologists of his generation, Beckles sees cricket in Barbados as the mirror of the society's soul. It reflects the society's ethos, aspirations, dreams and mores in a way in which no other single activity does or can do. Thus the career of a Sobers, for example, marks the flourishing of the national genius and creativity. A community in decline is incapable of producing a talent of this magnitude. By the same token, then, when the cricketing spark flickers but dimly (if it flickers at all) it is time for Barbadian cultural and political leaders to take critical and urgent stock. It must surely be an age of social crisis, in Beckles' view, when a Test match is being played in the Caribbean, between England and the West Indies, and there is not a single Barbadian in the eleven. Thus was the nadir reached at Antigua in April 1994 when, for the very first time in 303 Test matches, Barbados lacked representation on the international cricket stage.[25] It is true that Anderson Cummins and Roland Holder were often named to the final thirteen during the latest England tour of the Caribbean; and it is equally true that they played in most of the ODIs in 1994 and 1995. Desmond Haynes, however, was the lone Barbadian to participate in that Test series before injury forced his withdrawal from the final match.

Older Barbadians cannot relate easily to this state of affairs. They put it down to lack of discipline and dedication on the part of the current youth. Good batsmanship, especially, is the product of constant study, patient trial and error, and long hours of assiduous practice. These skills and virtues were once encouraged in the élite schools and the youngsters were compelled to face up to the best bowling available in the first division of the BCA. Clyde Walcott and Frank Worrell, for instance, were forced to counter the thunderbolts of the celebrated Empire four-pronged pace attack when they were only 12 or 13 years old.[26] By the time they were 17, they were both accomplished batsmen. Keith Walcott was already one of the most punishing batsmen in the colony by the time he was 14 years old. The same is true of Roy Marshall, who represented Barbados when he was only 15. In fact, prior to independence, no fewer than eight Barbadians made their first-class début before reaching the age of 17. Since then, there has not been a single case of such precociousness.[27] Derek Sealy, after a year of first-division competition, was still only seventeen when he gained his first Test cap for the West Indies in January 1930. In fact, had Combermere been promoted to the first division prior to 1928, he would most certainly have represented the school's senior team before the age of 14. Sealy and Sobers are still the only two West Indians to participate in Test cricket before reaching the age of 18.[28]

But the current generation of youngsters seem incapable of such effort and achievement. Nor do individual schools now have the opportunity of playing first-division cricket. Few promising batsmen, as a consequence, have surfaced in recent years before attaining their twentieth birthday. In fact, apart from Roland Holder, Barbados has not produced a middle-order batsman of any quality over the past 30 years. Prior to Holder's Test début in 1997, the last Barbadian middle-order batsman to represent the West Indies at this level was Seymour Nurse, who retired from the international scene in 1969. This is one of the major sources of Barbadian concern.

It would be improper to ask the schools to reshape their physical education programmes and return to the monolithic cultivation of cricketing skills. In any case, the majority of the current and recent coaches, such as Orlando Greene at Harrison College and Harcourt Wason at Combermere, have been trained in US colleges.[29] The national pride should also be touched by superior performances in other sports and a greater effort made to idolize such non-cricketing heroes as Albert Beckles, Elvis Forde, Leah Martindale, Obadele Thompson and Jim Wedderburn. Too few people in Barbados are aware of the exploits of their own Cecil Squires, who has been such a dominant force in world-class 'natural' body-building over the past 15 years.[30] Nor are many Barbadians conscious of the fact that their own Julia Sandiford was ranked among the best female middle-distance runners in North America during the mid 1990s. Had Sandiford and Squires been cricketers in the remotest parts of the Antarctic, their statistics would certainly have been common knowledge at home. Let the progress made in athletics, body-building, golf, hockey, soccer, swimming and tennis continue. It would be absurd to attempt to reverse the hands of the clock in those areas.

The sport that has profited most in recent times from the impact of satellite television and the promotion of American culture is basketball, which has captured the imagination of a number of Barbadian youth. Thus considerable energy has been deflected away from cricket. But while this is true, not many youngsters apparently see themselves as potential NBA stars in the same way that Barbadian lads once dreamed of emulating English professional cricketers. It is common knowledge that West Indians do not normally grow beyond 6 ft 4 in. and the NBA offers few models with Caribbean roots. One can point only to Kareem Abdul Jabbar (Trinidad), formerly of the Los Angeles Lakers, and Patrick Ewing (Jamaica) of the current New York Knicks as outstanding players whose parents were born in the West Indies. Moreover, some of the youth who participate in this sport (or in any of the others) continue to be active on the cricket field. While the new distractions might help to explain the Barbadian failure to dominate the Red Stripe competition (1987–97) as convincingly as they had done the Shell Shield (1965–87), it is still clear from all the evidence that no single sporting (or other) activity has yet replaced the island's fanatical devotion to cricket. Indeed, the competing sports have suffered much from the reluctance of the government and the commercial houses to fund them as generously as they still do cricket. What perhaps is even more significant still is the approach of the 'grass-roots' to all sports in general and to cricket in particular. Cricket continues to dominate the discussions on the Barbadian call-in radio programmes, especially when international teams are touring the Caribbean. This was by far the main topic of conversation in the early months of 1994 and 1995 when England and Australia visited. From all reports, the same was true when the New Zealand cricketers toured the West Indies in 1996 and when the Indians followed them in 1997.

The inescapable fact is that the cricket tradition has been too securely established as a major feature of the Barbadian heritage. Excellence on the cricket field seems destined to remain for many years as a positive plank in Barbadian nationalism. The establishment there in 1993 of the Centre for Cricket Research by the Cave Hill branch of the UWI is deliberately intended by its founder, Professor Hilary Beckles (himself an accomplished allrounder), to perpetuate the cult of cricket, which he proudly sees as "an area of conquest".[33] The fundamental link between cricket and nationalism is still too securely forged to allow the Barbadian cricketers to disappoint the nation indefinitely; and, indeed, the excellent form of such young stars as Adrian Griffith, Floyd Reifer and Patterson Thompson in recent Red Stripe competition augurs well for the future.[34]

SOME RECOMMENDATIONS

This future is assured so long as the society is prepared to invest more time, money, thought and energy in a coaching programme at all levels. West Indians should not remain oblivious to the fact that other cricketing powers have recently been establishing 'cricket academies', deliberately calculated to narrow the gap between their lads and those from the Caribbean. Such an institution, conceivably, could help to improve the general quality of batsmanship in Barbadian schools and clubs. But, against this proposal, it might also be argued that coaching on a nationwide scale has manifestly failed to improve the standard of English batting and too much of it has led palpably to the stifling of creative genius. The true charm of Barbadian batsmanship traditionally has resulted from the flourishing of unrestricted talent in unique and individual ways. When Barbadian batting was supreme, there were no coaches in Barbados at all. Challenor, Ince, the three Ws, Hunte, Sobers and Nurse, among others, prospered as batsmen precisely because they lacked the kind of coaching that would surely have stifled their natural bent for the unorthodox and the unusual. Their batting, in a very real sense, constituted free and unfettered expression of the individual will.

There are more coaches and physical education experts in Barbados now than ever before, and it is therefore possible to link the steady decline in batting with the gradual emergence of physical education specialists and cricket coaches. Perhaps the coaches are stressing orthodoxy at the expense of individualism. What the Barbadian community must do, therefore, is to ensure that the coaching programme is effective. If Barbadians were to invest in additional coaches, they ought to insist that, while teaching the obvious fundamentals of strokeplay, the coaches do not inhibit free expression or the urge to experiment and improvise. They must recognize that it is much more beneficial for the ball to strike the middle of the bat than for the right-hander's left elbow to be cocked at a particular angle before the moment of impact. Much better use, that is to say, can be made of such former batting stars as Nurse, Sobers and Weekes, who would be most unlikely to preach in an "English fashion".

Another recommendation is to urge both the BCA and the BCL to insist on the preparation of fair strips, which offer equal opportunity to batsman and bowler. It is arguable that Barbadian batsmanship has been strangled over the past quarter of a century by the constant production of lightning fast pitches, at the Kensington Oval and elsewhere, to favour the faster bowlers. In Challenor's day, great Barbadian fast bowling at the club level was certainly not the norm. The Bank Hall wicket was notoriously fast, it is true, but other grounds offered fewer hazards. When the three Ws, Sobers, Hunte, Lashley and Nurse were at their peak, they were not bombarded, Saturday after Saturday, by the galaxy of fast bowlers who have recently sprung up. Nor were they forced to bat, week after week, on strips that favoured the ball. There may be a message here that is well worth heeding.

On the other hand, it is possible to argue that Barbados' triumphs in the early days of the Shell Shield competition depended, to a large extent, on the quality of its fast bowling. Such speedsters as Gregory Armstrong, Keith Boyce, Sylvester Clarke, Wayne Daniel, Richard Edwards, Joel Garner, Vanburn Holder and Hallam Moseley had as much to do with the first ten territorial championships won by Barbados as did the local batsmen. Perhaps those fast bowlers might not have progressed as they did had they been discouraged by the groundsmen. The Barbadian wickets, after all, had been much too placid during the period 1940–65 to offer any encouragement to the men of speed. Hence the general dearth of Barbadian speedsters during that golden age of batsmanship. Even so, it is clear that a sensible balance is now lacking. While it would be an error to return to the policy of preparing batting paradises everywhere, it is still wrong to inhibit the production of scintillating strokes.

The period of Barbadian cricket decline has coincided with the removal of the so-called élite schools from the BCA first division competition. Does this mean that the BCA should revisit that decision? Perhaps yes, and perhaps no. The policy of exalting certain schools at the expense of others was not a very sound idea, even in the beginning. When, in 1878, the Barbados Government passed the famous Education Act, that statute was reflective of Victorian social attitudes and conditions.[35] It made a most invidious distinction between first-grade and second-grade secondary schools in the island. It was a deliberate attempt to segregate the classes and to exclude blacks, as much as possible, from Harrison College and the Lodge. The act was based on a system of élitism that had become outmoded by the 1940s. Quite rightly, the establishment was eventually challenged by the headmasters of Combermere and Foundation, who insisted that the sons of lower-middle income parents had every right to compete for the prestigious island and Barbados scholarships. The immediate result of their defiance was that R.D. (now Dr Robert) Thomas of Foundation won a Barbados Scholarship in 1954 and K.A.P. (now Professor Keith) Sandiford of Combermere reached government exhibition standing in

1955. Combermere, Foundation and St Michael could not indefinitely be restricted to Ordinary Level courses.[36]

By 1960, the distinction between first-grade and second-grade schools had broken down completely, and this *fait accompli* was duly acknowledged by a more sensible series of education statutes, beginning in 1961 and continuing throughout the period of independence.[37] The BCA could not then, in all conscience, have continued to restrict first division status to a mere three schools when so many institutions of relatively equal status had steadily come into being. Whereas there were only about half-a-dozen secondary schools in Barbados with a substantial enrolment in 1955, this number increased to well over 20 by 1980. There are now more than 30 secondary schools, in one way or another funded by the state, with enrolments far in excess of the old Combermere, Harrison and Lodge school statistics. The problem has also been complicated, from a purely cricketing standpoint, by the introduction of co-education during the 1970s. Physical education programmes once geared to meet the needs of a single sex must now be revamped. It was probably good policy on the BCA's part to introduce the notion of a composite Combined Schools' XI in 1978 and later to divide the schools into two zones. But with the steady increase in the number of academic institutions and the dramatic rise in the number of pupils, the time has obviously come to divide these schools into several zones with the view of introducing about four or more schoolboy teams into the senior ranks. It is not a major catastrophe if the school teams regularly finish at the bottom of the first division ladder. It is much more important to provide as many lads as possible with first division experience during their developing years. It is clear that the notion of a southern and a northern Combined Schools' XI has failed. Barbados has not produced a single schoolboy prodigy in years.

In the days when Combermere, Harrison and the Lodge participated in first division cricket, they served as three of the most successful cricket nurseries in the world. They provided Barbados with the bulk of its first-class players for about 100 years (1865 to 1965) and produced an incredibly large number of West Indian Test cricketers as well. For about 30 years now, these schools have done very poorly. There must be sounder reasons for this than the simple fact that more cricketers in recent years have emerged from the elementary ranks without any secondary training at all. This latter development indicates that the BCA is less snobbish in its methods of selection and is more willing than it once was to choose representatives from the lower income strata. That, of course, is a sign of social progress and the BCA must be congratulated. But why are the secondary schools, now almost 10 times as plentiful and about 20 times as populous, collectively less productive of promising cricketers? That is not an easy question, either for the BCA or the schools themselves, to answer. But it does seem strange that Carlisle Best and Sherwin Campbell remain the lone international stars produced by Ellerslie, while Foundation thus far can boast only Joel Garner and Norman Marshall.

Joel Garner, the greatest star produced by Foundation School

In the Final Analysis

What, then, should the community do, if it needs to do anything at all? It might be suggested that Barbadians should react more philosophically to cricket losses in a sport where success and failure have historically been cyclical. No one county has yet succeeded in dominating English cricket for unconscionably long spells, nor has any single state indefinitely monopolized the Sheffield Shield in Australia. Even New South Wales, with its 42 triumphs in the first 93 Australian seasons, has known its periods of slump. Lancashire, Middlesex, Nottinghamshire, Surrey and Yorkshire (by far the most successful of English county cricket clubs) have all experienced their ups and downs. Given the cricketing fire which still burns brightly within the community's soul, it is more than likely that Barbados will rise again from the ashes and dominate territorial and international cricket in the early years of the twenty-first century. If Jamaica and the Leeward Islands now appear to be enjoying a cricket renaissance, so be it. These things are but temporary aberrations. The cricketing balance will, in due course, be restored. Just give both bowling and batting a fair chance at the club level, employ more coaches with specific instructions not to aim at the mere reproduction of clones, and encourage more schoolboys to take part in first division cricket. These may well be the simple solutions to this awful "crisis of social culture".

NOTES

1 David Wallechinsky, *The Complete Book of the Summer Olympics* (New York, 1996), 105–6.

2 Personal knowledge. When I myself captained the Combermere team during 1953–56, we played 'friendly' matches only against the Combermere School Old Boys, Pickwick and the Polo Club. We played mainly on Thursday evenings but there was no regular season, schedule or competition. Most of these games were arranged by S. Jackson Adams, our senior mathematics teacher. See also Keith A.P. Sandiford and Earle H. Newton, *Combermere School and the Barbadian Society* (Kingston, 1995), 85.

3 See, for example, Hilary McD. Beckles, "The Origin and Development of West Indies Cricket Culture in the Nineteenth Century: Jamaica and Barbados", in *Liberation Cricket: West Indies Cricket Culture* edited by Hilary McD. Beckles and Brian Stoddart (Manchester, 1995), 33–43; C.L.R. James, *Beyond a Boundary* (London, 1964); and Brian Stoddart, "Cricket, Social Formation and Cultural Continuity in Barbados: A Preliminary Ethnohistory", *Journal of Sport History* 14 (Winter 1987): 317–40.

4 See, for example, *Barbados Globe*, 27 March 1899 and 27 December 1899.

5 Keith A.P. Sandiford, "Cricket and the Growth of Barbadian Nationalism Before Independence (1966) and Since", forthcoming.

6 *Wisden* 1996, 1227.

7 J.S. Barker, *In the Main: West Indies v MCC 1968* (London, 1969), 10.

8 The six Barbadians who toured England in 1950 were John Goddard (captain), Roy Marshall, Clyde Walcott, Everton Weekes, C.B. 'Boogles' Williams and Frank Worrell. See "West Indies in England, 1950", *Wisden 1951*, 207–56.

9 The seven Barbadians who toured England in 1957 were John Goddard (captain), Denis Atkinson, Wesley Hall, Garfield Sobers, Clyde Walcott, Everton Weekes and Frank Worrell. "West Indies in England, 1957", *Wisden 1958*, 227–76.

10 The six Barbadian cricketers who visited Australasia in 1951–52 were Goddard (captain), Atkinson, Marshall, Walcott, Weekes and Worrell. A.G. Moyes, *With the West Indies in Australia 1951–52* (London, 1952), 6–7.

11 The seven Barbadians who toured Australia in 1960–61 were: Wesley Hall, Conrad Hunte, Patrick Lashley, Seymour Nurse, 'Cammie' Smith, Garfield Sobers and Frank Worrell (captain). A.G. Moyes, *With the West Indies in Australia 1960–61* (London, 1961), 2–3.

12 *Wisden 1956*, 871–72.

13 *Wisden 1972*, 434.

14 *Wisden 1990*, 1134.

15 Philip Thorn, *Barbados Cricketers, 1865–1990* (West Bridgford, 1990), passim.

16 *Wisden 1980*, 303.

17 Keith A.P. Sandiford, "Everton Weekes: A Cricket Legend Comes to Winnipeg", *Winnipeg Tribune*, 28 July 1978.
18 See the files of these newspapers during the period 1870 to 1900.
19 *Barbados Advocate*, 1900–1930.
20 Ivo Tennant, *Frank Worrell: A Biography* (Cambridge, 1987), 93.
21 *Wisden 1994*, 1044–47.
22 Tony Cozier, ed., *Caribbean Cricket Quarterly* (August 1992), passim.
23 BCA, *Report and Statement of Accounts 1st April 1992 to 31st March 1993*, 13.
24 BCA, *100 Years*, 50–1.
25 Frindall, *Wisden Book of Test Cricket*, II, 453.
26 Clyde Walcott, *Island Cricketers* (London, 1958), 15. Frank Worrell, *Cricket Punch* (London, 1959), 24.
27 BCA, *100 Years of Organised Cricket in Barbados, 1892–1992* (Bridgetown, 1992), 51. They are Roy Marshall, Clyde Walcott, Derek Sealy, Gary Sobers, Robin Bynoe, Keith Walcott, Percy Goodman and Norman Marshall.
28 *Wisden 1996*, 173.
29 Personal observation and interviews.
30 Cecil is a resident of Winnipeg in Manitoba, Canada, and is a regular performer at the annual 'Bajan Night' festival, staged by the Barbados Association of Winnipeg in June.
31 *Barbados Nation*, 19 May 1995, 44.
32 Personal observation, February to April 1994 and February to April 1995.
33 Hilary Beckles, ed., *An Area of Conquest: Popular Democracy and West Indies Cricket Supremacy* (Kingston, 1994).
34 Tony Cozier, ed., *Red Stripe Caribbean Cricket Quarterly* (April/June 1996), 41, 47.
35 Keith A.P. Sandiford, "Education and the Barbadian Society", *Banja: A Magazine of Barbadian Life & Culture* (April 1989): 49–50.
36 Sandiford and Newton, *Combermere School and the Barbadian Society*, 86–8.
37 Sandiford, "Education and the Barbadian Society", 45–53.
38 *Wisden 1996*, 1205.
39 Robert Brooke, *A History of the County Cricket Championship* (London, 1991), passim.

Select Bibliography

I NEWSPAPERS AND MAGAZINES

Banja: A Magazine of Barbadian Life & Culture

Barbados Advocate

Barbados Agricultural Reporter

Barbados Annual Review

Barbados Bulletin

Barbados Globe

Barbados Herald

Barbados Nation

Barclays West Indies Players' Guide

Combermerian

Harrisonian

Lodge School Record

Pelican

Playfair Cricket Annual

Red Stripe Caribbean Cricket Quarterly

Wisden Cricketers' Almanack

II OTHER SOURCES

Advocate Year Book and Who's Who 1951. Bridgetown, 1951.

Advocate Year Book 1964. Bridgetown, 1964.

Aspinall, A.E., *The British West Indies: Their History, Resources and Progress*. London, 1912.

Bailey, P. et al., *Who's Who of Cricketers*. London, 1984.

Bailey, P., and P. Thorn, *Sussex Cricketers 1815–1990*. West Bridgford, 1991.

Bailey, T.E., *Sir Gary: A Biography*. London, 1976.

Bannister, A., *Cricket Cauldron: With Hutton in the Caribbean*. London, 1954.

Barbados, *Annual Estimates*. 1967–95.

Barbados Cricket Association, *100 Years of Organised Cricket in Barbados 1892–1992*. Bridgetown, 1992.

_______, *Report and Statement of Accounts*. Bridgetown, 1948–97.

Barker, J.S., *Summer Spectacular: The West Indies v. England 1963*. London, 1965.

_______, *In the Main: West Indies v. MCC 1968*. London, 1969.

Beckles, H., *A History of Barbados: From Amerindian Settlement to Nation State*. Cambridge, 1990.

_______, ed., *An Area of Conquest: Popular Democracy and West Indies Cricket Supremacy*. Kingston, 1994.

Beckles, H., and B. Stoddart, eds., *Liberation Cricket: West Indies Cricket Culture*. Manchester, 1995.

Bell, C., *West Indian Test Cricketers: A Complete Statistical Record 1928–1993*. Kingston, 1994.

Bell, G.O., *Sir Garfield Sobers*. London, 1978.

Bell, W., ed., *The Democratic Revolution in the West Indies*. Massachusetts, 1967.

Benaud, R., *A Tale of Two Tests*. London, 1962.

_______, *The New Champions: Australia in the West Indies 1965*. London, 1966.

Birbalsingh, F., and C. Shiwcharan, *Indo-Westindian* [sic] *Cricket*. London, 1988.

Blood, H., "West Indian Cricket and Cricketers". *Corona* (July 1957).

Bolt, C., *Victorian Attitudes to Race*. London, 1971.

Bowen, C.P., "English Cricketers in the West Indies". *Herald*, 25 April 1895.

Boycott, G., *In the Fast Lane: West Indies Tour 1981*. London, 1981.

Brooke R., *A History of the County Cricket Championship*. London, 1991.

Butt, D. S., *Psychology of Sport*. New York, 1976.

Callender, B.A., and K.A.P. Sandiford, "Growing Up in the Bay Land: Sir Garfield Sobers and His Roots". *The Greatest Cricketer Ever! Sir Garfield Sobers*, Souvenir Programme. Bridgetown, 1994.

Cameron, D.J, *Caribbean Crusade: New Zealand Cricketers in the West Indies*. Newton Abbot, 1974.

Canynge Caple, S., *England v The West Indies 1895–1957*. Worcester, 1957.

Cashman, R., Patrons, *Players and the Crowd: The Phenomenon of Indian Cricket*. New Delhi, 1980.

Chandos, J., Boys *Together: English Public Schools 1800–1864*. London, 1984.

Cenery, J.W.B., *The Revival of Sport in Barbados*. Bridgetown, 1920.

Clarke, J., and B. Scovell, *Everything That's Cricket: The West Indies Tour of 1966*. London, 1966.

Close, B., *The* M.C.C. *Tour of West Indies, 1968*. London, 1968.

Constantine, L., *Cricket in the Sun*. London, undated.

_______, *Colour Bar*. London, 1954.

Cotter, G., *England versus West Indies*. London, 1991.

Cozier, T., *The West Indies: Fifty Years of Test Cricket*. Newton Abbot, 1978.

Cozier, T., ed., *West Indies Cricket Annual*. Bridgetown, 1970–92.

Dale, H., *Cricket Crusaders*. London, 1953.

Dobson, D., *Records of West Indies First Class Cricket*. Victoria, 1994.

Duckworth, L., *The Story of Warwickshire Cricket*. London, 1974.

Dunning, E, ed., *Sociology of Sport*. London, 1970.

Eastmond, H., *The Handbook of Test Cricket Records*. Bridgetown, 1995.

Edmonds, F., *Another Bloody Tour: England in the West Indies 1986*. London, 1986.

Edwards, H., *Sociology of Sport*. Illinois, 1973.

Elias, N., and E. Dunning, *Quest for Excitement: Sport and Leisure in the Civilizing Process*. Oxford, 1986.

Empire Cricket Club, *The Empire Club, 1914–1989*. Bridgetown, 1989.

Eytle, E., *Frank Worrell: The Career of a Great Cricketer*. London, 1964.

Figueroa, J., *West Indies in England: The Great Post-War Tours*. London, 1991.

Foot, D., *Viv Richards*. Essex, 1982.

Frindall, B., *The Wisden Book of Test Cricket 1877–1984*. London, 1985.

_______, *The Wisden Book of Test Cricket 1977–1994*. London, 1995.

Garner, J., *'Big Bird' Flying High: An Autobiography*. London, 1988.

Giuseppe, U., *Sir Frank Worrell*. London, 1969.

Goodwin, C., *Caribbean Cricketers from the Pioneers to Packer*. London, 1980.

_______, *West Indians at the Wicket*. London, 1986.

Great Britain, *Annual Report on the Social and Economic Progress of the People of Barbados*. London, 1865–1966.

_______, *Colonial Estimates*. London, 1888–1966.

Greenidge, C.G., *The Man in the Middle*. Newton Abbot, 1980.

Griffith, C.C., *Chucked Around*. London, 1970.

Gruneau, R., *Class, Sports and Social Development*. Amherst, 1983.

Guttman, A., *From Ritual to Record: The Nature of Modern Sports*. New York, 1978.

Haley, B.E., *The Healthy Body and Victorian Culture*. Harvard, 1978.

Hall, W.W., *Pace Like Fire*. London, 1966.

Hamilton, B., *Cricket in Barbados*. Bridgetown, 1947.

Harragin, H., *Sixty Years of Cricket: Australia vs The West Indies 1930–1990*. Port-of Spain, 1991.

Harris, B., *West Indies Cricket Challenge 1957*. London, 1957.

Holmes, H.R., *The American Cricketers in the West Indies 1887–88*. London, 1975.

Holt, R., *Sport and the British: A Modern History*. Oxford, 1989.

Howat, G., *Learie Constantine*. London, 1975.

Hoyos, F.A, *Some Eminent Contemporaries*. Bridgetown, 1944.

_______, *Two Hundred Years: A History of the Lodge School*. Bridgetown, 1945.

_______, *Our Common Heritage*. Bridgetown, 1953

_______, *Grantley Adams and the Social Revolution*. London, 1974.

_______, *Barbados: A History from the Amerindians to Independence*. London, 1978.

_______, *The Quiet Revolutionary*. London, 1984.

Hunte, C.C., *Playing to Win*. London, 1971.

Hunte, G, *Barbados*. London, 1974.

Inniss, E., "West Indian Test Cricket and its Social Implications". UWI undergraduate paper, 1978.

Isaacs, V., and P. Thorn, *Hampshire Cricketers 1800–1982*. Retford, 1982.

James, C.L.R., *Beyond a Boundary*. London, 1963.

_______, *Cricket*. London, 1989.

Jones, B., *The Best of Cricket: West Indies vs England 1895–1974*. Port-of-Spain, 1974.

Kanhai, R, *Blasting for Runs*. London, 1966.

Keating, F., *Another Bloody Day in Paradise!* London, 1981.

Kraus, R., *Recreation and Leisure in Modern Society*. New York, 1971.

Landsberg, P., *The Kangaroo Conquers: West Indies v Australia, 1955*. London, 1955.

Lawrence, B., and R. Goble, *The Complete Record of West Indian Test Cricketers*. Leicester, 1991.

Lemmon, D., *Cricket Mercenaries: Overseas Players in English Cricket*. London, 1987.

Lewis, G.K., *The Growth of the Modern West Indies*. London, 1968.

Lindo, H., "The Social History of Cricket in Barbados". UWI undergraduate paper, 1974.

Lloyd, C., *Living for Cricket*. London, 1980.

Lowenthal, D., *West Indian Societies*. Oxford, 1972.

Loy, J., and G. Kenyon, eds., *Sport, Culture and Society*. Toronto, 1969.

Lynch, L., *The Barbados Book*. London, 1972.

Malec, M., *The Social Roles of Sport in Caribbean Societies*. New York, 1996.

Mangan, J.A., *Athleticism in the Victorian and Edwardian Public School*. Cambridge, 1981.

_______, *The Games Ethic and Imperialism*. London, 1986.

Mangan, J.A., ed., *Pleasure, Profit, Proselytism: British Culture and Sport at Home and Abroad 1700–1914*. London, 1988.

Manley, M., *A History of West Indies Cricket*. London, 1989.

Marshall, M., *Marshall Arts: Autobiography of Malcolm Marshall*. London, 1987.

Marshall, R., *Test Outcast*. London, 1970.

Marshall, T., "Race, Class and Cricket in Barbadian Society, 1800–1970", *Manjak* 11 (November 1973).

Marshall, W.K., "Gary Sobers and the Brisbane Revolution". *New World Quarterly* (1965).

Martin-Jenkins, C., *Testing Time: MCC in the West Indies 1974*. Newton Abbot, 1975.

_______, *The Complete Who's Who of Test Cricketers*. London, 1983.

_______, *World Cricketers: A Biographical Dictionary*. Oxford, 1996.

McIntosh, P.C., *Physical Education in England since 1800*. London, 1952.

_______, *Sport in Society*. London, 1963.

Metcalfe, A., "C.L.R. James' Contributions to the History of Sport". *Canadian Journal of the History of Sport* (1987).

Millar, W.B., *Reminiscences of Kensington*. Bridgetown, 1973.

Moyes, A.G., *With the West Indies in Australia, 1951–52*. London, 1952.

_______, *With the West Indies in Australia, 1960–61*. London, 1961.

Nicole, C., *West Indian Cricket*. London, 1957.

Parker, S., *The Sociology of Leisure*. New York, 1976.

Patterson, O.O. "The Ritual of Cricket". *Jamaica Journal* (March 1969).

Pilgrim, T., *The Sir Frank Worrell Pictorial*. New York, 1992.

Ramsay, M.C., "A Critical Examination of Factors affecting the Formation of Major Cricket Clubs in Barbados". UWI undergraduate paper, Cave Hill, 1979.

Richards, J., and M. Wong, *Statistics of West Indies Cricket 1865-1989*. Kingston, 1990.

Ross, A., *Through the Caribbean: The MCC Tour of the West Indies, 1959–1960*. London, 1960.

_______, *The West Indies at Lord's*. London, 1963.

Ross, G., *A History of West Indies Cricket*. London, 1976.

Sandiford, K.A.P., "Everton Weekes: A Cricket Legend Comes to Winnipeg". *Winnipeg Tribune*, 28 July 1978.

_______, "The Victorians at Play: Problems in Historiographical Methodology". *Journal of Social History* (Winter 1981).

_______ "Amateurs and Professionals in Victorian County Cricket". *Albion* (Spring 1983).

_______, "Cricket and the Victorian Society". *Journal of Social History* (Winter 1983).

_______, "The Professionalization of Modern Cricket". *British Journal of Sports History* (December 1985).

_______ "Cricket and the Barbadian Society". *Canadian Journal of History* (December 1986).

_______, "Cricket in Barbados". *Banja: A Magazine of Barbadian Life & Culture*. (April 1988).

_______, "Combermere School, 1926–46: Twenty Years of Rapid Growth". *Banja: A Magazine of Barbadian Life & Culture* (August 1988).

_______, "Combermere School under G.B.R. Burton (1897–1925)", *Journal of Caribbean Studies* (Spring 1989).

_______, "Education and the Barbadian Society". *Banja: A Magazine of Barbadian Life & Culture* (April 1989).

_______, "Barbados Then, and Barbados Now". *Banja: A Magazine of Barbadian Life & Culture* (1989/90).

_______, "The Spartan Cricket Club, 1893–1993". *Journal of the Cricket Society* (Autumn 1993).

_______, "Sir Garfield Sobers: An Appreciation". *Journal of the Cricket Society* (Autumn 1994).

_______, *Cricket and the Victorians*. Aldershot, 1994.

_______, *Everton DeCourcey Weekes: His Record Innings-by-Innings*. West Bridgford, 1995.

_______, " 'Sons in the Sun': The Cricket Story of The Lodge School of Barbados", *Cricket Lore* 2, no. 3 (1995).

_______, " 'Sons in the Sun': The Cricket Story of Harrison College of Barbados". *Cricket Lore*, 2, no. 4 (1995).

_______, " 'Sons in the Sun': The Cricket Story of Combermere School of Barbados". *Cricket Lore* 2, no. 5 (1995).

_______, *Clyde Leopold Walcott: His Record Innings-by-Innings*. West Bridgford, 1996.

_______, "Post-War West Indies Cricket: A Personal View". *Journal of the Cricket Society* (Spring 1996).

______, "The Cricketers of Barbados, 1865–1995", *Cricket Lore* (1997).

______, *Frank Mortimer Maglinne Worrell: His Record Innings-by-Innings*. West Bridgford, 1997.

______, "Cricket and the Growth of Barbadian Nationalism Before Independence and Since." Forthcoming in *Sporting Heritage*.

______, *John Douglas Claude Goddard: His Record Innings-by-Innings*. West Bridgford, forthcoming.

______, *Garfied St Aubrun Sobers: His Record Innings-by-Innings*. West Bridgford, forthcoming.

______, *Wesley Winfield Hall: His Record Innings-by-Innings*. West Bridgford, forthcoming.

Sandiford, K.A.P., and E.H. Newton, *Combermere School and the Barbadian Society* Kingston, 1995.

Sandiford, K.A.P., and B. Stoddart, "The Elite Schools and Cricket in Barbados: A Study in Colonial Continuity", *International Journal of the History of Sport* (December 1987).

Schumpeter, J.A., *Imperialism and Social Classes*. Oxford, 1951.

Smith, P., ed., *England v West Indies 1981*. London, 1981.

Sobers, G., *Cricket Crusader*. London, 1966.

———, *King Cricket*. London, 1967.

———, *Gary Sobers' Most Memorable Matches*. London, 1984.

———, *Twenty Years at the Top*. London, 1988.

———, *The Changing Face of Cricket*. London, 1996.

Spencer, F., and G. King, *Lost Ball – Six Runs*. Bridgetown, 1976.

Starkey, O.P., *Economic Geography of Barbados*. New York, 1939.

Steen, R., *Desmond Haynes: Lion of Barbados*. London, 1993.

Stoddart, B., "Cricket, Social Formation and Cultural Continuity in Barbados: A Preliminary Ethnohistory". *Journal of Sport History* (Winter 1987).

______, "Caribbean Cricket: The Role of Sport in Emerging Small-nation Politics", *International Journal* (1988).

______, "Cricket and Colonialism in the English-speaking Caribbean to 1914: Towards a Cultural Analysis". In *Pleasure, Profit, Proselytism: British Culture at Home and Abroad 1700–1914*, edited by J.A. Mangan. London, 1988.

Stollmeyer, J.B., *Everything under the Sun*. London, 1983.

St Pierre, M. "West Indian Cricket: A Sociocultural Appraisal". *Caribbean Quarterly* (1973).

Swanton, E.W., *West Indian Adventure: With Hutton's MCC Team 1953–54*. London, 1955.

______, *West Indies Revisited: The MCC Tour 1959/60*. London, 1960

Swanton, E. W., et al., eds., *Barclays World of Cricket*. London, 1986.

Tennant, I., *Frank Worrell: A Biography*. Cambridge. 1987.

Thompson, L. O'B., "How Cricket is West Indian Cricket? Class, Racial and Colour Conflicts". *Caribbean Review* (1983).

Thorn, P., *Barbados Cricketers 1865–1990*. West Bridgford, 1991.

Walcott, C.L., *Island Cricketers*. London, 1958.

Wickham, J., "Herman". *West Indies Cricket Annual* (1980).

Wanderers Cricket Club, *Wanderers Cricket Club Centenary, 1877–1977*. Bridgetown, 1977.

Warner, P.F., *Cricket in Many Climes*. London, 1900.

_______, *Long Innings: An Autobiography*. London, 1953.

Wallechinsky, D., *The Complete Book of the Summer Olympics*. New York, 1996.

Wolstenholme, G., *The West Indian Tour of England 1906*. Nelson, 1992.

Woolridge, I., *Cricket, Lovely Cricket: The West Indies Tour 1963*. London, 1963.

Worrell, F.M., *Cricket Punch*. London, 1959.

Wrigley, A., *The Book of Test Cricket 1876–1964*. London, 1965.

Wynne-Thomas, P., *England on Tour*. London, 1982.

_______, *The Complete History of Cricket Tours at Home and Abroad*. London, 1989.

Index

Accrington 133
Adams, Sir Grantley 7, 11, 21, 102
Adelaide 85
Africa 87
Albion 65
Alexander, Franz C.M. 149, 151
Allan, David W. 58, 61, 63, 66, 67. 95
Alleyne, Charles G. 23, 119, 122, 123, 138
Alleyne, Hartley 29
Alleyne, Peter 99
Alleyne, Theodore W. 47, 65
Alleyne, W.N. 39
Alleyne School 10, 107
Ambridge, Revd F.G. 74
Amstelveen 149
Amsterdam 149
Anglo-Saxonism 146, 147
Antarctic 154
Anti-Discrimination Laws (1957) 10, 11
Antigua 17, 18, 41, 64, 74, 75, 120, 126, 136, 153
Apartheid 150
Archer, David 139
Archers, the (YMPC) 21
Armstrong, Revd Arthur Evelyn 6, 73, 107, 108, 120
Armstrong, Gregory 29, 150, 157
Arnos Vale Ground 124
Arthurs, the (Wanderers) 8
Asgarali, Nyron 149
Ashby, Winslow 135–136
Athleticism 3
Athletics 2, 46, 48, 50, 51, 54, 63, 93, 107, 113, 119, 120, 128, 146, 148, 154
Atkinson, Denis St E. 22, 31, 128–129, 138, 140, 141, 142, 149
Atkinson, Eric St E. 128–129, 140, 141, 142
Atkinson, Richard 128
Atkinson, William 128, 138
Atkinson, W. St Eval 128
Atkinsons, the (Wanderers) 127, 128–129, 140
Atlanta Olympics 148
Austin, A.F.G. 'Frankie' 53–54
Austin, F.E.W.G. 78, 102
Austin, Francis Gardiner 3
Austin, Sir Harold B.G. 3, 9, 23, 53, 74, 77, 78,79, 100, 101, 102
Austin, Henry F. 111, 140
Austin, John Gardiner 3, 74
Austin, P.B. 74
Austins, the (Wanderers) 8
Australian Cup, the 139
Australia 1, 19, 31, 59, 78, 85, 101, 111, 126, 129, 133, 148, 149, 151, 155, 159
Australians 1, 32, 61, 126

Babb, Vendall S. 130
Bailey, Herbert 80
Bailey, Trevor E. 125
Bancroft, Clyde Keith 3, 78, 81, 101, 102

Bancrofts, the (Pickwicks) 9
Bank Hall 16, 32, 121, 126, 157
Banks Cricket Club 22
Barbados Advocate 13, 14, 15, 111, 139, 150
Barbados Agricultural Reporter 150
Barbados Bulletin 150
Barbados Colts 61, 96
Barbados Colts XV 47
Barbados Cricket Association (BCA) 4, 6, 13, 14, 18–22, 32, 50, 52, 54, 55, 56, 57, 58, 61, 62, 63, 64, 65, 66, 72, 82, 87, 90, 91, 92, 93, 95, 96, 97, 98, 99, 100, 117, 120, 122, 123, 124, 127, 128, 131, 133, 134, 135, 136, 137, 138, 140, 152, 153, 156, 157, 158, 159
Barbados Cricket Challenge Cup (BCCC) Committee 2, 4, 10–17, 18, 43, 72, 81, 107, 147
Barbados Cricketers 1865–1990 66, 100, 107
Barbados Cricket League (BCL) 4, 18–19, 21, 32, 58, 66, 107, 140, 156
Barbados Daily News 62
Barbados Globe 13–14, 150
Barbados Herald 40, 150
Barbados Labour Party 21, 22, 120
Barbados Rediffusion 139
Barbados Regiment 11
Barbados Scholarship 17, 47, 58, 60, 77, 157
Barbados Workers' Union 21, 22, 120
Barbados XI (1899) 15
Barbados XI (1939) 87
Barbados XI (1951) 123
Barbados Youth Team 135
Barclays, the (Pickwick) 9
Barker, Hughley 127, 141
Barker, J.S. 148
Barnes, Howell Wood 3, 80, 81
Barnes, Theorold 21
Barrera, J. 53
Bartlett, E. Lawson 30, 83, 85, 100, 101
Basketball 146, 148, 154–155
Basseterre 62
Batson Dr Richard E. 81, 82
Bay, the 8, 10, 17, 84, 122, 123
Bay Estate 8, 9, 10
Bay Land 8, 28, 128
BBC Sunday cricket 88
Beaumont Cup Competition 88
Beckles, Albert 154
Beckles, Professor Hilary 146, 153, 155
Beckles Road 8
Belize 87
Belleplaine 26
Belleville 44, 107
Belleville Cricket Club 7, 11, 12, 73
Benn, Joe 82
Benson & Hedges Competition 135
Best, Carlisle 22, 27, 151, 159
BET 32
Bethell, Arthur 58, 59, 60–61, 63, 65, 67
Bethell, T.E. 96
Birkett, Lionel S. 83, 85, 87, 100, 101, 139
Birkett, Theodore S. 87, 89, 130
Blackman, Roger G. 53, 54, 67, 83, 100
Blades, Charlie 43
Blades, Colin F. 63–64
Body-building 148, 154
Bourne, Hilary B. 53, 54, 67
Bourne, William 99
Bowen, B. Keith 57, 58, 67, 129
Bowen, C.P. 73
Bowen, Eustace 38
Bowring, William 9
Boxing 56
Boyack, R.A.J. 47
Boyce, Keith David 29, 121, 157
Boyce, Walter 75
Boycott (1992) 138, 152
Boycott, Geoffrey 30
Boys' Central School 128
Bradman, Sir Donald 25
Bradshaw, Cecil 55
Brancker, Rawle C. 56, 120, 131, 132–133, 138, 140–141, 142
Branker, Kenneth A. 'Honey' 130
Brathwaite, C.P. 59
Brathwaite, Chris 16, 18, 21, 138, 140
Brathwaite, Leonard 63, 64

Brazilians 1
Brewster, Hal H. 123
Brewster, Harold Gittens 6, 109, 119, 120, 122, 123
Brewster, Lisle 123
Bridgetown 10, 20, 37, 45, 50, 53, 57, 82, 83, 92, 100, 106, 119, 121, 126, 127, 129
Brisbane 134
British Columbia 125
British Commonwealth, the 106
British Empire XI 88
British Guiana 10, 47, 51, 52, 54, 57, 63, 73, 78, 81, 83, 85, 90, 92, 96, 110, 111, 118, 121, 123, 124, 127, 149
British West Indian Federation 11, 146
Brookes, Vere H.C. 58–59
Browne, A DeV. 59
Browne, Alfred 3, 74
Browne, Allan 81
Browne, Chester A. 'John' 3, 80
Browne, Clement 3, 13, 74
Browne, Clement F. 78
Browne, Courtney 22
Browne, Cyril R. 'Snuffie' 3, 80–82, 100, 101, 102, 139
Browne, Oliver M. 94
Browne, Robert 74
Brownes, the (Pickwick) 9
Brownes, the (Spartan) 11
Brydens, the (Wanderers) 8
Burke, John 135, 136, 140
Burkes, the (YMPC) 21, 140
Burnham, Chetwyn 99
Burslem, William 2, 4, 38, 73
Burton, Sir Carlisle A. 90–91
Burton, G.B.R. 5, 73, 107–108
Burton, W.T. 13, 14, 23, 90–91
Butcher, Basil 92
Bynoe, Michael Robin 25–26, 96, 97, 100, 101, 102, 111

Cable & Wireless 32, 92, 133
Callender, Bertram A. 94
Callender, R.G. 150
Callender, Victor 131, 132
Camacho, Stephen 111
Campbell, Sherwin 27, 159
Campbell, Trevor 99
Cambridge University 54, 78, 84, 95, 97
Canada 62, 63, 78, 130, 131, 132, 150
Carew, George McD. 27, 49, 116, 117, 121, 138, 140, 141
Carleton University 62
Carlton Cricket Club 20–21, 57, 60, 66, 73, 93, 98, 127, 136, 140
Carrington, the (Wanderers) 8
Carter, William H. 21
Cave, E.W. 57
Cave Hill Campus 155
Central Cricket Club 43
Central Lancashire League 127
Centre for Cricket Research (CCR) 29, 155
Ceylon 77, 78
Challenge Cup competition 10–17, 41–42, 78, 84, 100, 108, 110, 111, 112, 114
Challenor, Brigadier General Edward Lacy 74, 80
Challenor, G.R. 39
Challenor, George 3, 6, 23–25, 26, 27, 28, 39, 41, 44, 74, 78, 79–80, 81, 100, 101, 102, 134, 147, 156, 157
Challenor, Robert L. 'Laddie' 80
Challenor, Vicary Clive 80
Challenors, the 8, 80
Chandlers, the (Wanderers) 8
Christ Church 37, 42
Christianity 1, 3, 5
CIBC Schools Under 19 competition 135
Clairmonte, Frederick A.C. 81, 100
Clairmontes, the (Spartan) 11
Clarke, Carl 106
Clarke, Carleton Howell 3
Clarke, Dr Carlos Bertram 87, 88–89, 100, 102
Clarke, Revd Charles 73, 78
Clarke, Howell 74
Clarke, M.I.C. 87, 89
Clarke, Nolan 149–150

Clarke, Sylvester 29, 150, 157
Clarke, Revd Theodore G. 2, 74, 102
Clarke, Revd Thomas 39
Clarkes, the (YMPC) 21
Classics 1, 7, 17, 46, 50, 75, 84, 90
CLICO International Life Insurance Company 29
Codrington College 5, 10, 11, 37, 46, 50, 73, 75, 90
Cole, Hallam 3, 76
Coleridge and Parry School 107
Coles, the (Pickwick) 9
Collymore, Eric 45, 84, 85, 87
Collymore, Sir Ernest Allan 81, 82, 100
Collymore, Frank Appleton 108, 112, 114–115, 116, 119
Collymore, the (Wanderers) 8
Combermere School 1, 5, 6, 10, 12, 13, 17, 32, 33, 39. 49. 50, 51, 54, 56, 64, 66, 73, 76, 85, 87, 99, 100, 106–145, 146, 154, 157, 158
Combermere School Cadet Corps 108
Combermere School Magazine 115
Combermerian 121
Combined Schools XI 58, 59–60, 63, 96, 99, 135, 158
Combined Islands 64
Compton, Denis 30
Constantine, Lord Learie 31, 39, 81, 129
Constantine, Lebrun 39
Constitution Hill 107, 122, 135
Coppin, O.S. 139
Corbin, Pedro 135, 136, 140
Cornwall College 85
Cox, Alan Pile 42
Cox, G.B.Y. 'Gussie' 3, 5, 73, 74, 75–76, 77, 82, 108, 109, 110, 116
Cox, Hampden Tudor 42
Cox, Percy Ince 42, 43, 66, 67
Cozier, Tony 59, 62
Crawford, Wynter 21
Crichlow, L. 55
Crichlow, P.McD. 5
Crick, Cuthbert O'Brien 49, 119, 122, 123, 124. 141
Cricket in Barbados 84
Culloden Road 8
Cumberbatch, Archie 14, 15
Cumberbatch, Chester St C. 76, 83, 87
Cumberbatch, Graham Trent 11, 13
Cumberbatch, H. St C 123
Cumberbatch, Julian St C. 76, 87
Cummins, Anderson 29, 32, 135, 137, 138, 140, 142, 152, 153
Curling 1
Cutting, Revd E.A. 74

DaCosta, Darnley 100
DaCostas, the (Wanderers) 8
D'Ade, L.S. 76
Dalton, Dr Herbert A. 75, 78–79
Daniel, Wayne 29, 157
Dare, J. St F. 47
Davidson, Alan 96
Dayrell's Road 8
Deane, Colin 56
Deane, N. 39
DeCaires, C. 149
Deighton, Horace D. 2–6, 9, 10, 45, 72–75, 78, 79, 108
Demerara 10, 12, 14, 17, 23, 38, 39, 41, 43, 110
Democratic Labour Party 106, 133
Depeiza, Clairemont 19, 129, 140, 149
Derbyshire 51, 57
Dewdney, Tom 149
Dominica 126
Dorset 136
Downes, Othniel 'Hitler' 19, 29
Drakes, Vasbert 29, 32
Drill Hall 7
Dunedin 138
Durham 138

Edgbaston 99
Edgehills, the (Carlton) 21
Education Act (1878) 37, 91, 106, 157
Edwardian era 16–17
Edwards, J.R. 'Bunny' 83, 86
Edwards, N. 94
Edwards, Richard M. 'Prof' 29, 49, 58, 61–62, 63, 64, 66, 67, 157
Ellcock, Ricardo 29, 135, 136, 142

Ellerslie School 159
Elliott, Gilbert 74
Elliott, Greenidge 74
Empire, (British) 3, 40, 79
Empire Cricket Club 4, 16, 21, 27, 48, 55, 56, 59, 64, 76, 87, 89, 92, 93, 98, 109, 111–112, 114, 117, 118, 120, 121, 122, 123, 124, 127, 129, 130, 131, 132, 133, 135, 137, 138, 139–140, 153
Emtage, B. 116
Emtage, Herbert 10
Emtage, James Bernard 47–48
Emtage, Oliver DeCourcey 5, 6, 40, 45–46, 73
England 1, 9, 18, 23, 28, 29, 37, 39, 42, 45, 48, 50, 57, 61, 62, 72, 76, 77, 78, 79, 80, 81, 82, 83, 86, 88, 97, 101, 111, 113, 117, 118, 119, 121, 125, 133, 135, 136, 139, 148, 149, 150, 153, 155
England XI 149
Englishmen 32
English Young Cricketers 51
Eric Inniss Stand 20, 90
Essex 88, 121
Estwick, Owen 'Nobbie' 58, 66
Estwick, Roddy 29
Eton College 2
Europe 19
European Economic Community 132
Evans, T.L. 58
Evelyn, D. 55
Evelyn, Edward 74
Evelyn, John 58
Evelyn, Thomas Birt 8
Evelyns, the (Wanderers) 8
Ewing, Patrick 155

Farmer, Stephen 40, 47, 55, 60, 64, 65, 67
Farmer, W.A. 5, 40, 46–47, 48, 50, 55, 63
Farmer, Capt. Wilfred A. 21, 40, 46–47, 53, 54–55, 66, 67, 83
Farr, Revd S. 2, 37
Felsted 78
Fenwick Cricket Club 13, 14, 15, 147
Ferguson, W. 149
Field, Frankie 87
'Fitz Lily Affair' 12–14
Flannigan, Fred 24
Fontabelle 9
Forde, Elvis 154
Foster, C.S. 121
Foster, Geoffrey 95
Foster, Leon 117
Foster, Teddy 64, 65
Foster, W.M. 88, 89
Fosters, the (YMPC) 140
Foundation Boys' School 42, 66, 99, 107, 157, 158, 159
Frame Food Competition 15, 18, 21
Francis, George Nathaniel 14, 23, 31
Franklyn, Warwick 106
Franks, G.F. 73
Frank Worrell Day 126
Frank Worrell Grounds 126
Frank Worrell Mementos 126
Frank Worrell Memorial Gardens 126
Farnk Worrell Pavilion 126
Frank Worrell Trophy 126
Frederick, Michael 50, 55, 57, 66, 67, 83
Fredericks, Roy C. 117
Frost, C. 116
Frost, Patrick D. 58, 59, 60

Games Committee (Lodge) 45–46
Ganteaume, Andrew G. 117, 149
Garner, Joel 7, 29, 157, 159
Garrison, the military 7, 10, 11, 37, 39, 73
Garrison Sports Club 11, 21
George Challenor Stand 20
George Street 107
Georgetown 52, 110, 149
George VI, King 118
Gibson, Ottis 29, 32
Gilchrist, Roy 149
Gilkes, Benjamin 16, 111–112, 114
Gill, Ossie 131, 132, 141
Gill, Shirley 88, 89

Gittens, Lionel L. 109, 122
Gittens, Lionel O. 16
Gittens, Stanton O'Connor 6, 23, 83, 87, 100, 102, 108, 109, 120, 122, 124, 139
Glasgow, E.W. 59
Gleeville Cricket Club 15
Goddard, John D.C. 22, 48, 50, 51–52, 53, 55, 63, 65, 66, 67, 77, 82, 83, 100, 126, 130, 149
Goddard, Kenneth 19, 50
Goddard, Randall 63
Goddards, the (Pickwick) 9
Golf 146, 148, 154
Gomez, Gerald E. 31
Gooding, Harry Beaujon 73
Goodman, Clifford E. 13, 38, 40–41, 49, 66 67, 75
Goodman, Flavius 39, 41
Goodman, Sir Gerald Aubrey 3, 10, 13, 41, 74
Goodman, Percy Arnold 41–42, 66, 67
Goodman, W. Evan 41
Goodmans, the (Pickwick) 9, 13, 16, 40–42, 66
Goodwill tournament 48
Goodwill tours (1939–45) 51, 89, 90
Goonesena, Gamini 93
Gore, Hugh 64
Gower, David 30
Grace, Dr W.G. 25, 79
Graham, Ormond 19
Grant, E. Winston 127
Grant, G.C. 'Jackie' 119
Grant, G. Neville B. 130–131, 140
Graveney, Tom 30
Greaves, Herbert 39
Greaves, H.F.K. 85
Greek 110
Greene, Orlando 154
Greene, Victor 29
Greendige, Geoffrey 99, 100, 101, 102, 150
Greenidge, Gordon 7, 27, 44, 100, 136, 149
Greenidge, Malcolm 39
Greenidges, the (Carlton) 21
Grenada 17, 18, 51, 64, 139
Griffith, Adrian 155
Griffith, Charles C. 19, 20, 23, 29, 31, 53, 59, 62, 133, 140
Griffith, E.H.C. 'Teddy' 25–26, 95–96, 101
Griffith, George H.C. 94–95, 102
Griffith, Harold L.V. 23, 92, 94, 123
Griffith, Herman Clarence 11, 16, 23, 31, 55, 92, 113–114, 118, 121, 124, 138, 140, 141, 142
Griffith, Kenneth H.C. 94, 114
Griffiths, Russell 117
Gunn, George 50
Gunn, John 79
Guyana 30, 60, 65, 92

Hadley, W.B. 59
Hall, Wesley Winfield 7, 20, 29, 30–32, 56, 59, 62, 106, 117, 120, 131, 132, 133–134, 135, 138, 140, 141, 142, 149
Hall & Griffith Stand 20
Hallam, A.W. 79
Hamilton, Dr Bruce 37, 84
Hampshire 56, 136, 149
Hannay's 10
Harris, Arnott 117, 121
Harris, C. 74
Harris, H. 116
Harris, L.F. 'Shell' 88, 89
Harrison College 1, 1–6, 9, 10, 11, 16, 17, 33, 37, 39, 40, 41, 43, 45, 46, 47, 50, 54, 58, 60, 64, 66, 72–105, 106, 107, 108, 109, 110, 112, 114, 115, 116, 120, 122, 128, 134–135, 154, 157, 158
Harrisonian 2, 73, 81–82
Harrow 2, 100
Haskell, Harold Noad 93
Hassell, Albert 'Runty' 95, 96, 102
Hawke, Lord 40
Haynes, Desmond 7, 22, 27, 44, 100, 136, 151, 152, 153
Headley, George 16, 31, 79, 86
Headley, Philip 63

Headley, Sam A. E. 51
Headley, Samuel A. 49, 50, 55, 57, 58, 63, 66, 83
Hendren, Patsy 79
Hewitt, J. Mitchie 18, 140
Hinds, Delmont 11–15, 147
Hinkson, Ernest A. 3, 74, 76
Hinkson Ernest Stephen 29, 58, 60, 66
Hinksons, the (Wanderers) 8
Hirst, George 41
Hoad, E.L.G. Jnr 93, 102, 113
Hoad, E.L.G. Snr 100, 112–113, 120, 121, 122, 139, 140, 141, 142
Hoad, John S. 111, 112, 140
Hoad, William C. 80, 93
Hoads, the (Pickwick) 9, 13, 112
Hockey 50, 52, 146, 148, 154
Holder, Adzil 58, 93, 129, 141
Holder, Gladstone 109
Holder, John 135, 136, 139, 149
Holder, Roland 22, 135, 137–138, 140, 141, 151, 153, 154
Holder, Vanburn 19, 22, 29, 41, 157
Holford, David 22, 41, 96, 98, 101, 102, 139, 152
Holland 65, 149
Holy Trinity Cricket Club 15
Hong Kong 83
Hooper, Carl 30
Horse-racing 146
Hove 113
Howell, William M. 74, 81
Hoyoses, the (YMPC) 21
Hughes, Ronald G. 56, 109–110, 131–132
Humpage, Geoffrey 99
Hunte, Conrad 19, 25–26, 27, 66, 97, 140, 156, 157
Hunte, G.B. 87
Hunters Cricket Club 15
Hurley, Kenneth 120, 141
Hutchinson, Geoffrey St C. 58, 60, 63, 66, 100
Hutchinson, W. St Clair 21
Hutchinsons, the (Carlton) 21
Hutson, J. 55
Hutson, Dr John 8, 10, 39
Hutson, Dr Lionel 81
Hutton, Sir Leonard 30
Hyde Park Cricket Club 15
Hyderabad 137
Hylton, L.G. 119

Ince, Douglas 10
Ince, Harry W. 30, 56, 81, 82, 101, 102, 156
Inces, the (Wanderers) 8
Independence (1966) 28, 64, 106, 146, 147, 154, 158
India 1, 52, 80, 91, 98, 125, 126, 137, 139, 148
Indians 155
Industrial Revolution 7
Inniss, Bruce DeL. 83, 87
Inniss, Sir Clifford 83, 86–87, 101
Inniss, Eric D. 20, 88, 90, 100
Inniss, Errie 131, 132
Inniss, Michael 64
Instant Money Game 20, 134
Intermediate division 19, 63
International Cricket Council (ICC) 66, 92, 136
Inter-School Athletic Championships 6, 46, 54, 120, 123, 128
Ishmael, Alan F. 119, 122, 124, 141
Island Scholarship 17, 157

Jabbar, Kareem Abdul 155
Jackman, Edward Clarence 74
Jackmans, the (Wanderers) 8
Jamaica 17, 18, 41, 47, 55, 57, 63, 85, 93, 94, 95, 96, 100, 126, 137, 148, 155, 159
Jamaicans 146
James, C.L.R. 73, 146
John, George 31
John Goddard Gates 52
Johnson, Hines 31
Johnson, H. Laurie 50, 51, 55, 57, 67, 84
Jones, A.N. 21
Jones, Prior 31
Jones, William 15
Jordan, Harold 88, 89, 102, 130

Jordan, H.B. DeC. 88
Jordan, Oscar W. 58, 59–60
Julien, Shane 64

Kanhai, Rohan 92, 149
Kennington Oval 42
Kensington Oval 9, 10, 12, 15, 20, 26, 43, 47, 48, 52, 53, 54, 57, 58, 60, 62, 64, 75, 76, 83, 90, 92, 95, 119, 122, 125, 139, 152, 156
Kent 78, 82
Kidney, Harold 88, 111
Kidney, John MacColl 88, 111, 138, 140
King, Anthony St E. 96, 98, 99
King, Collis 150
King, Ernest 38
King, Frank McD. 13, 19, 31, 123, 131, 140, 149
King, Hampton 130
King, Horace A. 58, 93, 98, 102, 129, 139
Kingston 117
Knight, Alfred 96
Knight, Rudolph H. 'Huffie' 130

Laker, James C. 121, 125
Lancashire 133, 159
Lara, Brian C. 30
Lashley, 'Peter' D. 23, 25–26, 56, 131, 132, 134, 138, 140, 141, 157
Latin 110
Laurie, C.W.F. 47
Lavine, Mark 29, 32
Lawless, C.B. 94
Lawless, David I. 94
Lawless, R.A. 94
Layne, Oliver 14–15, 82, 147
Learmond, George 12, 39, 110–11, 140–141
Lee Kow, Eric 88
Leeward Cricket Club 7, 10, 11, 43, 66, 118
Leeward Islands 62, 100, 159
Leicestershire 80
Lewis, Harcourt 106
Lindwall, Ray 30, 31
Lobo, Frank C. 117, 140
Lodge School, The 1, 3, 5, 9, 10, 11, 17, 33, 37-71, 73, 83, 86, 87, 91, 95, 99, 100, 106, 107, 110, 115, 134–35, 139, 157, 158
Lodge School Cadet Corps 56
Lodge School Debating Society 56
Lodge School Guild 58
Lodge School Record 45, 46, 47, 57,58, 63
Lodge School XIII (1960) 63
Logie, Augustine 151–152
London 78, 88
'Long Leg' 111
Lord's Cricket Ground 13, 98, 126
Los Angeles Lakers 155
Loughborough 123
Low, Andrew 75
Lucas, John H. 21, 49, 109, 119, 122, 124–125, 130, 141, 142
Lucas, Noel S. 'Brickie' 49, 119, 127, 140
Lucases, the (YMPC) 21, 140
Lynch, J. Challenor 11

Madray, Ivan 92
Magdalen College 48
Manning, Dr Charles G. 88
Maple Cricket Club 22
Marlar, Robin 93
Marshall, C.A. 150
Marshall, D. DaC. 90
Marshall, Harold A. 94
Marshall, Malcolm 7, 29
Marshall, Norman 149, 159
Marshall, Roy 27, 44, 50, 53, 55, 56–57, 66, 67, 84, 121, 149, 154
Marshall, Tony 23, 100
Marshalls, the (Carlton) 21
Martindale, Leah 148, 154
Martindale, E.A. 'Mannie' 7, 31, 49, 55, 109, 114, 117–118, 119, 121, 122, 140, 141, 142
Martinez, Frederick N. 15
Marylebone Cricket Club (MCC) 13, 18, 24, 42, 47, 50, 52, 79, 80, 82, 86, 88, 92, 119, 121, 130

Mason, Kenneth 78, 101, 102
Masons, the (Wanderers) 8
Massiah, H. 55
Mayers, Anthony C. 58, 59–60, 63, 67
Mayers, Michael Spencer 43
Mayers, Trevor L. 58, 59, 63
Maynard, Dayne 29, 32
McComie, Val 90, 91, 123
McGill University 54, 88
Mead, Philip 79
Medford, W.H.L. 'Golly' 84–85
Meckiff, Ian 96
Mendez, H. 55
Middlesex 136, 159
Miller, Keith 31
Minor Counties 136
Moe, Thomas A. 112, 114, 140
Morris, E. 16
Morris, Robert E. 95
Moseley, Ezra 29, 150
Moseley, Hallam 29, 157
'Mother Country' 9
Mullins, Carl 55
Murray, David 150
Murray, Deryck 61, 92

Nascimento, R. 131
Natal 80
National Basketball Association 155
Netherlands 149
New Jersey 74
Newsam, Arthur Ralph Vernon 5, 48, 53, 85–86
New South Wales 159
New World 7
New York Knicks 155
New Zealand 1, 52, 62, 63, 97, 137, 148, 149, 155
Noott, Major Cecil 13, 108, 124, 131
Norris, Anton 29, 131, 142
Northamptonshire 42, 88
Norville, Rodney 131, 132, 141
Nottinghamshire 159
Nurse, Seymour 19, 23, 25–26, 27, 53, 140, 154, 156, 157

Old Combermerians 4, 12, 106, 114, 120, 121, 122, 136, 138, 140–141, 142
Old Harrisonians 4, 5, 6, 48, 73, 80, 100–102, 112, 113, 139
Old Lodge Boys 4, 65, 66, 108
Ollivierre, C.A. 42
O'Neall, E. 116
One-Day Internationals (ODIs) 136, 137, 138, 139, 149, 153
Otago 97, 138
Ottawa 62
Outram, B.H.V. 43
Outram, Walter 39
Oxford and Cambridge certificates 79
Oxford University 2, 4, 38, 40, 47, 48, 60, 72, 75, 77, 78, 82, 86, 87

Packer, C.R. 53
Packer, Freddie 81
Padmore, Albert 150
Pairaudeau, Bruce 149
Pakistan 59, 96, 97, 136, 138, 139, 148
Parris, J.L. 'Puss' 116, 117, 121, 122, 139, 140, 141
Parris, Richard 38
Parris, Stanton 138
Parris, T. 39
Patterson, W.G. 57
Peirce, T. 63
Peirce, Thomas N.M. 88, 89–90, 100, 102, 149
Perkins, D. Ralph 109
Perkins, Eddie 58, 67, 95, 129
Phadkar, Dattu 91
Phillips, Fred D. 'Washer' 94, 102
Phillips, Dr Joseph Evelyn 47
Phillips, Randall 39
Phillips, Stephen 39
Pickwick Cricket Club 6, 7, 9–10, 11, 12, 13, 15, 16, 17, 20, 21, 22, 24, 39–40, 41–42, 43, 44, 45, 50, 52, 53, 54, 59, 61, 64, 66, 73, 74, 76, 80, 82, 83, 84, 85, 87, 88, 89, 91, 93, 95, 108, 110, 112, 113, 115, 116, 117, 122, 124, 125, 140, 146

Pickwick Pavilion 20
Pickwick Second XI 45, 115
Pierre, Lance 31
Piles, the (Wanderers) 8
Pilgrim, H.F. 112
Pilgrim, John Frere 39
Pilgrim, Owen A. 'Graffie' 46, 47, 48–49, 51, 65, 66, 67, 108–109, 125
Pilgrim, Torrey 50, 51, 55, 57
Pilgrim School 10
Pilgrims, the (Spartan) 11
Police (Frame Food) 15
Police Boys' Club 55
Police Cricket Club 20, 55, 66, 87, 96, 98, 123
Polo Club 146
Port Mourant 92
Port-of-Spain 57, 82, 87, 88, 98, 117, 129, 137
Prideaux, Revd W.H. 40
Priestley, Arthur 41, 74, 76
Printers Cricket Club 15
Proverbs, Gordon 93
Punjab University 126
Putney 88

Quakers Cricket Club 15
Queensland 133
Queen's Park, Barbados 107
Queen's Park Oval 88, 89
Queen's Royal College 38, 73
Queree, E.C. 21

Radcliffe 126
Rae, Alan F. 66
Railway Cricket Club 15
Ramadhin, Sonny 93, 101, 116–117, 149
Ramsay, J.T.C. 18, 140
Red Stripe Caribbean Cricket Quarterly 62
Red Stripe Cup competition 19, 65, 137, 151, 153, 155
Reece, Courtenay W. 82–83
Reeves, Sir Conrad 11, 110
Reifer, Floyd 64–65, 67, 155
Regiment, 35th 5
Rest of Barbados (1951) 123
Rest of the World (1967) 148, 151
Richards, I. Vivian A. 30, 151
Richardson, Richie 151
Roberts, G.C. 78
Roberts, T.F.C. 78
Roberts, Thomas Webb 77–78
Robinson, O. Merton 27, 120, 121, 141
Rock, George 29
Roett, Ishmael 135
Rogers, Cecil C. 117
Rogers, Hubert M. 117
Rome Olympics, 1960 146
Ronald Tree Cup 63, 135
Rowe, Lawrence G. 30, 117
Rowes, the (Lodge) 39
Rudder, Stephen 3, 13, 74, 76
Rudders, the (Spartan) 11
Rugby School 100

Sabina Park 28, 57, 93, 128
Sandiford, Julia N. 154
Sandiford, Professor Keith A.P. 157–158
Sandiford, L. Erskine 95
Schools Under 19 competition 135
Scotland 47, 82, 97, 131
Scots 1
Scott, Francis 131, 132
Scottish League Cricket 137
Seale, A.G.F. 48
Seale, Beresford 39
Sealy, Arthur E. 110
Sealy, G. Harry 110, 122, 123–124
Sealy, Glenroy R. 150
Sealy, J.E. Derek 6, 49, 109, 116, 118–120, 121, 122, 124, 140, 141, 142, 154
Sealy, R. 116
Second division competition 17, 19, 45, 46, 47, 48, 50, 58, 63, 76, 81, 88, 91, 107, 111, 112, 115, 123–124
Shand, J. 53
Sharjah 139
Sheffield Shield competition 133, 159
Shell Shield competition 19, 64, 98, 134, 148, 155, 157
Shepherd, John 150

Shepherd, William 14, 15, 82, 147
Short, Peter D.B. 22–23, 55, 56, 65
Simmons, David A. 59
Simmons, Dr Erskine A. 132
Simmons, Henderson 135, 137
Simmons, Keith 106
Simmons, Philip 151
Sir Garfield Sobers Pavilion 20
Skeete, Elliot 38
Skeete, Dr Harold E. 47, 81
Skeete, John Brathwaite 39
Skeete, Sammy 29, 32
Skeete, Torrence 39
Skeetes, the (Wanderers) 8
Skinner, Anthony O'N. 50, 53–54
Skinner, Clarence 116–117, 140
Slade Lucas XI 13, 75
Slavery 7, 28
Small, Gladstone 29, 135, 136, 142
Small, Milton 29
Smith, Augustus E. 38, 39
Smith, Cameron W. 23, 25–26, 27, 32, 59, 95, 96, 100, 101, 102, 139
Smith, C.C. 58, 59
Smith, C.E. Aurelius 5
Smith, D. 116
Smith, Frederick Bonham 10, 39
Smith, Frederick G. 110
Smith, Howard 38
Smith, O.G. 'Collie' 149
Smith, Richard Henry 38, 75
Smith, Samuel Ivan 110
Smith, Vernon O. 94
Sobers, Sir Garfield 7, 19, 20, 22, 25–26, 27–29, 30, 55, 58, 93, 96, 97, 98, 124, 128, 129, 140, 147, 149, 153, 154, 156
Soccer 1, 2, 4, 5, 6, 7, 50–51, 52, 54, 56, 64, 75, 79, 85–86, 90, 93, 96, 108, 109, 113, 114, 119, 120, 121, 124, 125, 127, 128, 132, 146, 148, 154
Social Darwinism 3
Solomon, George 110
Solomon, Joseph 92
Somers Cocks, Arthur 4–5, 9, 16, 75, 76, 77, 82
South Africa 19, 80, 101, 138, 139, 150, 152
South Africans 18
South Caribbean Force 11
Spartan Cricket Club 7, 11–14, 16, 21, 30, 39, 44, 45, 49, 51, 54, 57, 59, 60, 65. 73, 74, 76, 82–83, 84, 85, 87, 88, 89, 90, 91, 94, 96, 98, 108, 110, 112, 113, 114, 116, 117, 119, 120, 122, 130, 134, 137, 140
Speed, Arthur 39
Speed, Revd T. Lyall 2, 5, 6, 38, 39, 66, 107, 108, 139
Spooner, C.D. 'Pampie' 49, 55, 114, 117, 118, 121, 142
Sportsmans Cricket Club 15
Springer, Henderson 135, 137
Springer, Sir Hugh 21
Squires, Cecil 154
Sri Lanka 77
St Andrews's Cricket Club 10
St Ann's Cricket Club 6, 7, 10, 37, 51, 86, 108, 117
St Augustine campus 126
St Catherine Cricket Club 22
St Edward's School 78
St Hill, A.B. 13, 15
St Hill, Clinton 64
St John 10, 37, 49
St John's, Antigua 138
St Kitts 41, 51, 62, 74
St Lucia 45, 124
St Lucy 10
St Martins Cricket Club 15
St Michael 12, 37
St Michael's Cricket Club 7, 10, 38
St Michael's Girls' School 158
St Vincent 17, 18, 42, 74, 118, 124
Statham, Brian 30, 31, 125
Stephenson, Franklyn 29, 150
Stoddart, Andrew E. 41
Stoddart, Dr Brian 146
Stokes, H.B. 74
Stollmeyer, Jeffrey 66
Stow, Sir John 22
Stroudes, the (Spartan) 11
Stuart, Harold A. 120

Stuart, Lionel 83, 86
Stuart, N. 116
Sumpter, A.G. 63
Surrey 42, 159
Surrey County Cricket Club 92
Sussex 99, 100, 113
Swanton, E.W. 63
Swanton XI (1956) 58, 61, 93, 95, 96
Swimming 148, 154
Sydney 96

Taitt, Brantford 106
Tarilton, Percy H. 'Tim' 24–25, 26, 27, 44–45, 48, 65, 66, 67, 79, 92
Tariltons, the (Pickwick) 9
Taylor, Alfred M. 53, 63, 64, 67
Taylor, A.M. 'Charlie' 27, 50, 52–53, 63, 64, 67, 121
Tennis 146, 148, 154
'The Tub' 107
Thomas, F.G. 'Fluffie' 49, 119, 122, 124
Thomas, Dr Robert D. 157
Thompson, David 106
Thompson, Obadele 148, 154
Thompson, Patterson 29, 32, 155
Thorn, Philip 66, 100, 107
(Three) Ws, the 7, 20, 21, 25–26, 27, 31, 55, 92, 156, 157
Three Ws stand 20, 92
Tiffen, H.J. 74
Toronto 130
Tracey, Charles 2, 4, 38
Trent Bridge 79, 125
Trinidad 6, 10, 13, 14, 15, 17, 21, 24, 26, 30, 38, 41, 42, 43, 44, 47, 48, 50, 51, 53, 54, 57, 61, 72, 73, 76, 78, 82, 83, 84, 85, 86, 87, 88, 89, 90, 98, 110, 116, 117, 118, 119, 121, 124, 125, 126, 151, 155
Trinidad & Tobago 133, 139, 148
Trueman, Fred 30, 31, 125
Tudor, D. 55
Tyson, Frank H. 30, 31, 93

United Cricket Club 15
United States of America (USA) 43, 74, 126, 130, 131, 132, 154
University College of the West Indies 94, 95
University of Edinburgh 47, 59, 60, 82, 86, 97
University of Toronto 56
University of the West Indies (UWI) 29, 94, 95, 126, 155

Valentine, Alfred 93, 101, 149
Valentine, John 150
Vaughan, J.C.B. 150
Victorians 3
Volunteers 139
Von Glatz , R. 46

Walcott, Clyde A. 139
Walcott, Sir Clyde Leopold 7, 21, 25, 27, 32, 44, 45, 91–92, 100, 101, 102, 121, 123, 126, 139, 149, 153, 156, 157
Walcott, Frank 21
Walcott, Keith 21, 23, 91, 100, 123, 139, 153–154
Walcott, Leslie A. 'Bessie' 49–51, 53, 83–87, 90, 101, 102, 121, 139
Walcott, Michael A.C. 92, 99
Walcott, Victor 29, 32
Walker, Audley L. 58, 59
Walker, Cyril 106
Wallace, Philo 22, 27
Walton, George 13
Wanderers Cricket Club 7, 8–10, 11, 16, 17, 20, 22, 23, 24, 25, 28, 37, 39–40, 42, 43, 47, 48, 51, 54, 56, 58, 61, 62, 65, 66, 73, 74, 76, 77, 78, 79, 82, 84, 86, 87, 88, 89, 93, 97, 110, 117, 122, 128–129, 140
Wanderers Second XI 112
Warner, Charles William 72
Warner, Sir Pelham 18, 72, 100, 101
Warren, K.N. 'Tootie' 127, 140
Warwickwshire 97, 99, 136
Wason, Harcourt 154
Wass, Tom 79
Waterford 126, 135

Watts, Revd T. 2, 37
Webb, Revd W.T. 2, 37
Webster, Dr Rudi Valentine. 96, 97, 101, 102
Wedderburn, Jim 'Lolly' 146, 154
Weekes, Donald 131, 132
Weekes, Sir Everton DeCourcey 7, 19, 21, 22, 23, 25–26, 27, 28, 53, 61, 63, 80, 92, 95, 134, 140, 149, 150, 156, 157
Wellington 62
Western Province 80
West Indian XI 76, 82
West India Regiment Cricket Club 15
West Indies 1, 18, 23, 29, 30, 31, 32, 39, 41, 42, 43, 44, 45, 49, 50, 52, 55, 56, 57, 59, 62, 65, 66, 74, 76, 77, 78, 79, 81, 82, 83, 85, 86, 88, 91, 92, 95, 96, 100, 110, 111, 113, 114, 116, 117, 118, 119, 121, 122, 125, 126, 128, 129, 131, 133, 137, 138, 139, 140, 141, 148, 151, 153, 154, 155
West Indies Cricket Annual 62
West Indies Cricket Board (of Control) (WICBC), 43, 56, 66, 77, 90, 92, 96, 98, 111, 134, 151, 152
West Indies Youth Team 135
Westshire (Cricket Club) 21
Weymouth 107, 135
Wickham, C.W. 'Billy' 110
Wickham, Clennell 21
Wilkes, Graham 63
Wilkie, N. Gray 58, 67, 129
Wilkinson, Sam 139
Williams, Albert 4
Williams, Cecil B. 'Boogles' 21, 58, 92–93, 94, 101, 102, 129
Williams, Denys A. 94
Williams, Earle 135
Williams, E.A.V. 'Foffie' 7, 31, 49, 55, 109, 114, 120, 121, 138, 140, 141, 142
Williams, G.C. 16
Williams, James A. 94
Williams, Lionel 56, 131, 142
Williams, Vernon 138
Williams, Vincent B 'Bull' 108, 115–116, 119
Wilson, H.D. 94
Winchester College 79
Windward Cricket Club 7, 10, 11, 12, 66, 115
Windward Islands 51, 64, 124, 139
Winter, Mr 75
Wood, Gerald L. 43, 93–94, 102, 121
Wood, Lear O. 43, 93
Wood, Rupert 50
Wood, Bishop Wilfred Denison 132
Woods, J. 'Float' 13, 14
Woolley, Frank 25, 82
Worcestershire 136
World Cup 1979 150
World Cup 1987 139
World Cup 1996 133–134
World War I 39, 43, 47, 64, 84, 111, 112, 116
World War II 11, 20, 21, 22, 23, 25, 30, 31, 83, 88, 93, 149
Worme, Aubrey 43
Worme, Joe 82
Worme, Stanley Mills 43, 49, 67
Worrell, Sir Frank 7, 21, 25, 28, 29, 30, 31, 45, 49, 51, 80, 109, 119, 122, 124, 125–127, 136, 140, 141, 142, 149, 151, 153, 156, 157
Worrell, Lawrence R. 135, 136, 149
Wranglers Cricket Club 15

Yachting 146
Yearwood, L.T. 43
Yorkshire 41, 42, 159
Young Men's Progressive Club (YMPC) 20–21, 89, 125, 127, 138, 139, 140

Zimbabwe 137